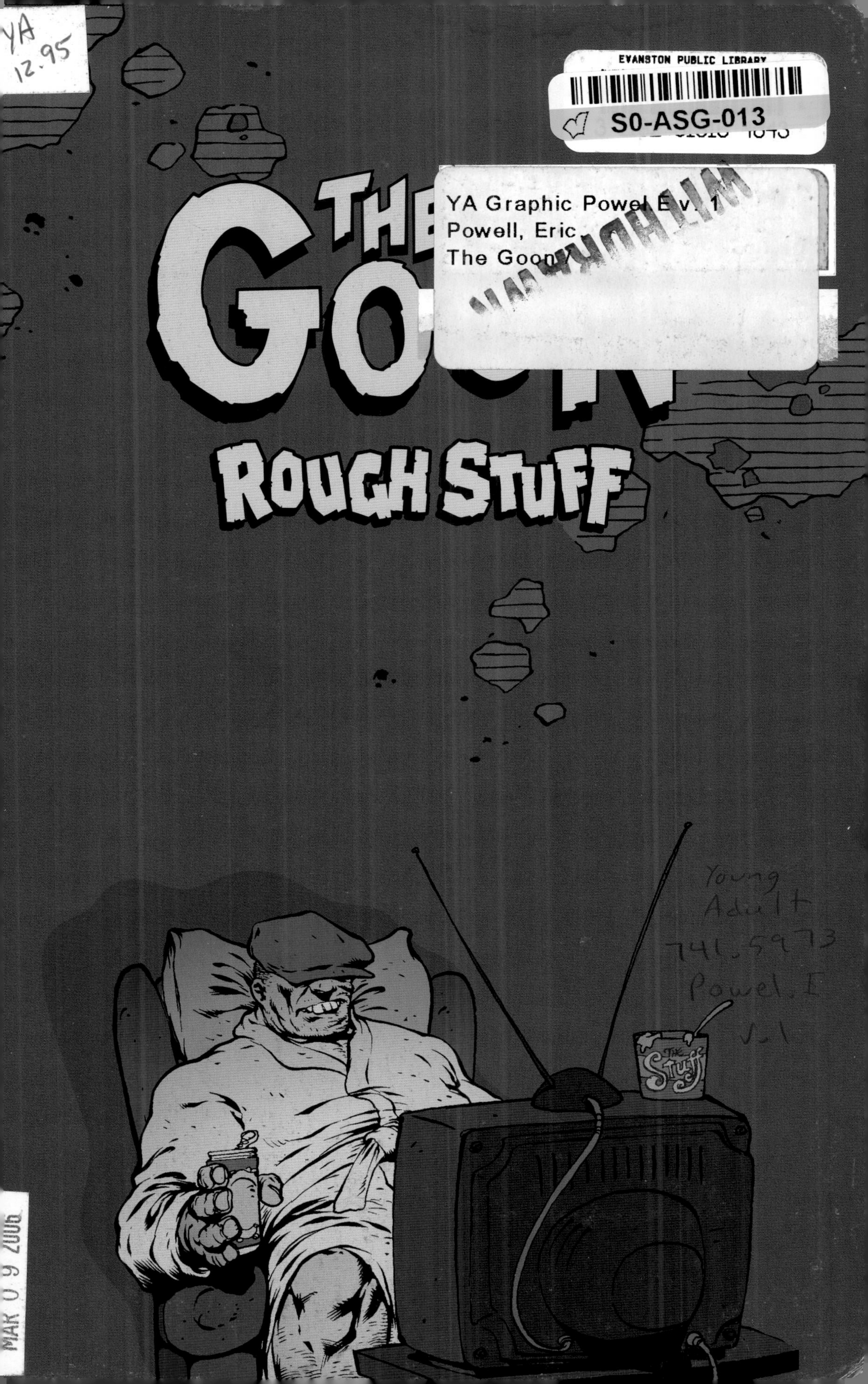
THE GOON
ROUGH STUFF
The Stuff

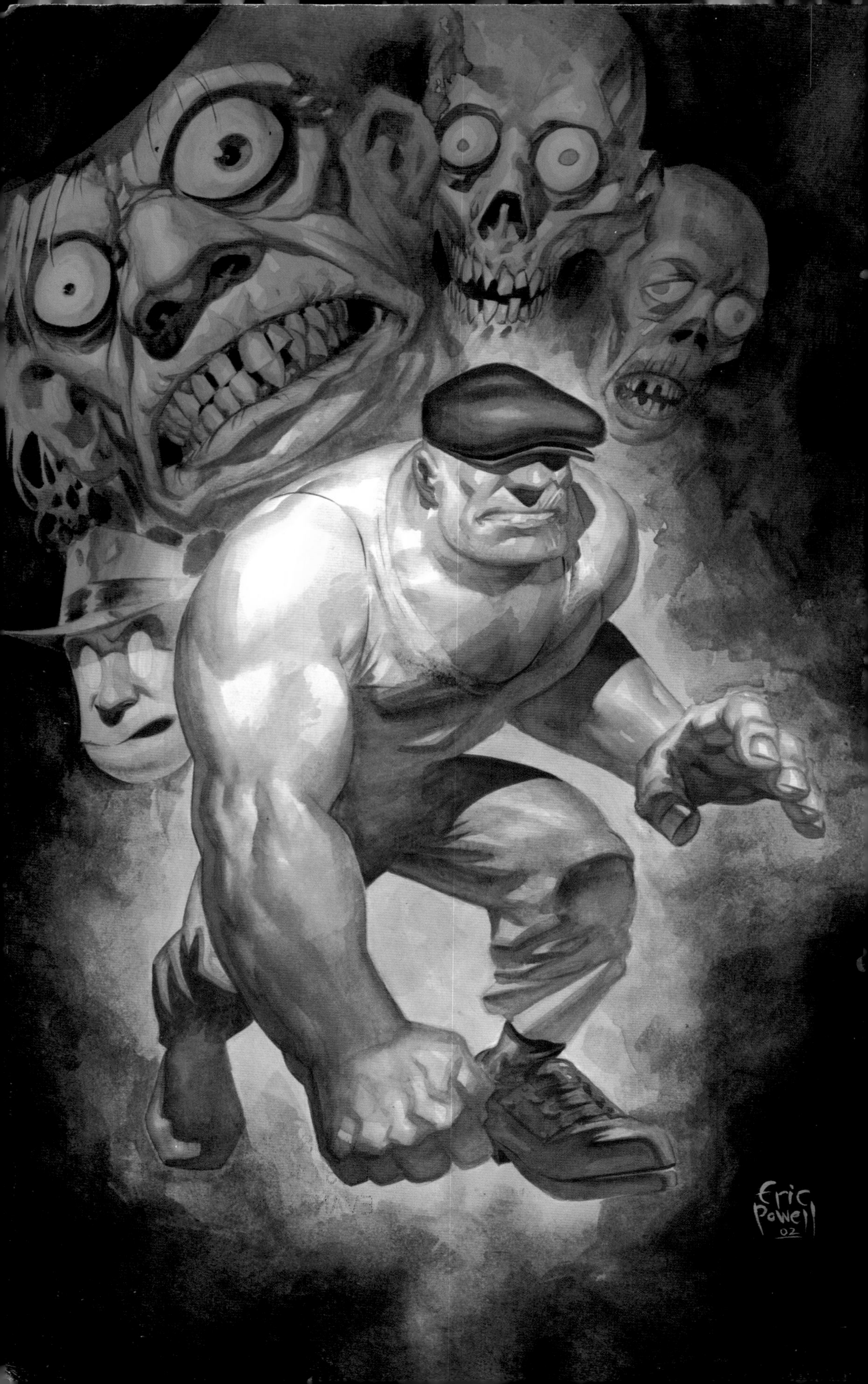
Eric Powell 02

# THE GOON™
## ROUGH STUFF

### by Eric Powell

### colors by Dave Stewart

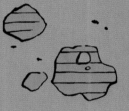

**editors**
**Scott Allie and Matt Dryer**

**designer**
**Amy Arendts**

**art director**
**Lia Ribacchi**

**publisher**
**Mike Richardson**

Zombies provided by Jethro & Earl Zombie Wranglerin' Inc.
and The Adopt-A-Zombie Foundation

**Dark Horse Books™**

No chimpanzees were harmed in the making of this comic ... except for that one
that we strapped to a table and bludgeoned with a baseball bat.
But honest injun, that was the only one.

SPECIAL THANKS TO-
Robin, Gage, and Cade, Bill and Alicia Schenk, Kyle Hotz, Mark Ballard, Mike Mignola,
Ben Cocke, Tom Sniegoski, Chuck Angel, Larry Underwood, Randy Bowen,
Frank Cho, Joe Bob Briggs, Steve Niles, Barry Gregory, Shaynne Corbett,
and everyone at Dark Horse Comics.

The Goon™: Rough Stuff. Published by Dark Horse Comics, Inc., 10956 SE Main Street, Milwaukie, OR, 97222. The Goon™
& © 2004 Eric Powell. The Albatross Exploding Funny Book Studio™ Logo is a trademark of Eric Powell. All rights reserved.
The stories, institutions, and characters in this publication are fictional. Any resemblance to actual persons (living, dead, or
undead), events, institutions, or locales, without satiric intent, is purely coincidental. No portion of this book may be reproduced,
by any means, without express written permission from the copyright holder. Dark Horse Books™ is a trademark of Dark Horse
Comics, Inc. Dark Horse Comics® is a trademark of Dark Horse Comics, Inc., registered in
various categories and countries. All rights reserved.

This volume collects issues 1-3 of *The Goon*, Volume 1, originally published in 1999, and collected in 2003
as *The Goon Rough Stuff* from Albatross Exploding Funny Books.

Published by
Dark Horse Books
A division of
Dark Horse Comics, Inc.
10956 SE Main Street
Milwaukie, OR 97222

First Dark Horse Edition: February 2004
ISBN: 1-59307-086-1

3 5 7 9 10 8 6 4 2
Printed in China

# FOREWORD TO THE ALBATROSS EDITION

This collection of my first three-issue series of *The Goon* is entitled *Rough Stuff* for a reason. If you're looking for the clean, refined work of an artist at the peak of his ability, or the steady, compelling storytelling of an established writer, you've come to the wrong place. Now, if you, like me, are a freak about wanting to see each step along the way of the process a creator takes in developing his skill, you may find this book entertaining. Before *The Goon* #1, I had not written a full-length comic, and my art, to say the least, was a bit crude. It looks like I inked some of this stuff with an electric toothbrush. You'll probably find some of this material pretty stupid. I'm inclined to agree. But it was never my intention to make an intellectual comic. In my humble opinion there are too many people trying (note that I said trying) to do that already. *The Goon* was always intended to be one thing … fun. Even in this rough stage, I believe it accomplishes that.

Oh, and by the way, if this is your first exposure to *The Goon*, pick up the new series. It makes this stuff look like crap.

Eric Powell
2002

# REGARDING THIS EDITION

Well, thanks for buying this crap again. If it's for the first time, my deepest apologies. First off, I'd like to thank the best colorist in the business, Dave Stewart, for working this project into his extremely busy schedule. Although I feel the quality of my drawings in this book are not up to snuff, it's still great to collaborate with someone of his ability.

When I was working on the first *Goon* book in '98, it seemed pretty unrealistic to think anything would come of it. I drew it anyway. Due to unfortunate circumstances, the first run only lasted the three issues that are collected in this book. After the rights reverted back to me I decided to commit sure financial suicide and self-publish it. Fortunately it went well, Dark Horse picked it up, and 2003 was an unbelievably surreal break-out year.

What I'm getting at is that I just had to do this comic. If there is anything to divine cosmic destiny, which I doubt, then I'm destined to draw a funny book about a buck-toothed guy who punches zombies and hoboes. Hopefully that makes you feel a little better about yourselves.

My deepest and sincerest thanks to all you *Goon* fans!

Eric Powell
Somewhere in the woods of middle Tennessee
2003

# ROUGH STUFF: MILKING-IT-FOR-ALL-IT'S-WORTH EDITION, A SPECIAL INTRODUCTION BY MR. GOON AND MR. FRANKY

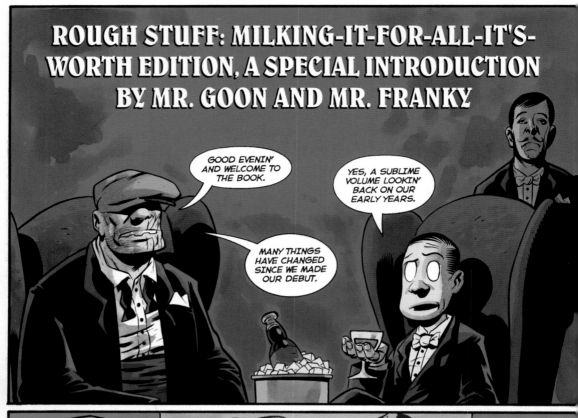

GOOD EVENIN' AND WELCOME TO THE BOOK.

YES, A SUBLIME VOLUME LOOKIN' BACK ON OUR EARLY YEARS.

MANY THINGS HAVE CHANGED SINCE WE MADE OUR DEBUT.

FOR ONE, I NO LONGER LOOK LIKE A SHAVED MULE.

AND I NO LONGER LOOK LIKE A BEADY EYED WEINER-HEAD.

THAT'S DEBATABLE.

QUIET, YOU!

BUT THE BIGGEST CHANGE HAS BEEN OUR FINANCIAL SITUATION.

YES, NOW THAT WE IS AT DARK HORSE, WE IS ALL HIGH CLASS AND DRINK ALL MANNERS OF WINES AND CHARDONNAYS, AS WELL.

AND YOU MAY NOTICE OUR NEW BOOKS IS A LITTLE DIFFERENT THAN WHAT'S IN THIS ONE.

YEAH, LIKE WE DON'T HAVE TALKIN' CHAINSAWS NO MORE.

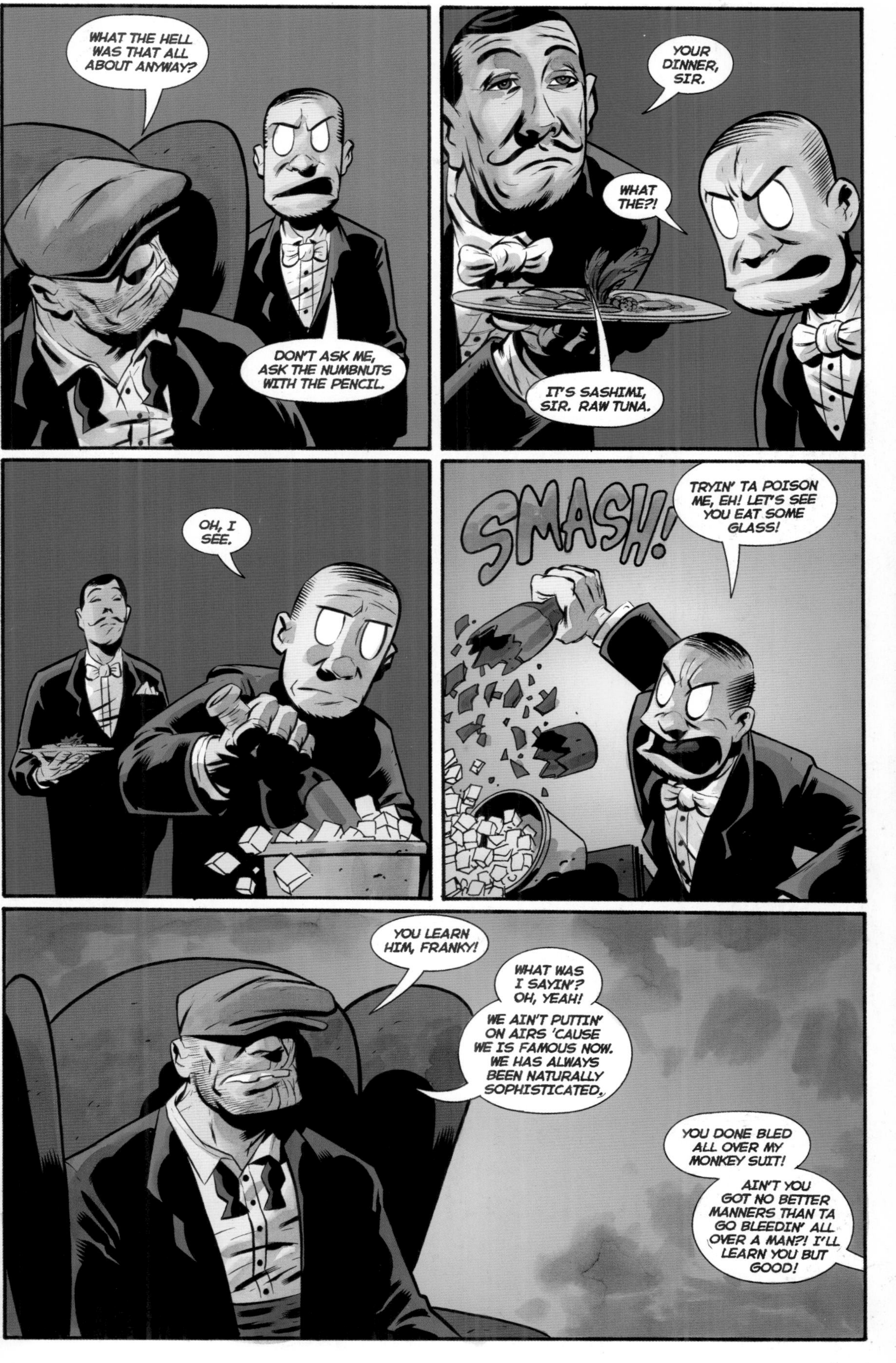
WHAT THE HELL WAS THAT ALL ABOUT ANYWAY?
DON'T ASK ME, ASK THE NUMBNUTS WITH THE PENCIL.
YOUR DINNER, SIR.
WHAT THE?!
IT'S SASHIMI, SIR. RAW TUNA.
OH, I SEE.
SMASH!
TRYIN' TA POISON ME, EH! LET'S SEE YOU EAT SOME GLASS!
YOU LEARN HIM, FRANKY!
WHAT WAS I SAYIN'? OH, YEAH!
WE AIN'T PUTTIN' ON AIRS 'CAUSE WE IS FAMOUS NOW. WE HAS ALWAYS BEEN NATURALLY SOPHISTICATED.
YOU DONE BLED ALL OVER MY MONKEY SUIT!
AIN'T YOU GOT NO BETTER MANNERS THAN TA GO BLEEDIN' ALL OVER A MAN?! I'LL LEARN YOU BUT GOOD!

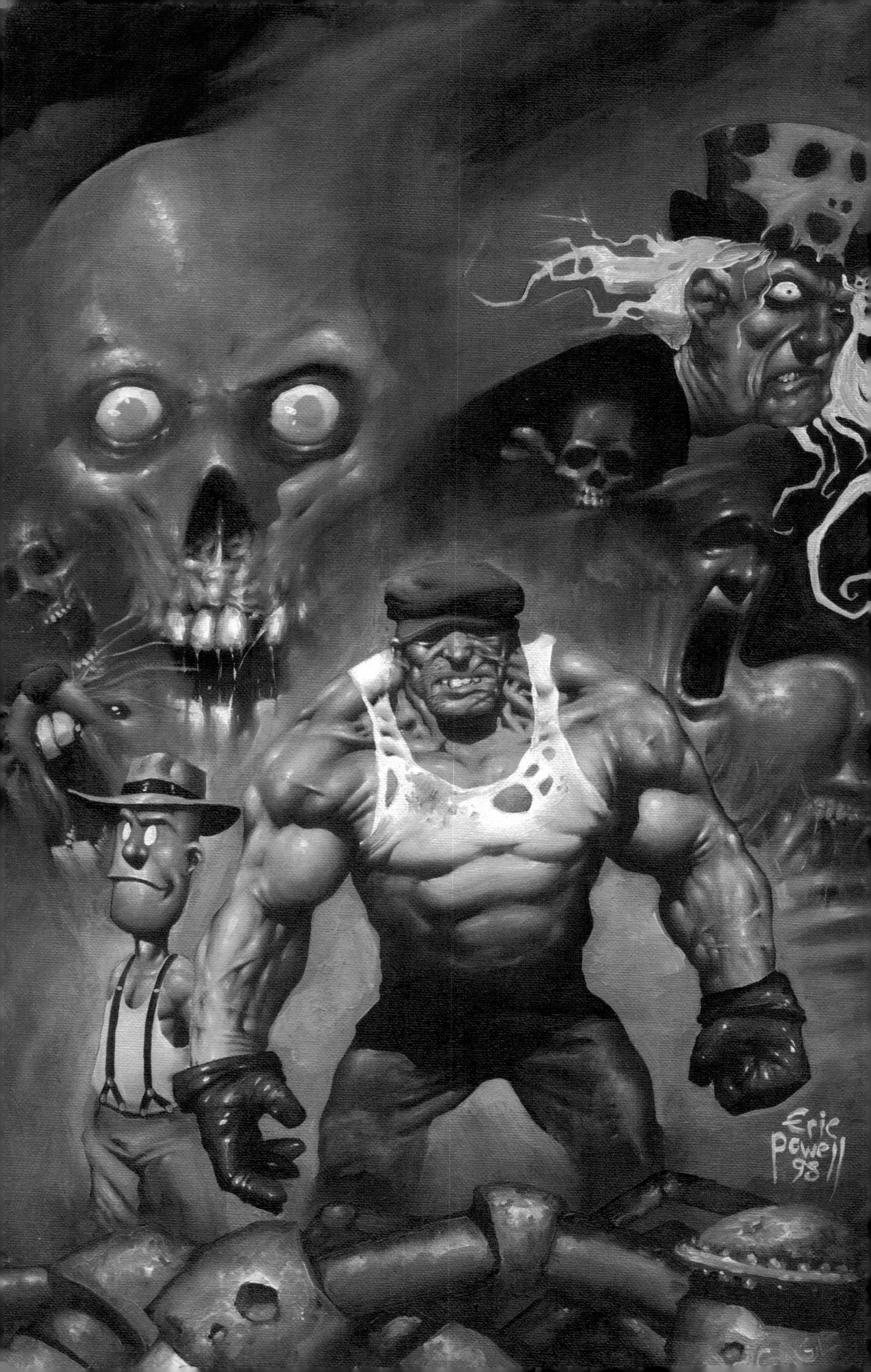
Eric Powell 98

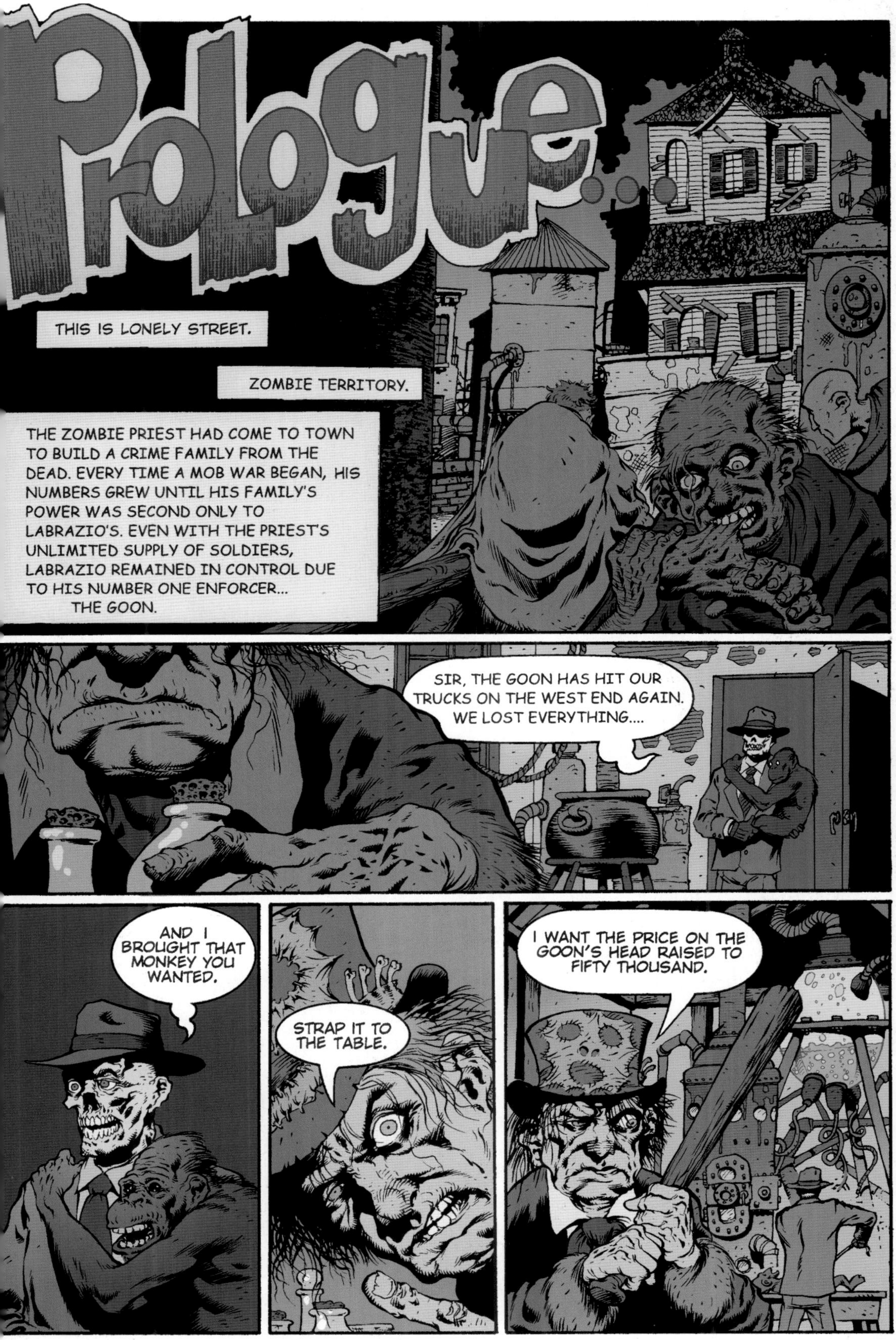
Prologue...
THIS IS LONELY STREET.
ZOMBIE TERRITORY.
THE ZOMBIE PRIEST HAD COME TO TOWN TO BUILD A CRIME FAMILY FROM THE DEAD. EVERY TIME A MOB WAR BEGAN, HIS NUMBERS GREW UNTIL HIS FAMILY'S POWER WAS SECOND ONLY TO LABRAZIO'S. EVEN WITH THE PRIEST'S UNLIMITED SUPPLY OF SOLDIERS, LABRAZIO REMAINED IN CONTROL DUE TO HIS NUMBER ONE ENFORCER... THE GOON.
SIR, THE GOON HAS HIT OUR TRUCKS ON THE WEST END AGAIN. WE LOST EVERYTHING....
AND I BROUGHT THAT MONKEY YOU WANTED.
STRAP IT TO THE TABLE.
I WANT THE PRICE ON THE GOON'S HEAD RAISED TO FIFTY THOUSAND.

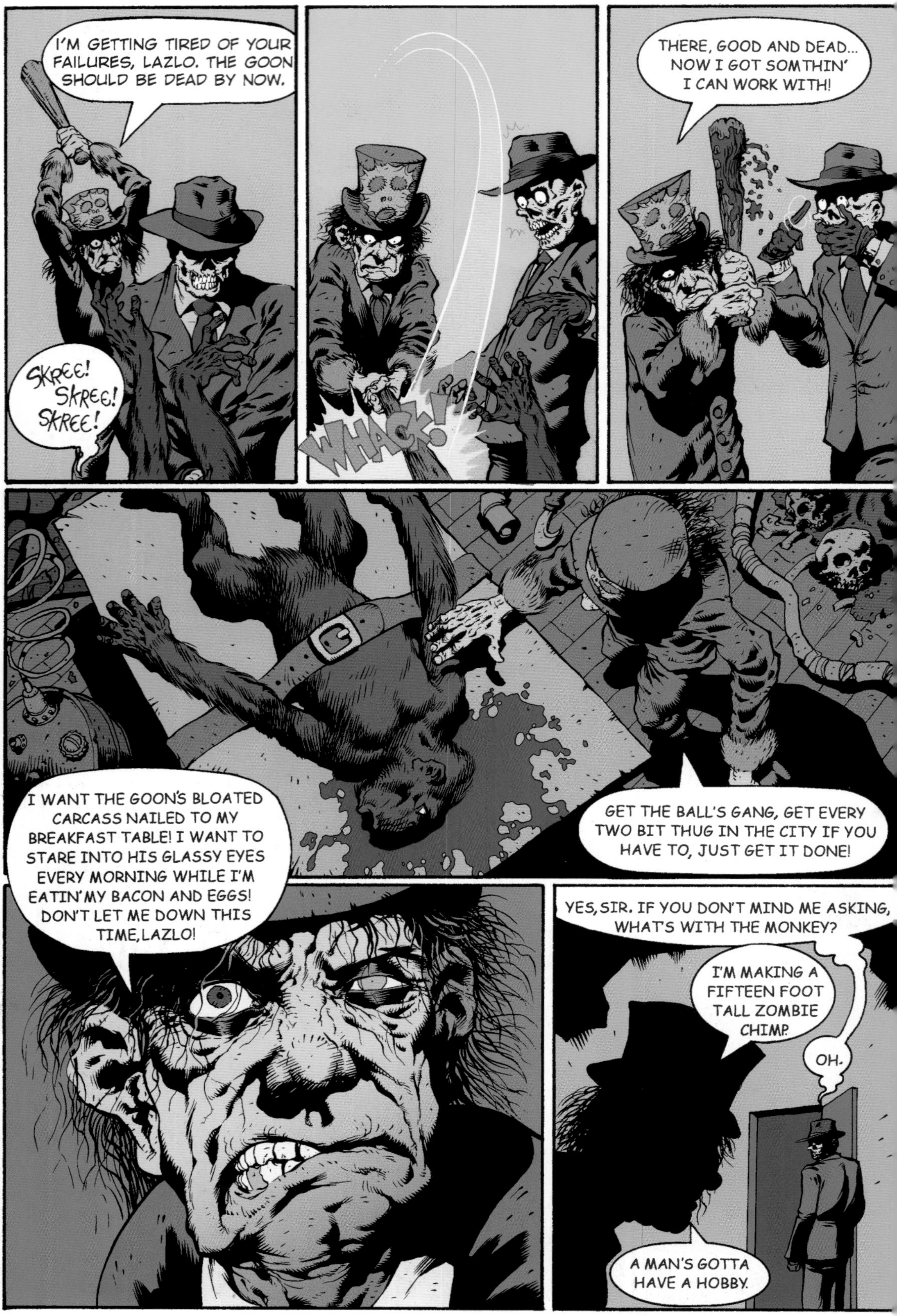
I'M GETTING TIRED OF YOUR FAILURES, LAZLO. THE GOON SHOULD BE DEAD BY NOW.
SKREE! SKREE! SKREE!
WHACK!
THERE, GOOD AND DEAD... NOW I GOT SOMTHIN' I CAN WORK WITH!
GET THE BALL'S GANG, GET EVERY TWO BIT THUG IN THE CITY IF YOU HAVE TO, JUST GET IT DONE!
I WANT THE GOON'S BLOATED CARCASS NAILED TO MY BREAKFAST TABLE! I WANT TO STARE INTO HIS GLASSY EYES EVERY MORNING WHILE I'M EATIN' MY BACON AND EGGS! DON'T LET ME DOWN THIS TIME, LAZLO!
YES, SIR. IF YOU DON'T MIND ME ASKING, WHAT'S WITH THE MONKEY?
I'M MAKING A FIFTEEN FOOT TALL ZOMBIE CHIMP.
OH.
A MAN'S GOTTA HAVE A HOBBY.

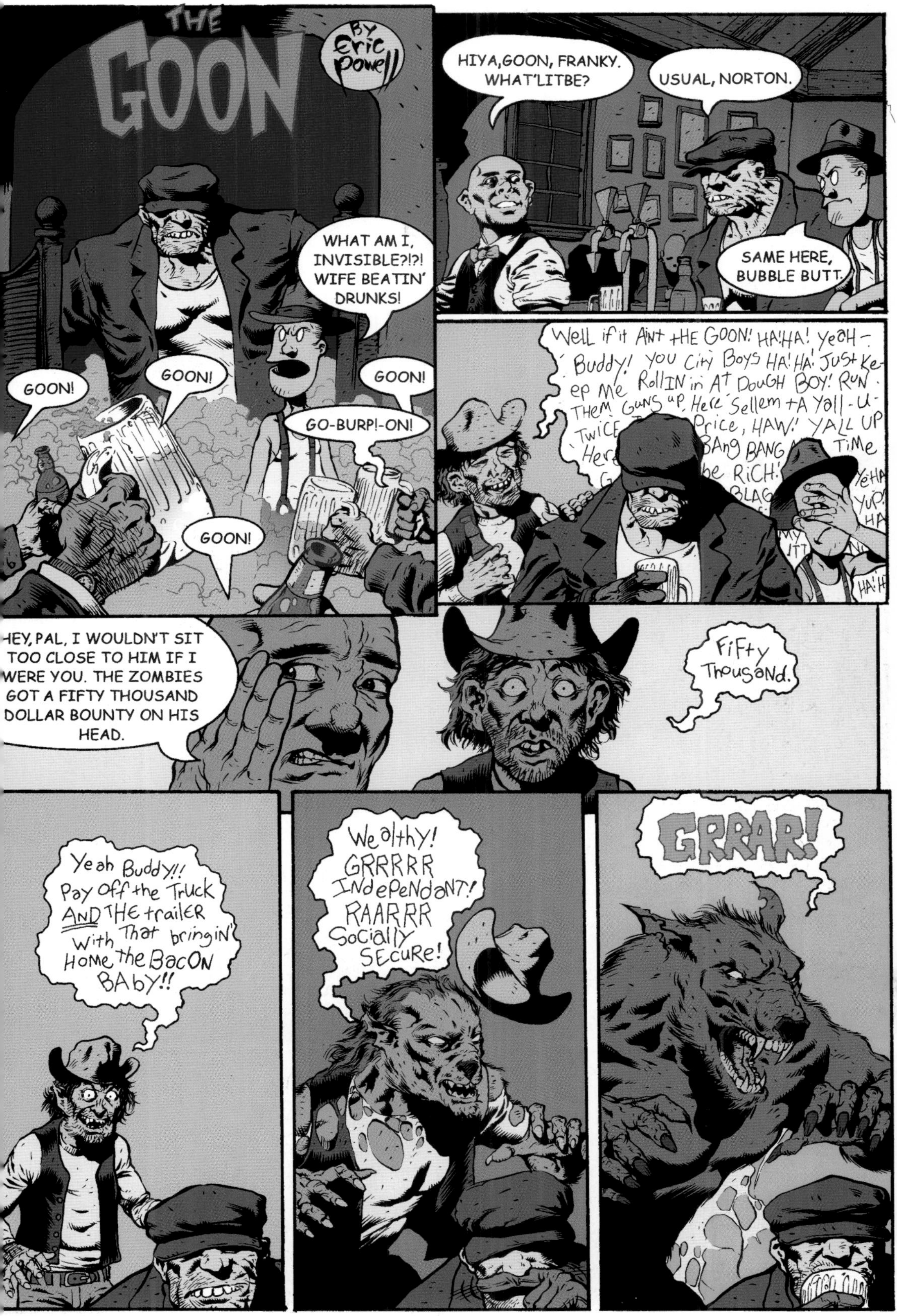
THE GOON
By Eric Powell
WHAT AM I, INVISIBLE?!?! WIFE BEATIN' DRUNKS!
GOON!
GOON!
GOON!
GO-BURP!-ON!
GOON!
HIYA, GOON, FRANKY. WHAT'LITBE?
USUAL, NORTON.
SAME HERE, BUBBLE BUTT.
Well if it Aint the GOON! HA!HA! yeah- Buddy! you City Boys HA! HA! Just keep me Rollin in at Dough Boy! Run them Guns up, Here Sellem tA Yall-u- Twice Price, HAW! YALL UP BAng BANG Time be RiCH!
YeHA YUP! HA
HA! H
HEY, PAL, I WOULDN'T SIT TOO CLOSE TO HIM IF I WERE YOU. THE ZOMBIES GOT A FIFTY THOUSAND DOLLAR BOUNTY ON HIS HEAD.
FiFty Thousand.
Yeah Buddy!! Pay off the Truck AND THE trailer with That bringin' Home the BacON BAby!!
Wealthy! GRRRRR Independant! RAARRR Socially SEcuRe!
GRRAR!

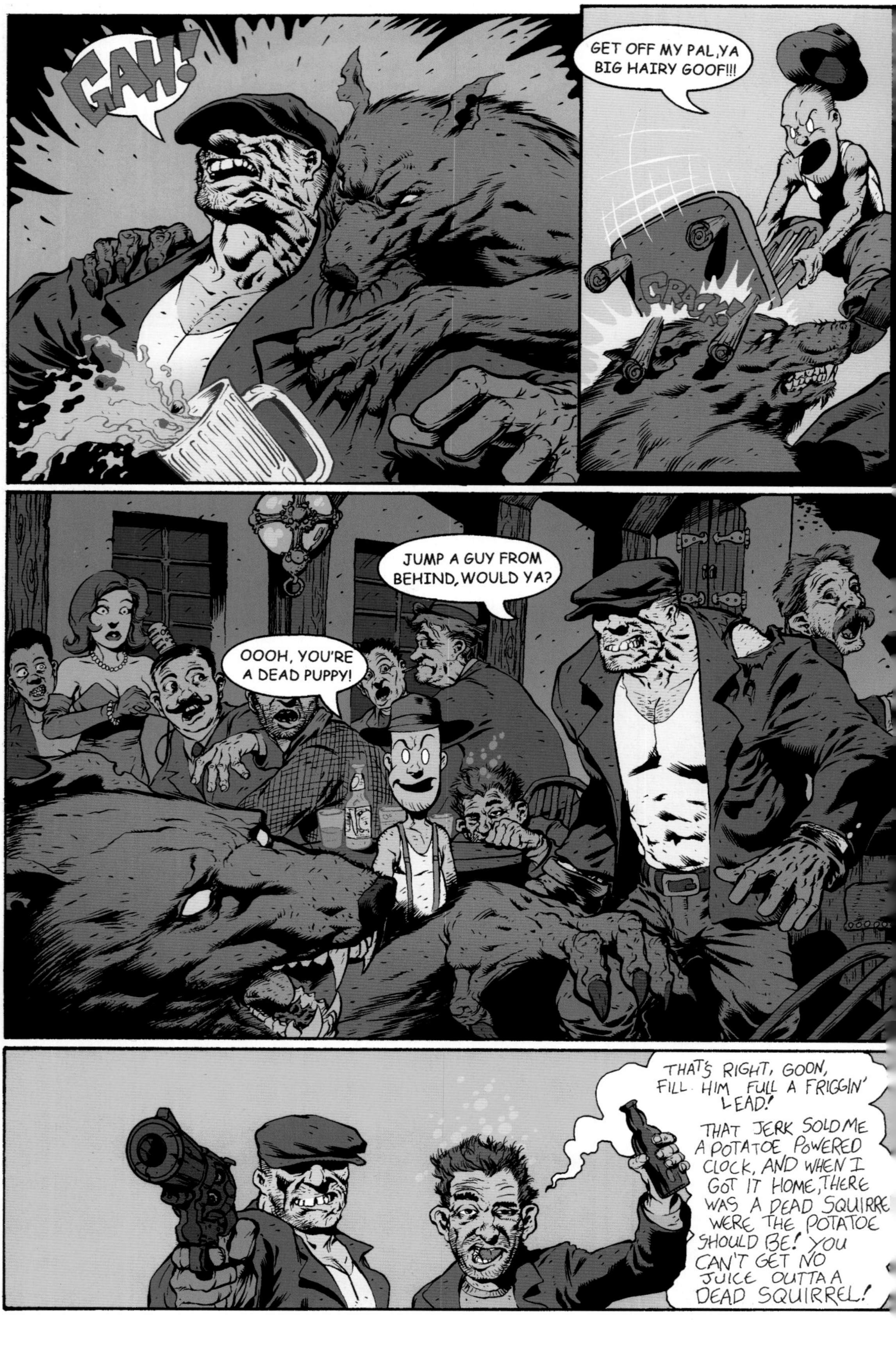
GAH!
GET OFF MY PAL, YA BIG HAIRY GOOF!!!
CRACK!
JUMP A GUY FROM BEHIND, WOULD YA?
OOOH, YOU'RE A DEAD PUPPY!
THAT'S RIGHT, GOON, FILL HIM FULL A FRIGGIN' LEAD!
THAT JERK SOLD ME A POTATOE POWERED CLOCK, AND WHEN I GOT IT HOME, THERE WAS A DEAD SQUIRREL WERE THE POTATOE SHOULD BE! YOU CAN'T GET NO JUICE OUTTA A DEAD SQUIRREL!

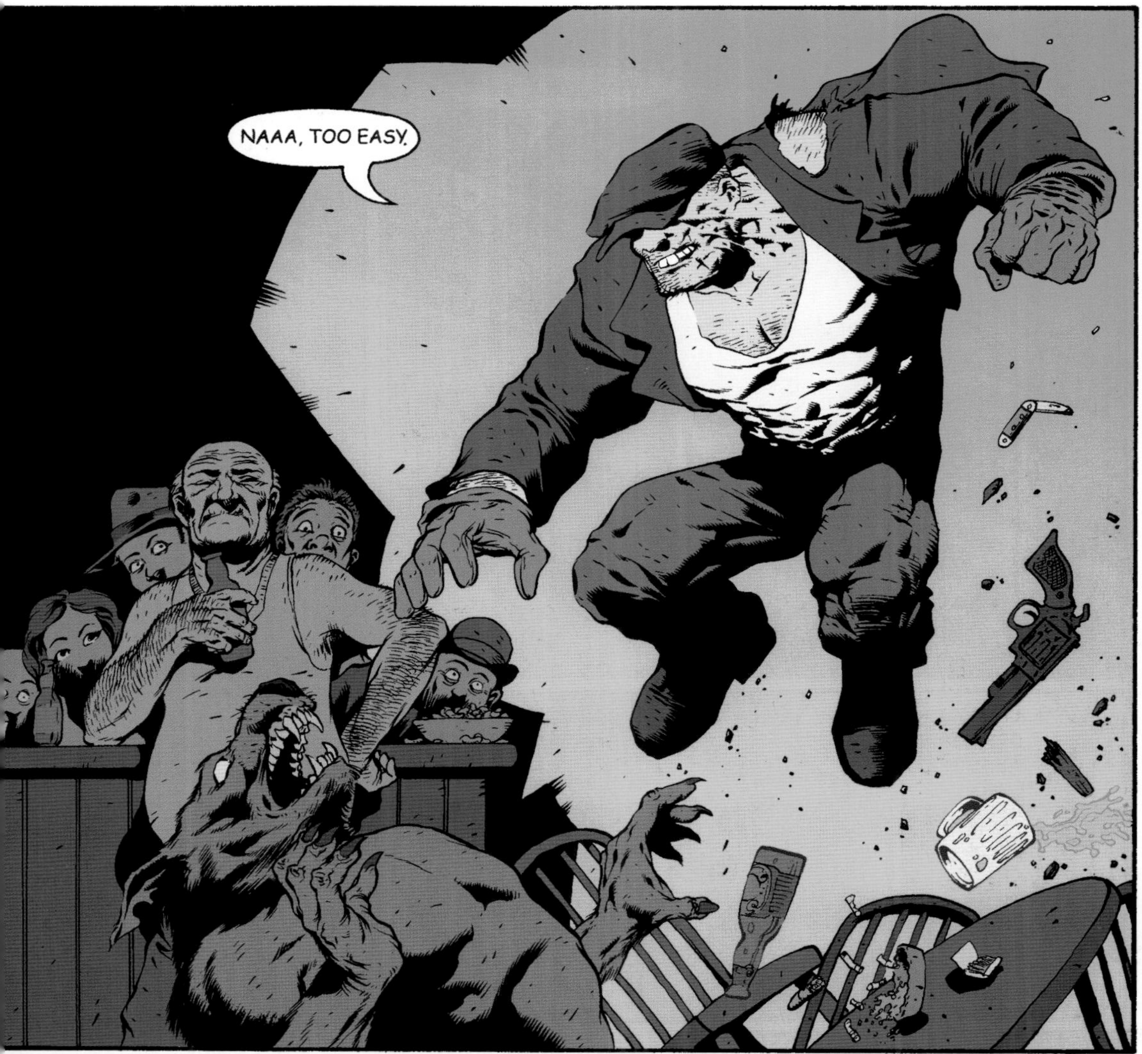
NAAA, TOO EASY.

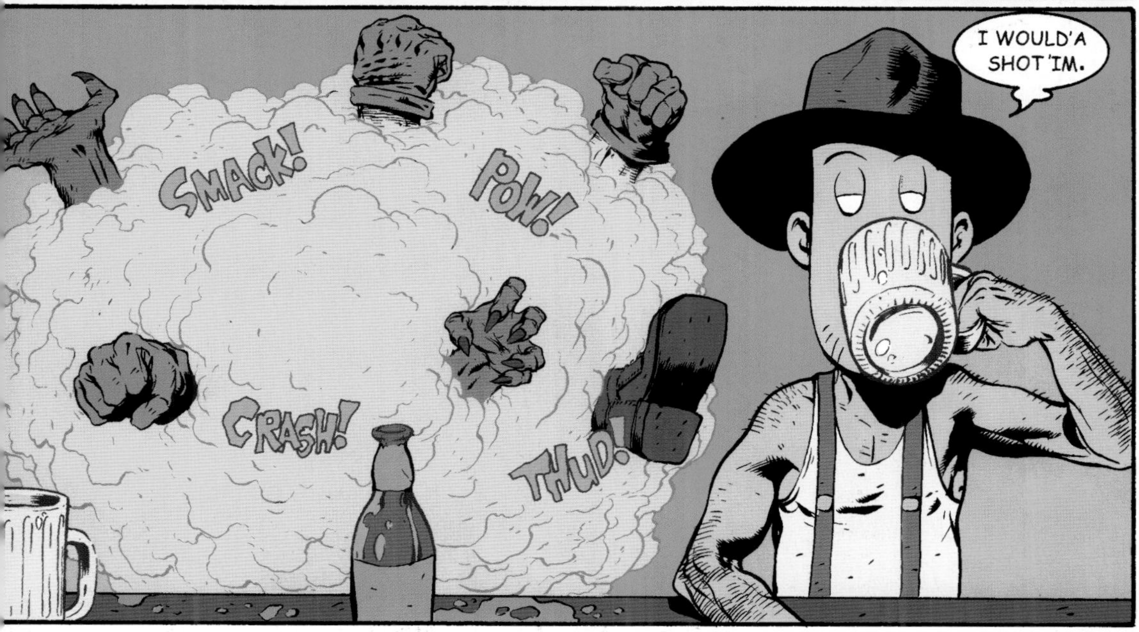
I WOULD'A SHOT 'IM.
SMACK!
POW!
CRASH!
THUD!

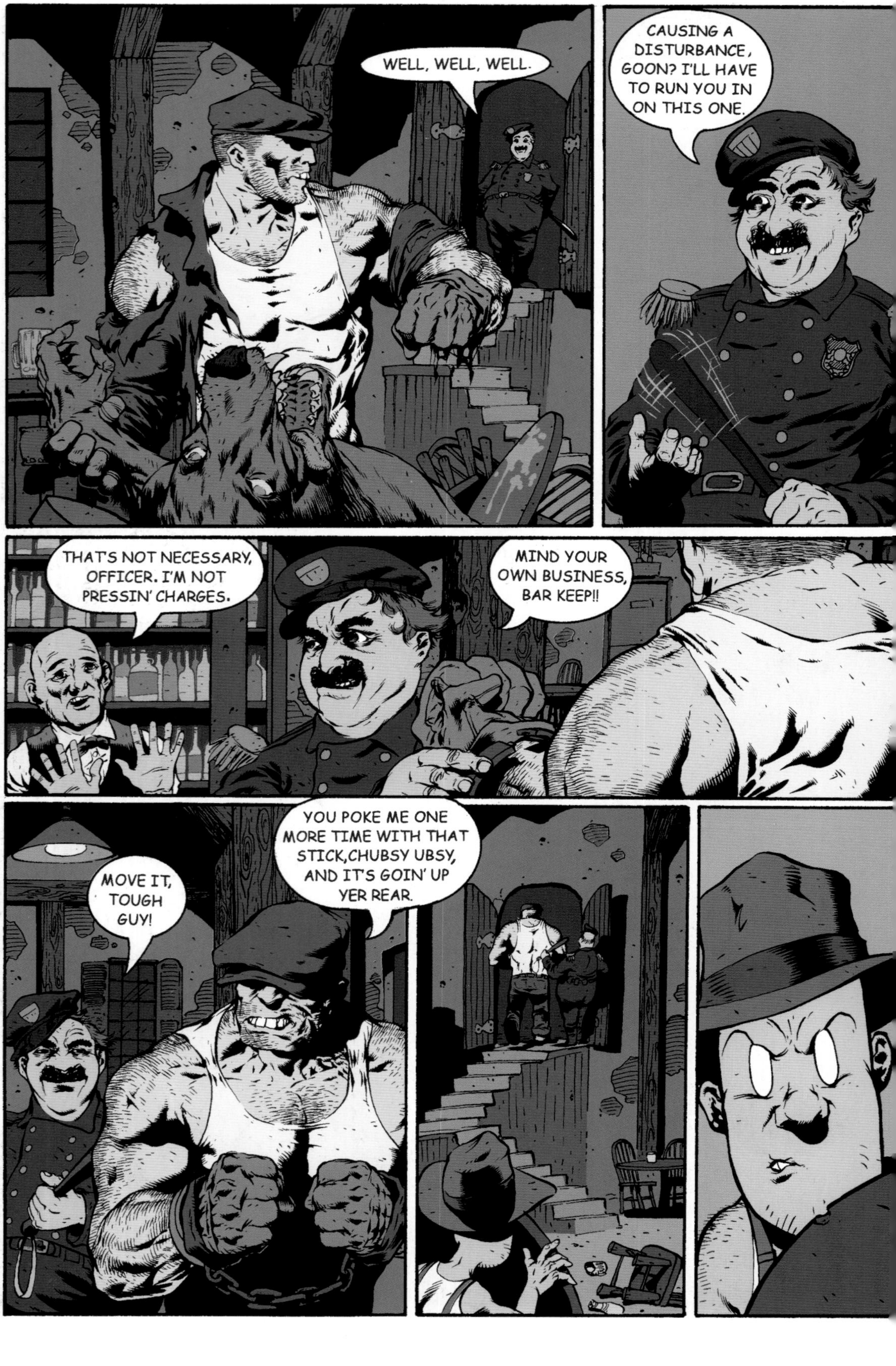
WELL, WELL, WELL.
CAUSING A DISTURBANCE, GOON? I'LL HAVE TO RUN YOU IN ON THIS ONE.
THAT'S NOT NECESSARY, OFFICER. I'M NOT PRESSIN' CHARGES.
MIND YOUR OWN BUSINESS, BAR KEEP!!
MOVE IT, TOUGH GUY!
YOU POKE ME ONE MORE TIME WITH THAT STICK,CHUBSY UBSY, AND IT'S GOIN' UP YER REAR.

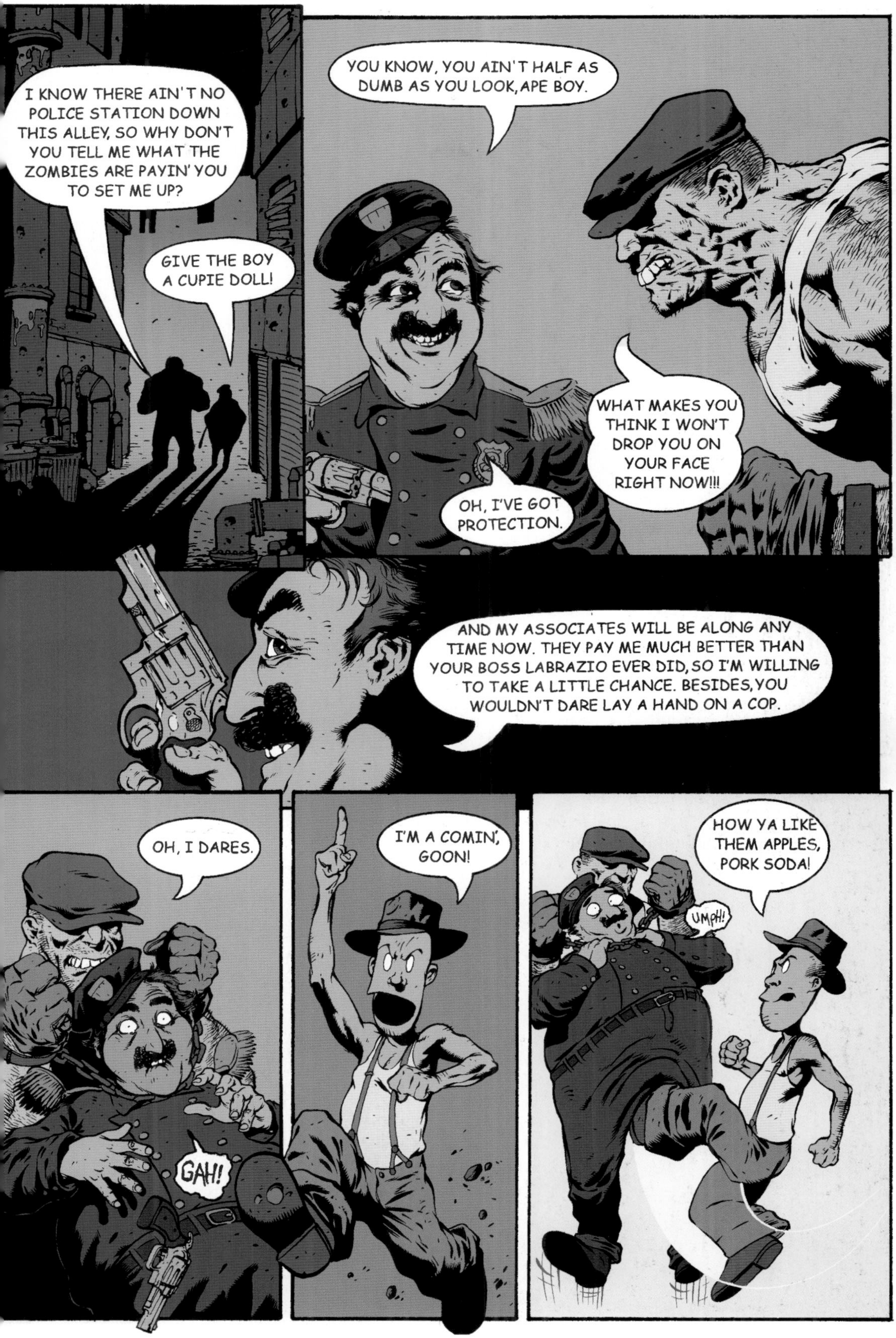
I KNOW THERE AIN'T NO POLICE STATION DOWN THIS ALLEY, SO WHY DON'T YOU TELL ME WHAT THE ZOMBIES ARE PAYIN' YOU TO SET ME UP?
GIVE THE BOY A CUPIE DOLL!
YOU KNOW, YOU AIN'T HALF AS DUMB AS YOU LOOK, APE BOY.
WHAT MAKES YOU THINK I WON'T DROP YOU ON YOUR FACE RIGHT NOW!!!
OH, I'VE GOT PROTECTION.
AND MY ASSOCIATES WILL BE ALONG ANY TIME NOW. THEY PAY ME MUCH BETTER THAN YOUR BOSS LABRAZIO EVER DID, SO I'M WILLING TO TAKE A LITTLE CHANCE. BESIDES, YOU WOULDN'T DARE LAY A HAND ON A COP.
OH, I DARES.
GAH!
I'M A COMIN', GOON!
HOW YA LIKE THEM APPLES, PORK SODA!
UMPH!

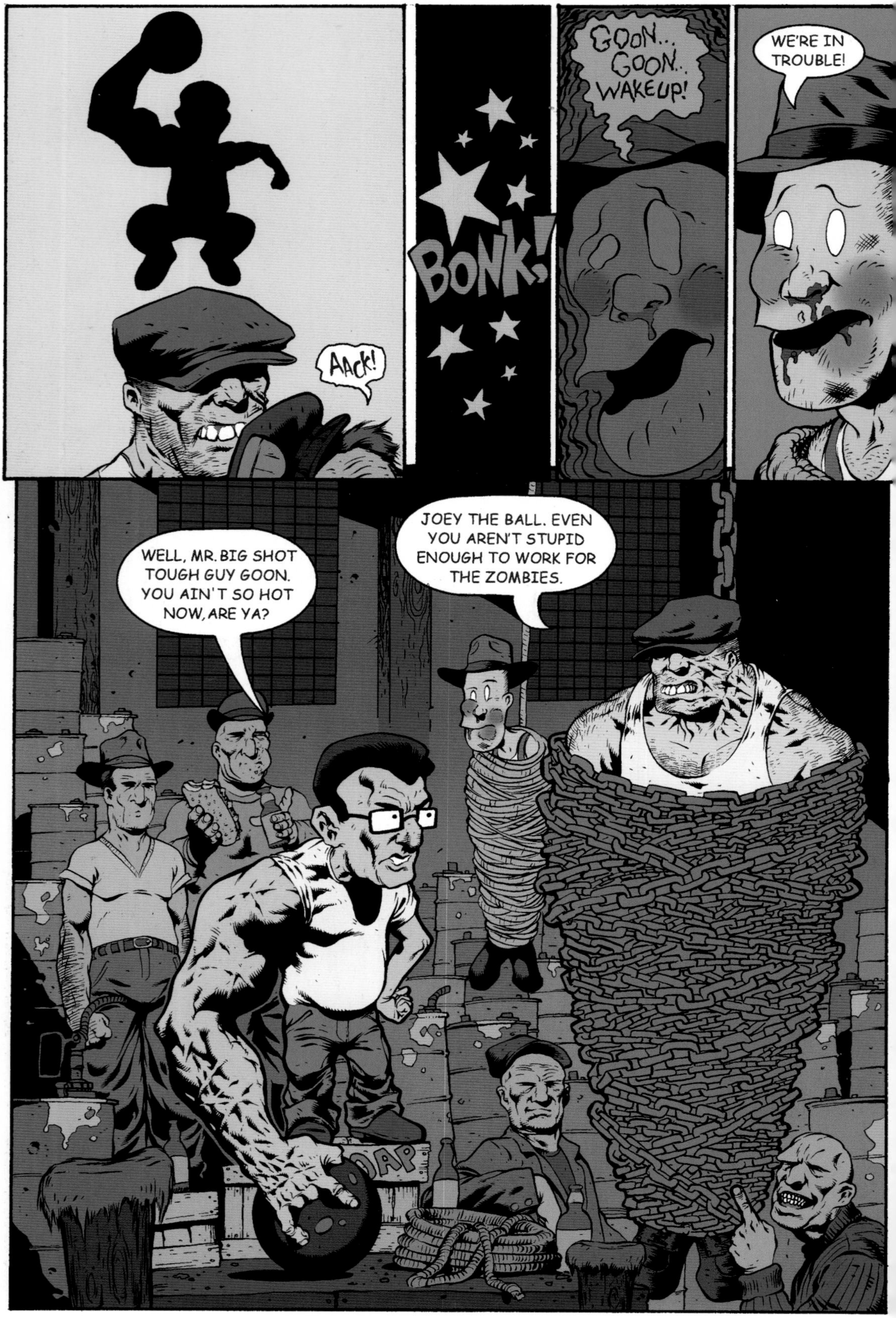
AACK!
BONK!
GOON... GOON.. WAKEUP!
WE'RE IN TROUBLE!
WELL, MR. BIG SHOT TOUGH GUY GOON. YOU AIN'T SO HOT NOW, ARE YA?
JOEY THE BALL. EVEN YOU AREN'T STUPID ENOUGH TO WORK FOR THE ZOMBIES.

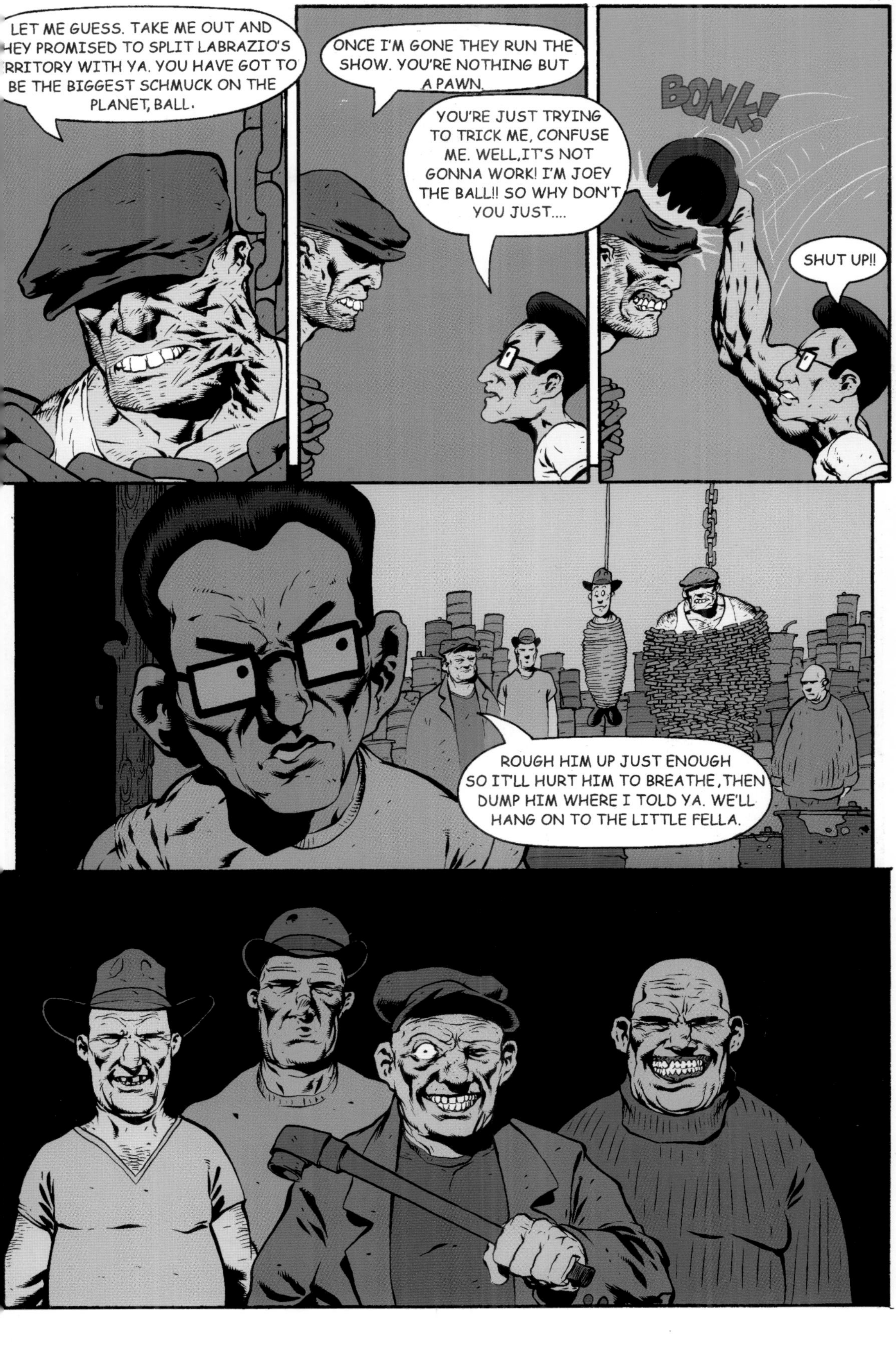
LET ME GUESS. TAKE ME OUT AND HEY PROMISED TO SPLIT LABRAZIO'S RRITORY WITH YA. YOU HAVE GOT TO BE THE BIGGEST SCHMUCK ON THE PLANET, BALL.
ONCE I'M GONE THEY RUN THE SHOW. YOU'RE NOTHING BUT A PAWN.
YOU'RE JUST TRYING TO TRICK ME, CONFUSE ME. WELL, IT'S NOT GONNA WORK! I'M JOEY THE BALL!! SO WHY DON'T YOU JUST....
BONK!
SHUT UP!!
ROUGH HIM UP JUST ENOUGH SO IT'LL HURT HIM TO BREATHE, THEN DUMP HIM WHERE I TOLD YA. WE'LL HANG ON TO THE LITTLE FELLA.

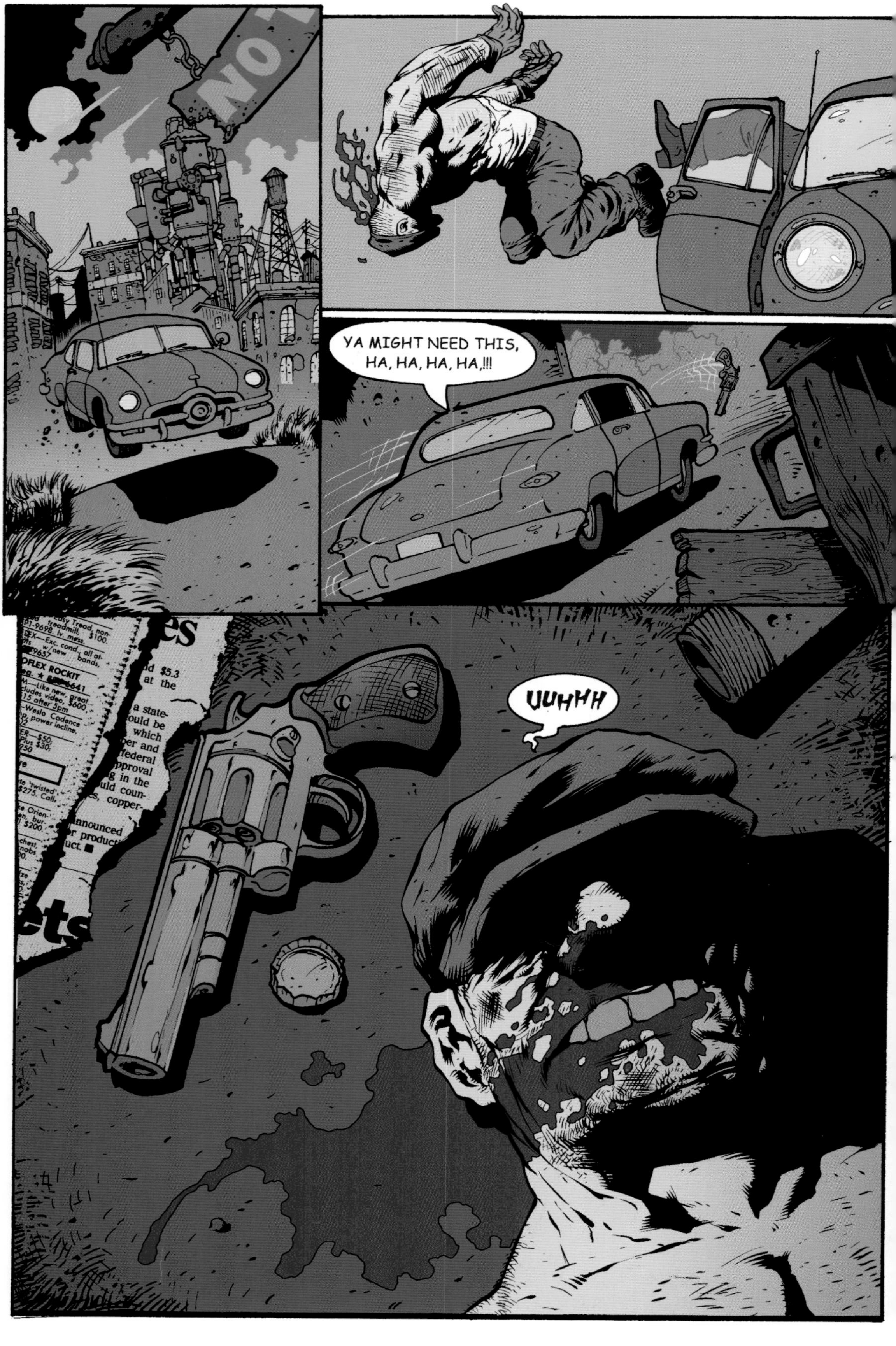
YA MIGHT NEED THIS, HA, HA, HA, HA,!!!
UUHHH

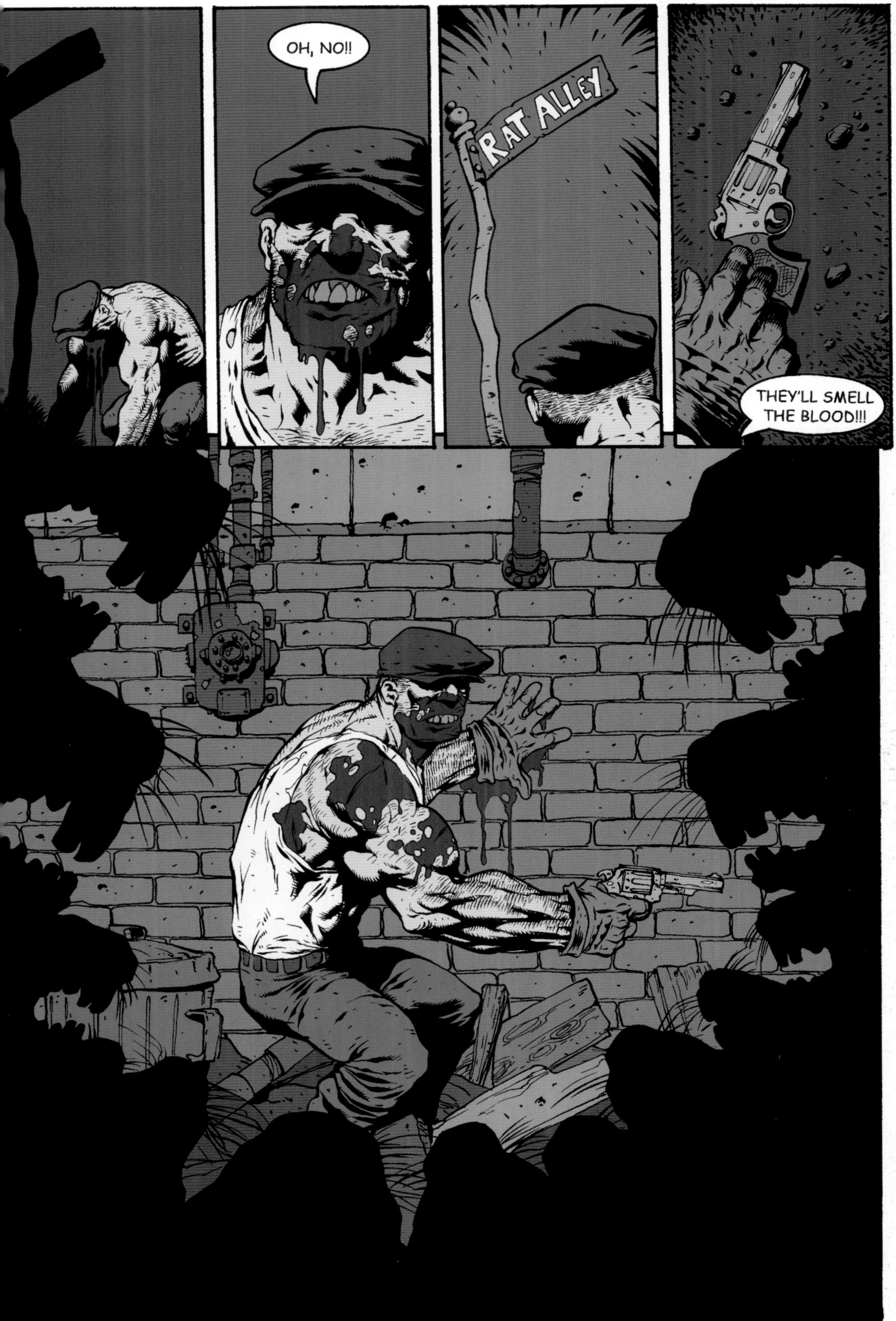
OH, NO!!
RAT ALLEY
THEY'LL SMELL THE BLOOD!!!

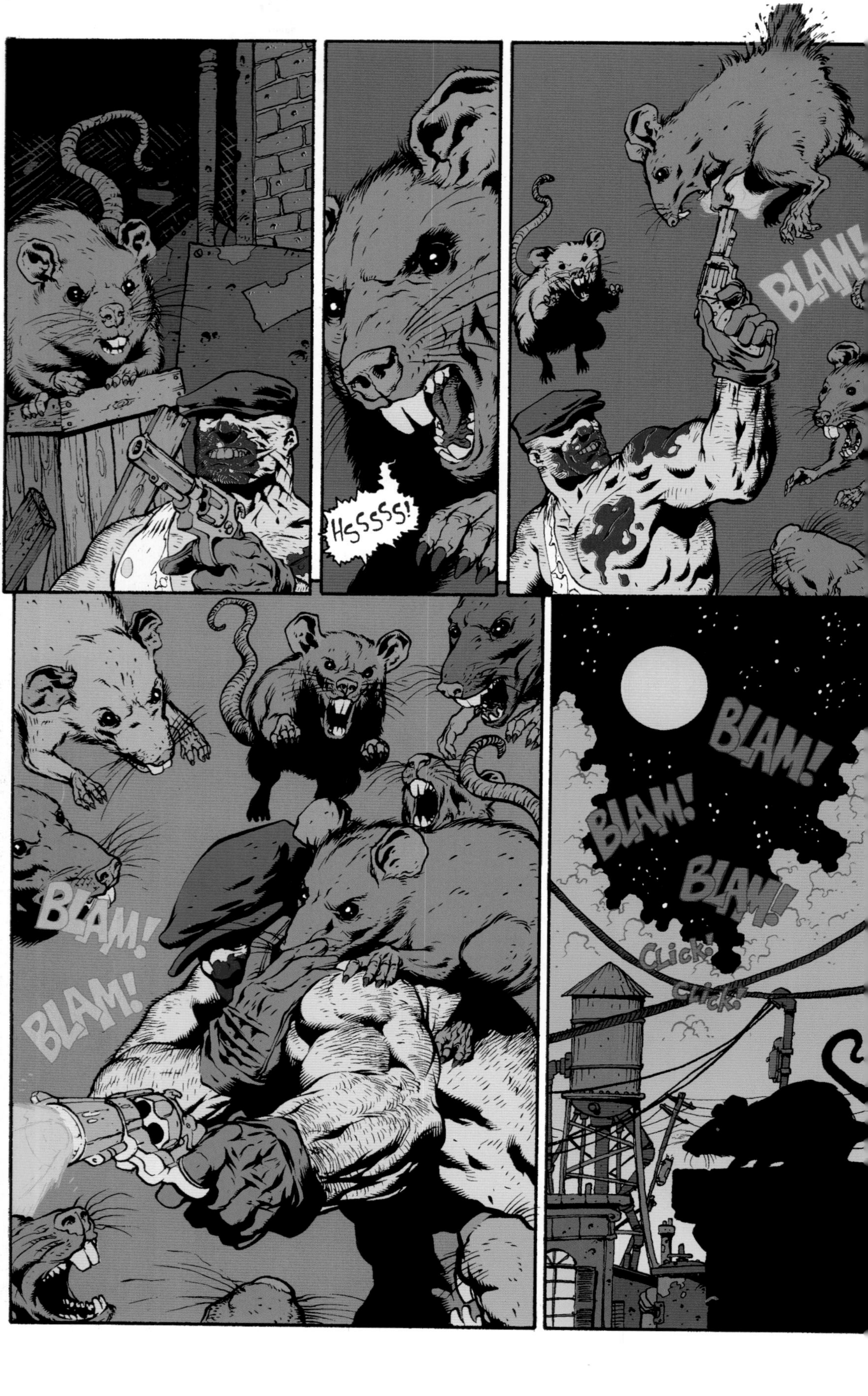

HSSSSS!
BLAM!
BLAM!
BLAM!
BLAM!
BLAM!
BLAM!
CLICK!
CLICK!

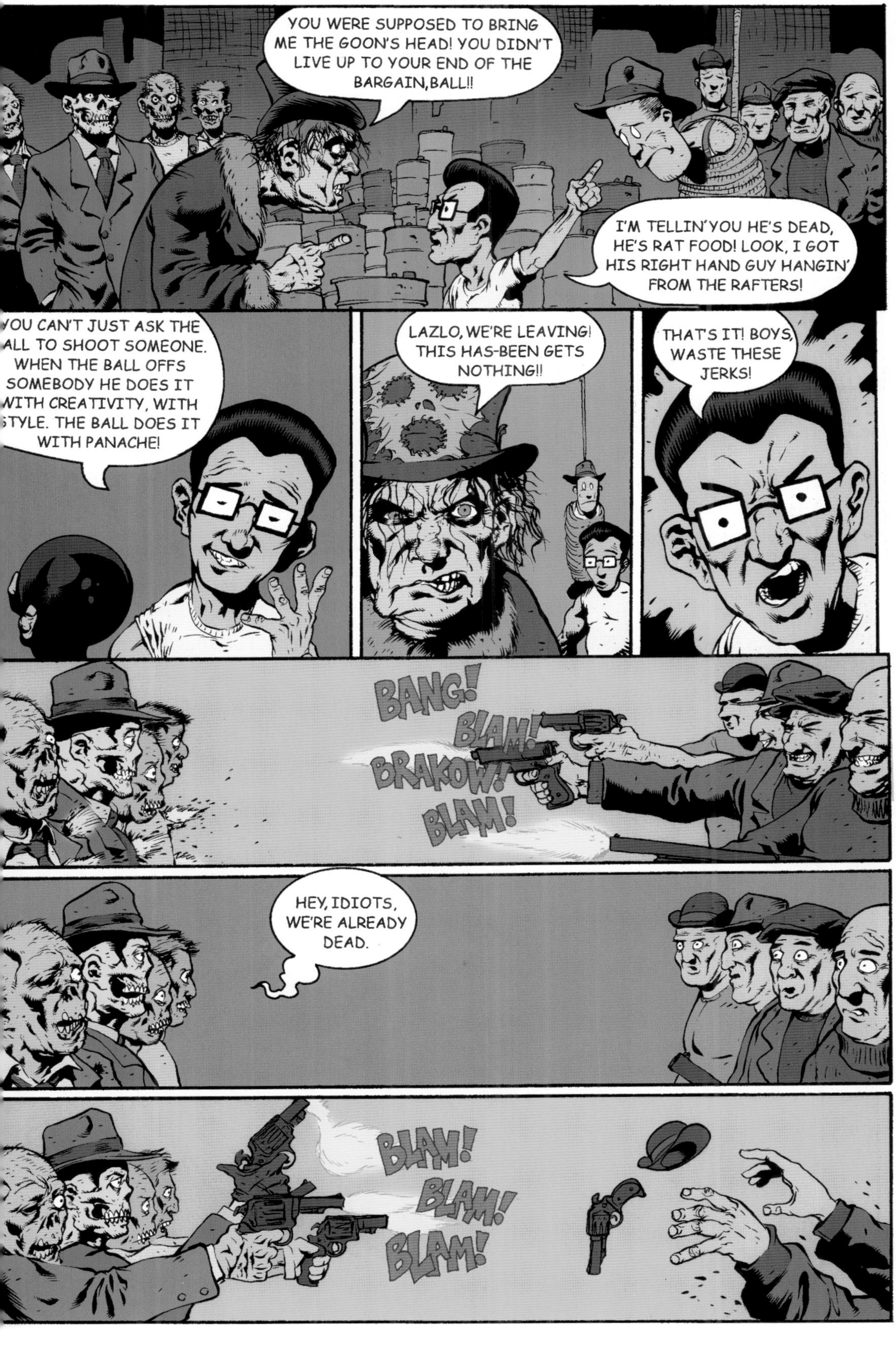
YOU WERE SUPPOSED TO BRING ME THE GOON'S HEAD! YOU DIDN'T LIVE UP TO YOUR END OF THE BARGAIN, BALL!!
I'M TELLIN' YOU HE'S DEAD, HE'S RAT FOOD! LOOK, I GOT HIS RIGHT HAND GUY HANGIN' FROM THE RAFTERS!
YOU CAN'T JUST ASK THE BALL TO SHOOT SOMEONE. WHEN THE BALL OFFS SOMEBODY HE DOES IT WITH CREATIVITY, WITH STYLE. THE BALL DOES IT WITH PANACHE!
LAZLO, WE'RE LEAVING! THIS HAS-BEEN GETS NOTHING!!
THAT'S IT! BOYS, WASTE THESE JERKS!
BANG!
BLAM!
BRAKOW!
BLAM!
HEY, IDIOTS, WE'RE ALREADY DEAD.
BLAM!
BLAM!
BLAM!

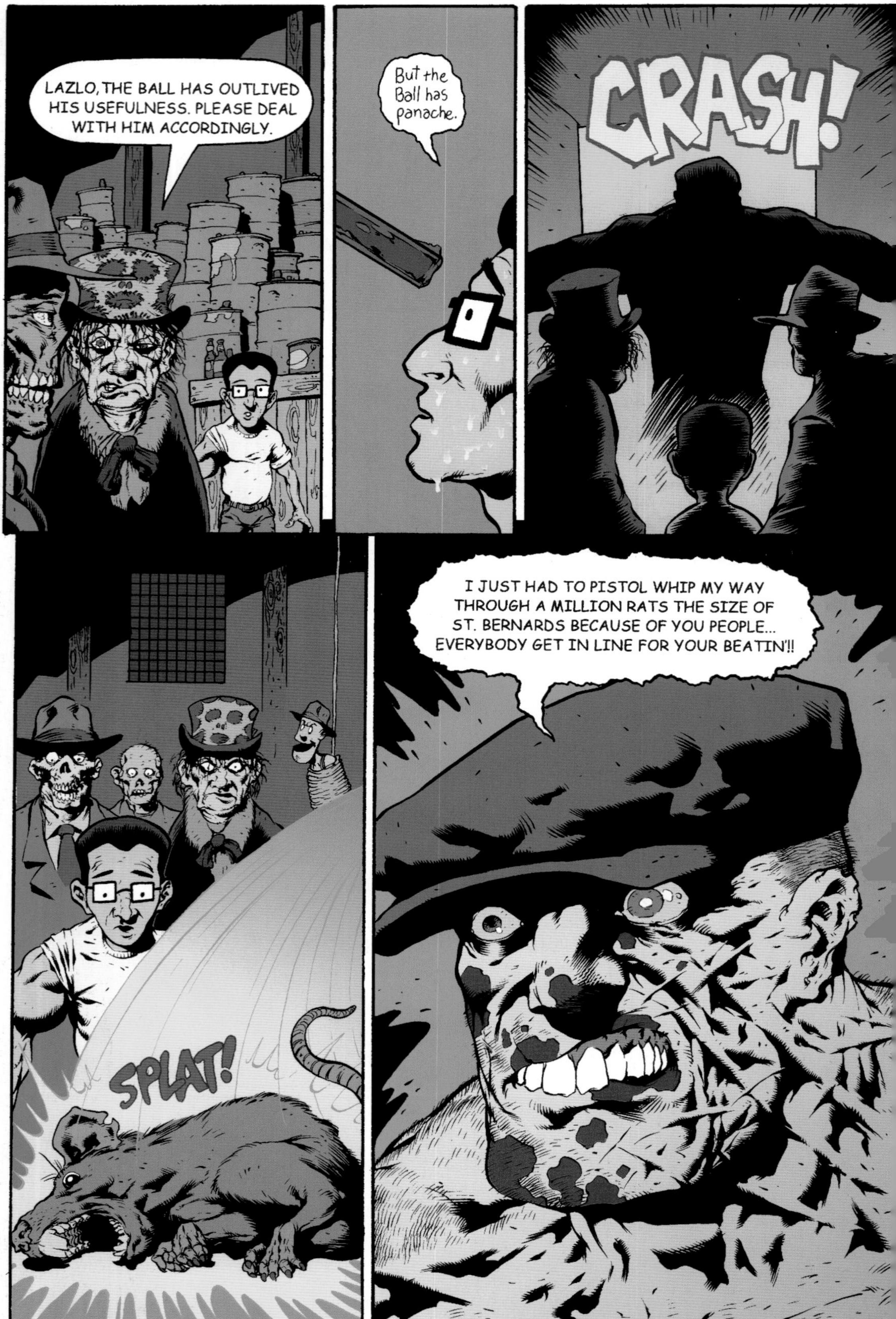
LAZLO, THE BALL HAS OUTLIVED HIS USEFULNESS. PLEASE DEAL WITH HIM ACCORDINGLY.
But the Ball has panache.
CRASH!
SPLAT!
I JUST HAD TO PISTOL WHIP MY WAY THROUGH A MILLION RATS THE SIZE OF ST. BERNARDS BECAUSE OF YOU PEOPLE... EVERYBODY GET IN LINE FOR YOUR BEATIN'!!

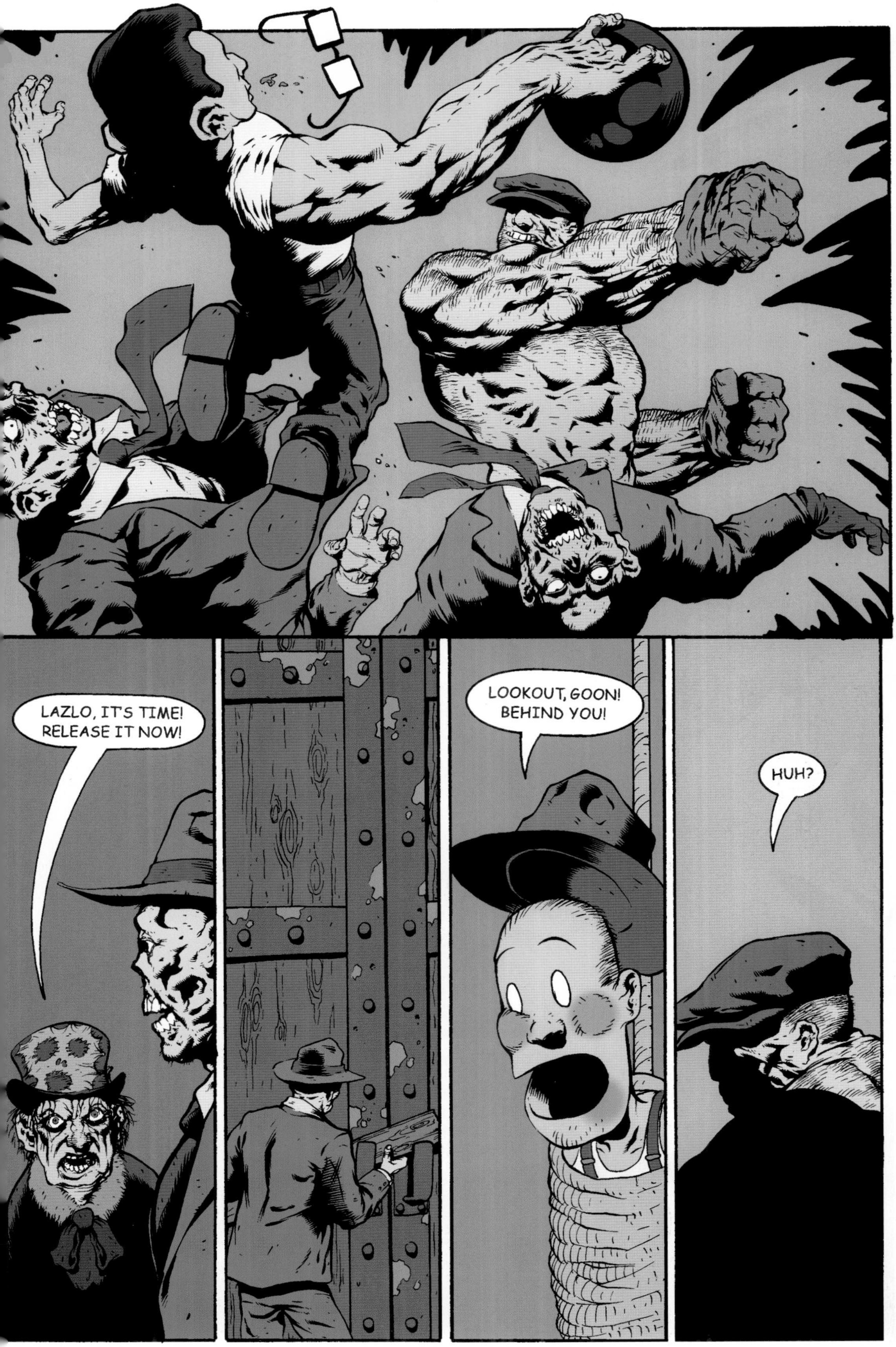
LAZLO, IT'S TIME! RELEASE IT NOW!
LOOKOUT, GOON! BEHIND YOU!
HUH?

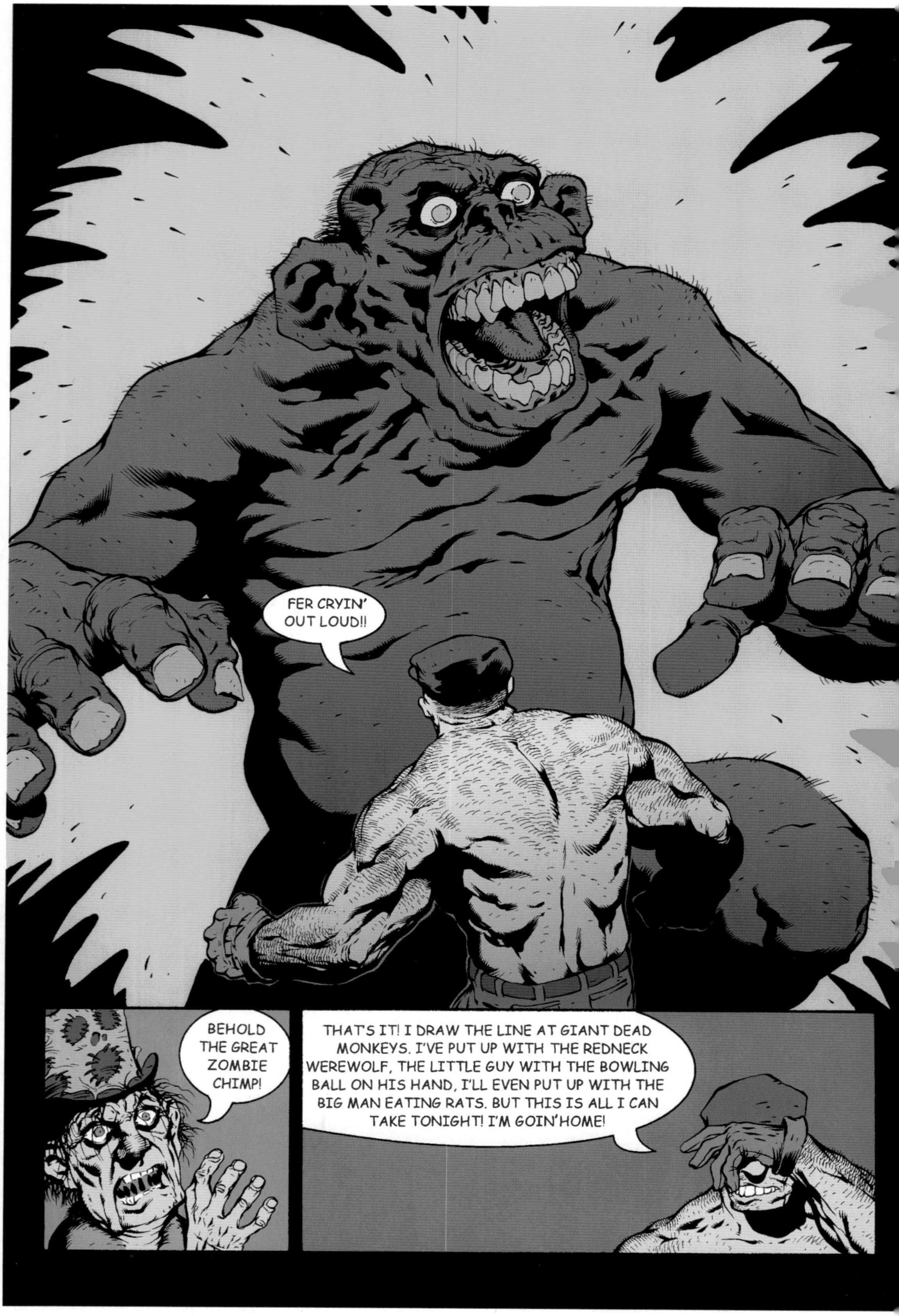
FER CRYIN' OUT LOUD!!
BEHOLD THE GREAT ZOMBIE CHIMP!
THAT'S IT! I DRAW THE LINE AT GIANT DEAD MONKEYS. I'VE PUT UP WITH THE REDNECK WEREWOLF, THE LITTLE GUY WITH THE BOWLING BALL ON HIS HAND, I'LL EVEN PUT UP WITH THE BIG MAN EATING RATS. BUT THIS IS ALL I CAN TAKE TONIGHT! I'M GOIN' HOME!

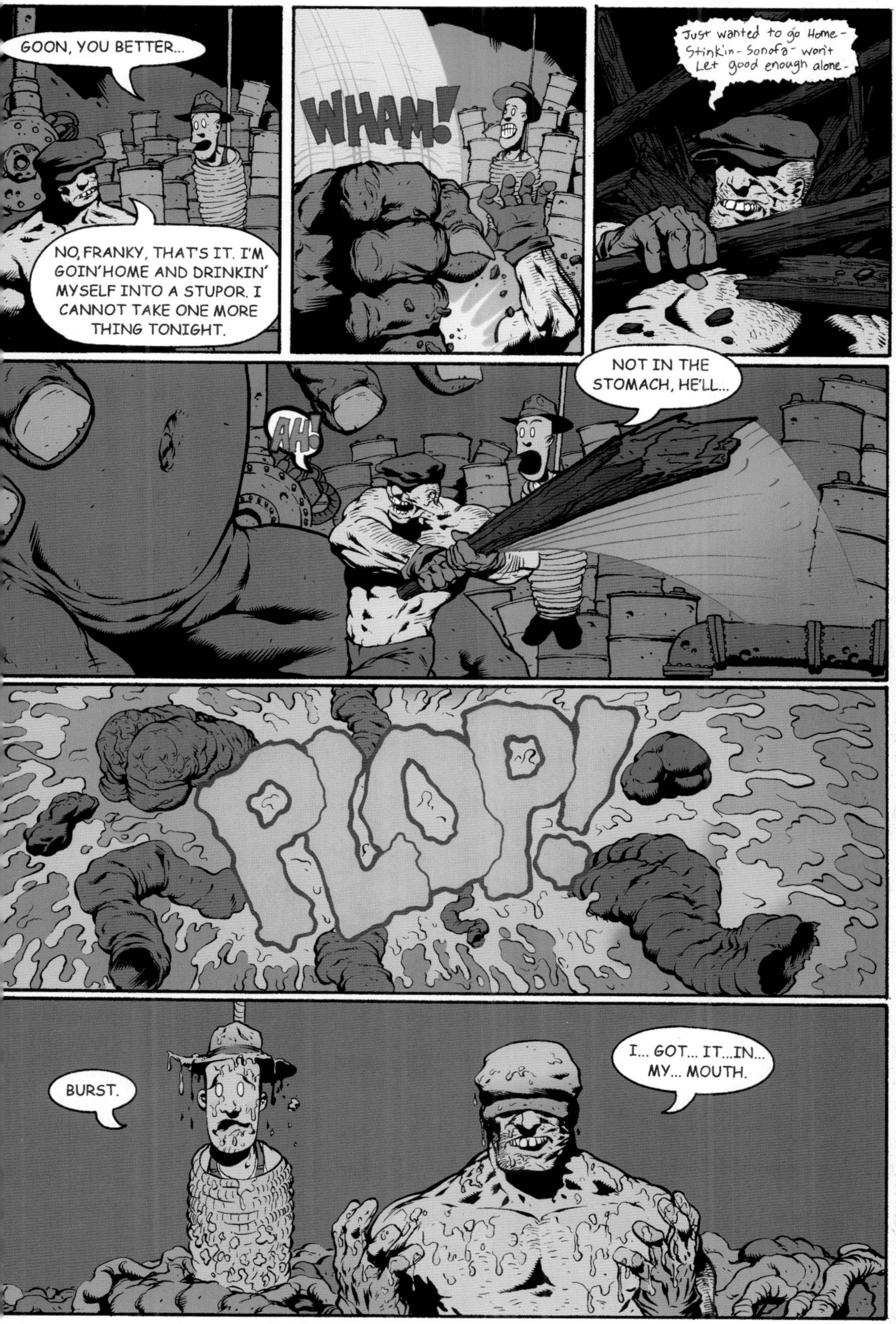
GOON, YOU BETTER...
NO, FRANKY, THAT'S IT. I'M GOIN' HOME AND DRINKIN' MYSELF INTO A STUPOR. I CANNOT TAKE ONE MORE THING TONIGHT.
WHAM!
Just wanted to go Home- Stinkin- Sonofa- won't Let good enough alone-
NOT IN THE STOMACH, HE'LL...
AH!
PLOP!
BURST.
I... GOT... IT...IN... MY... MOUTH.

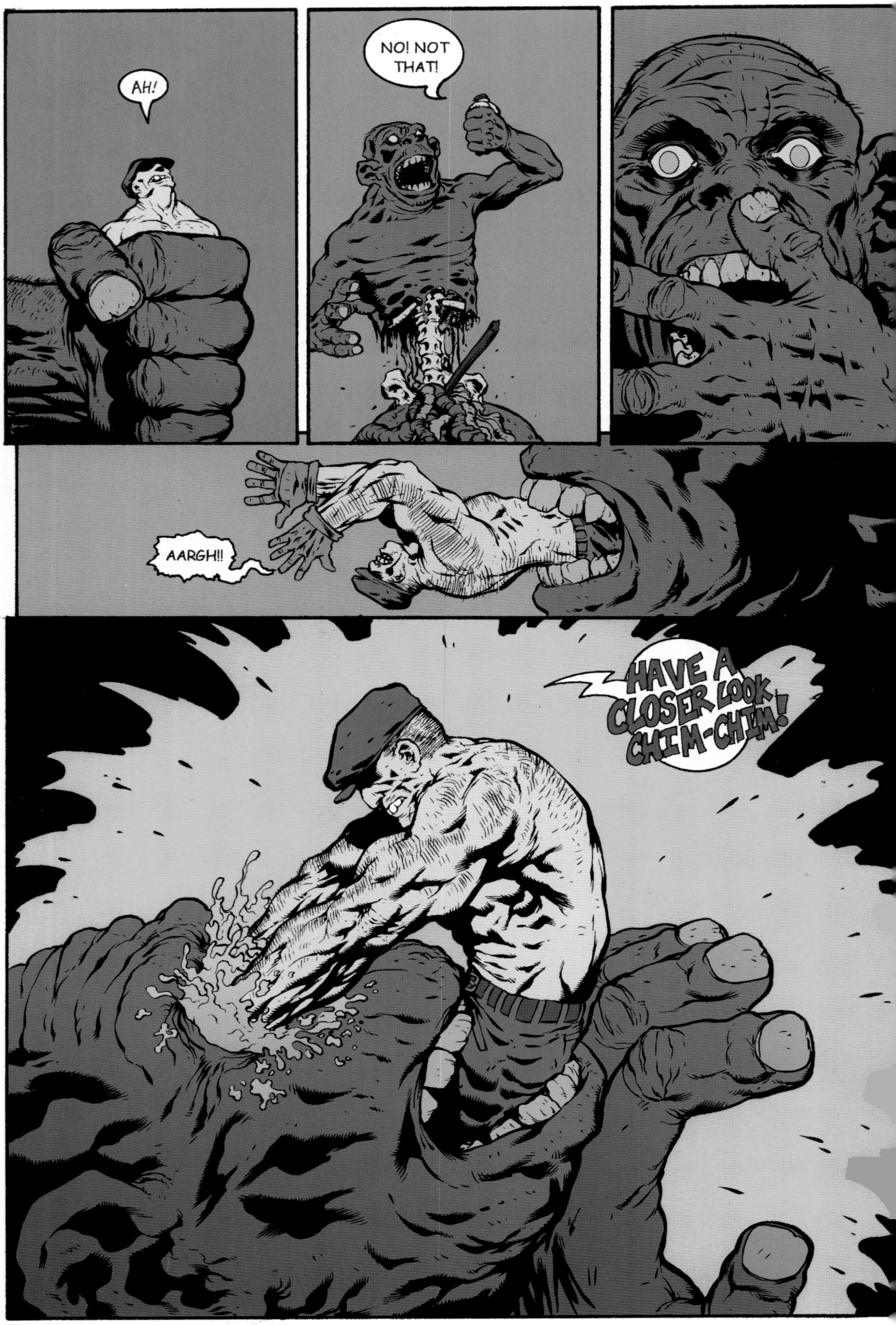
AH!
NO! NOT THAT!
AARGH!!
HAVE A CLOSER LOOK CHIM-CHIM!

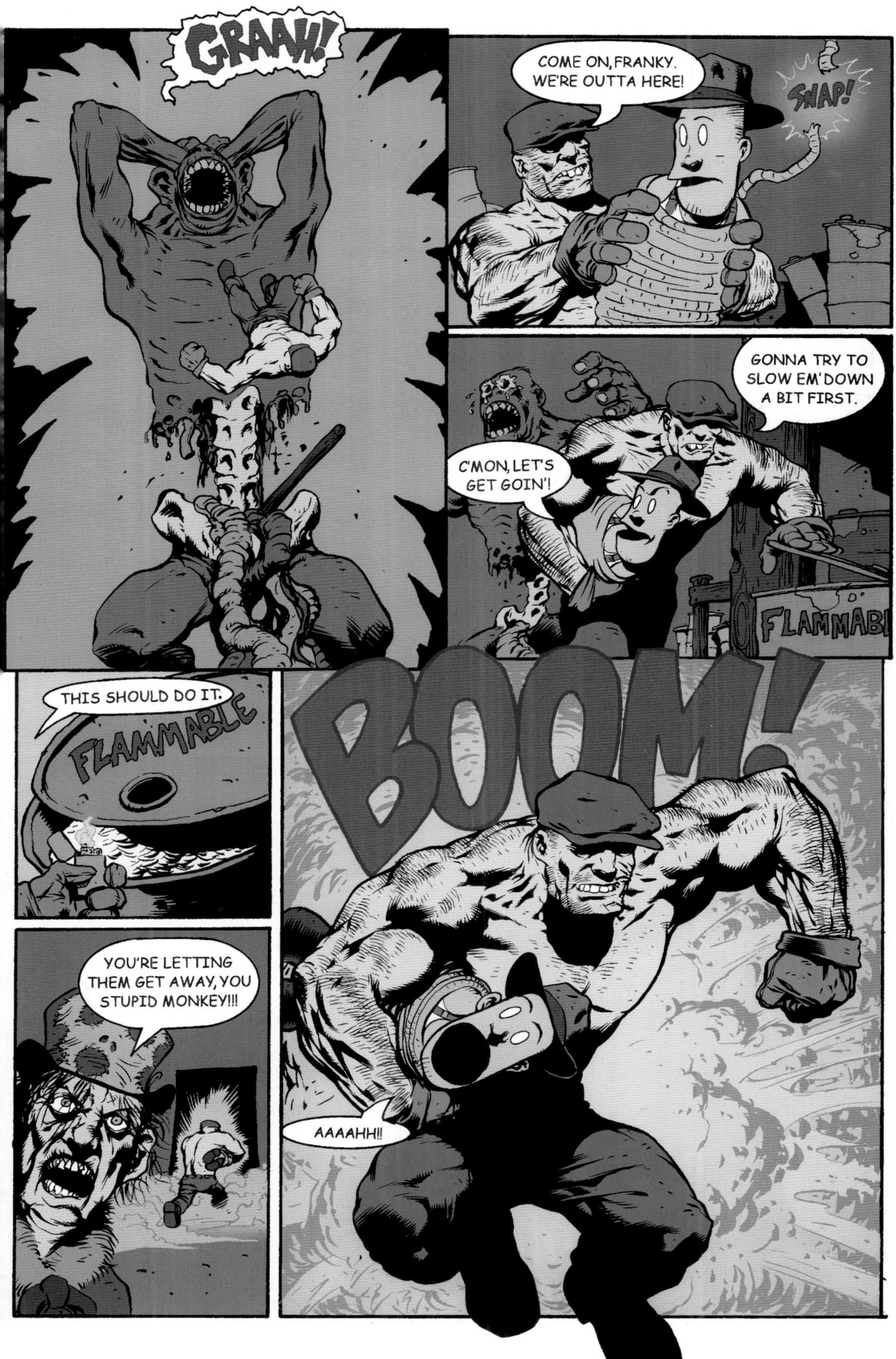
GRAAH!
COME ON, FRANKY. WE'RE OUTTA HERE!
SNAP!
GONNA TRY TO SLOW EM' DOWN A BIT FIRST.
C'MON, LET'S GET GOIN'!
FLAMMABL
THIS SHOULD DO IT.
FLAMMABLE
YOU'RE LETTING THEM GET AWAY, YOU STUPID MONKEY!!!
BOOM!
AAAAHH!!

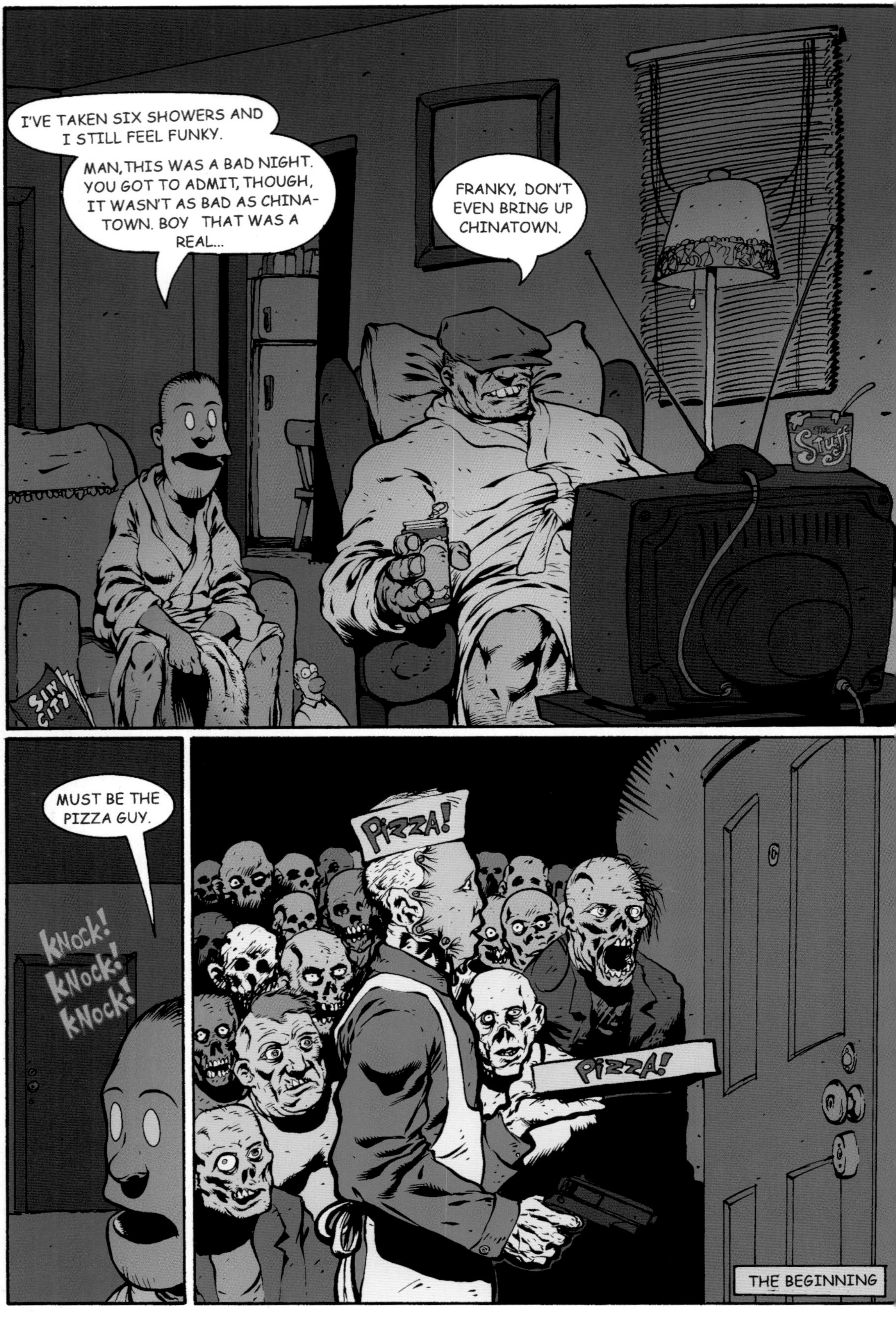
I'VE TAKEN SIX SHOWERS AND I STILL FEEL FUNKY.
MAN, THIS WAS A BAD NIGHT. YOU GOT TO ADMIT, THOUGH, IT WASN'T AS BAD AS CHINA-TOWN. BOY THAT WAS A REAL...
FRANKY, DON'T EVEN BRING UP CHINATOWN.
SIN CITY
MUST BE THE PIZZA GUY.
KNOCK! KNOCK! KNOCK!
PIZZA!
PIZZA!
THE BEGINNING

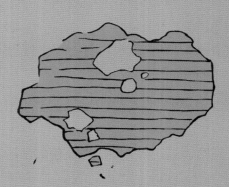
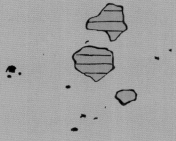

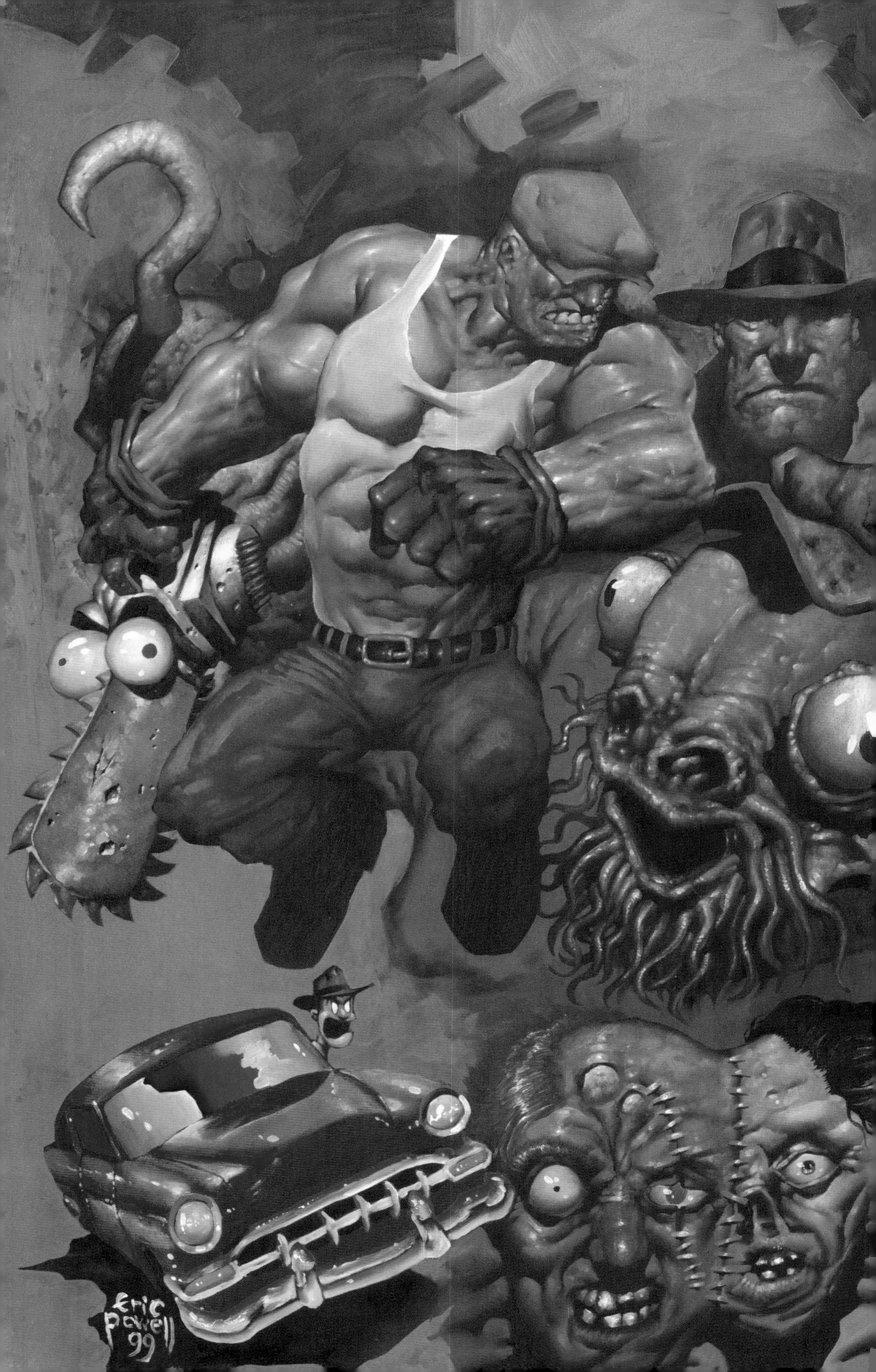
Eric
Powell
99

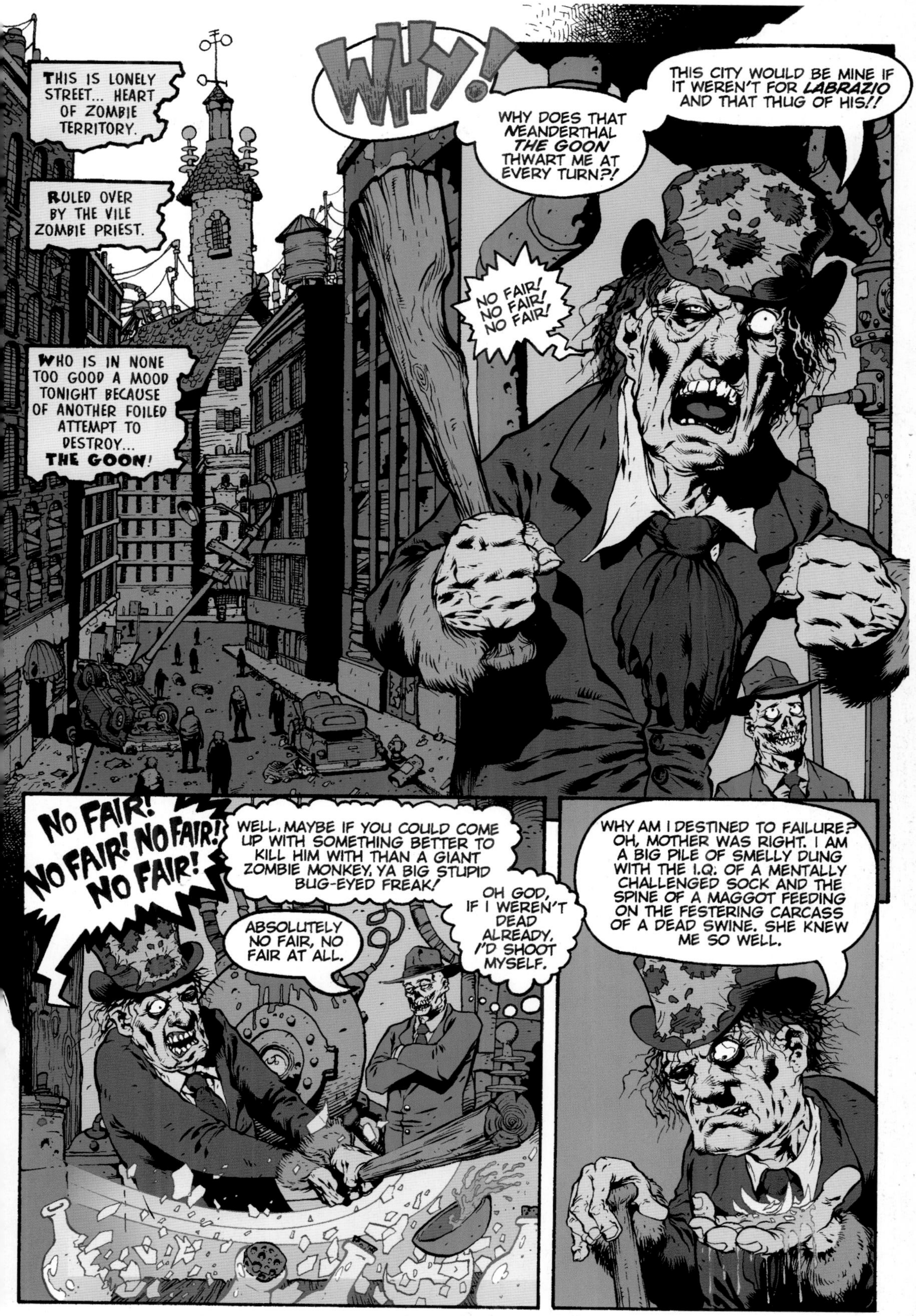
THIS IS LONELY STREET... HEART OF ZOMBIE TERRITORY.
RULED OVER BY THE VILE ZOMBIE PRIEST.
WHO IS IN NONE TOO GOOD A MOOD TONIGHT BECAUSE OF ANOTHER FOILED ATTEMPT TO DESTROY... THE GOON!
WHY!
WHY DOES THAT NEANDERTHAL THE GOON THWART ME AT EVERY TURN?!
THIS CITY WOULD BE MINE IF IT WEREN'T FOR LABRAZIO AND THAT THUG OF HIS!!
NO FAIR! NO FAIR! NO FAIR!
NO FAIR! NO FAIR! NO FAIR! NO FAIR!
WELL, MAYBE IF YOU COULD COME UP WITH SOMETHING BETTER TO KILL HIM WITH THAN A GIANT ZOMBIE MONKEY, YA BIG STUPID BUG-EYED FREAK!
ABSOLUTELY NO FAIR, NO FAIR AT ALL.
OH GOD, IF I WEREN'T DEAD ALREADY, I'D SHOOT MYSELF.
WHY AM I DESTINED TO FAILURE? OH, MOTHER WAS RIGHT. I AM A BIG PILE OF SMELLY DUNG WITH THE I.Q. OF A MENTALLY CHALLENGED SOCK AND THE SPINE OF A MAGGOT FEEDING ON THE FESTERING CARCASS OF A DEAD SWINE. SHE KNEW ME SO WELL.

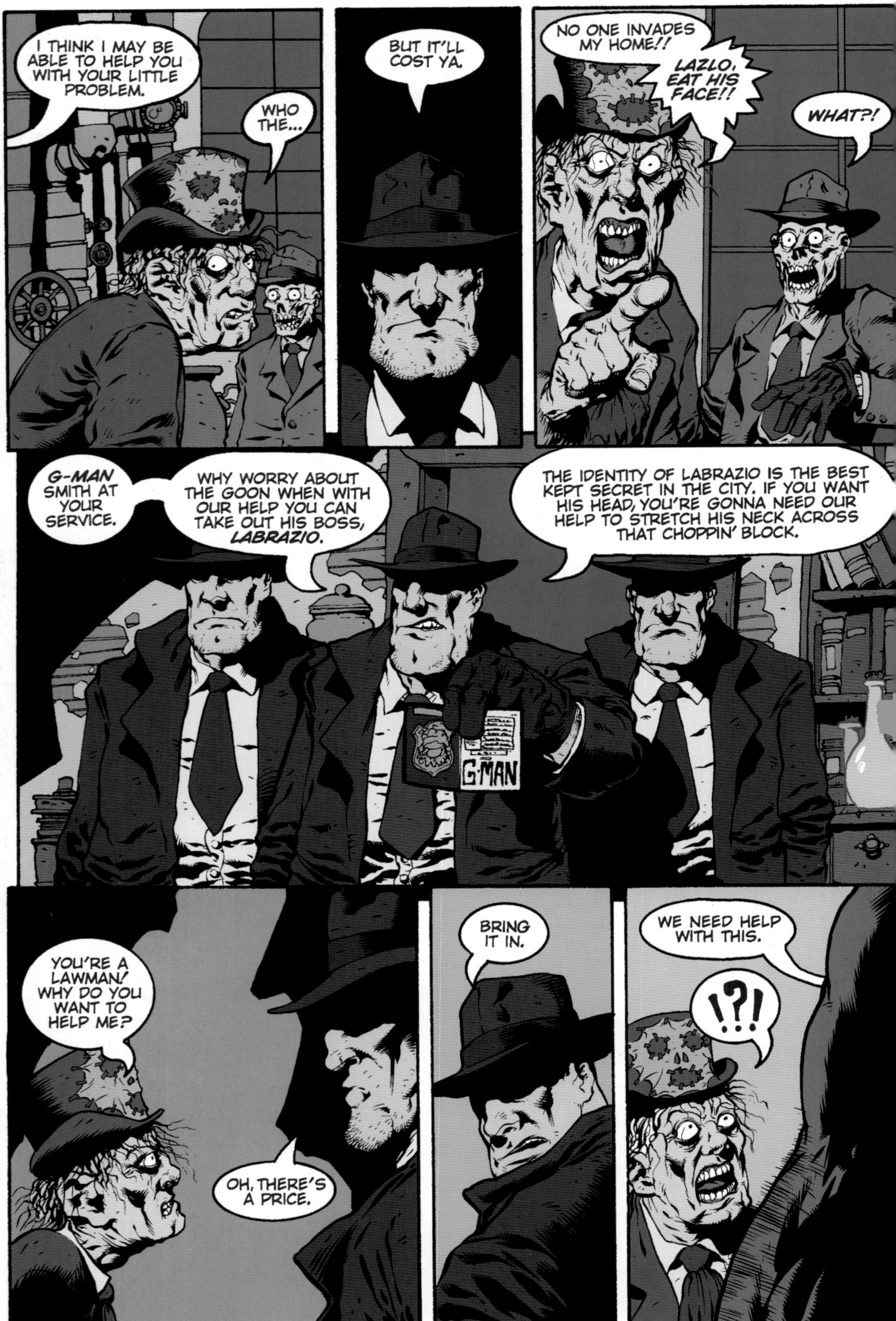
I THINK I MAY BE ABLE TO HELP YOU WITH YOUR LITTLE PROBLEM.
WHO THE...
BUT IT'LL COST YA.
NO ONE INVADES MY HOME!!
LAZLO, EAT HIS FACE!!
WHAT?!
G-MAN SMITH AT YOUR SERVICE.
WHY WORRY ABOUT THE GOON WHEN WITH OUR HELP YOU CAN TAKE OUT HIS BOSS, LABRAZIO.
THE IDENTITY OF LABRAZIO IS THE BEST KEPT SECRET IN THE CITY. IF YOU WANT HIS HEAD, YOU'RE GONNA NEED OUR HELP TO STRETCH HIS NECK ACROSS THAT CHOPPIN' BLOCK.
G-MAN
YOU'RE A LAWMAN! WHY DO YOU WANT TO HELP ME?
OH, THERE'S A PRICE.
BRING IT IN.
WE NEED HELP WITH THIS.
!?!

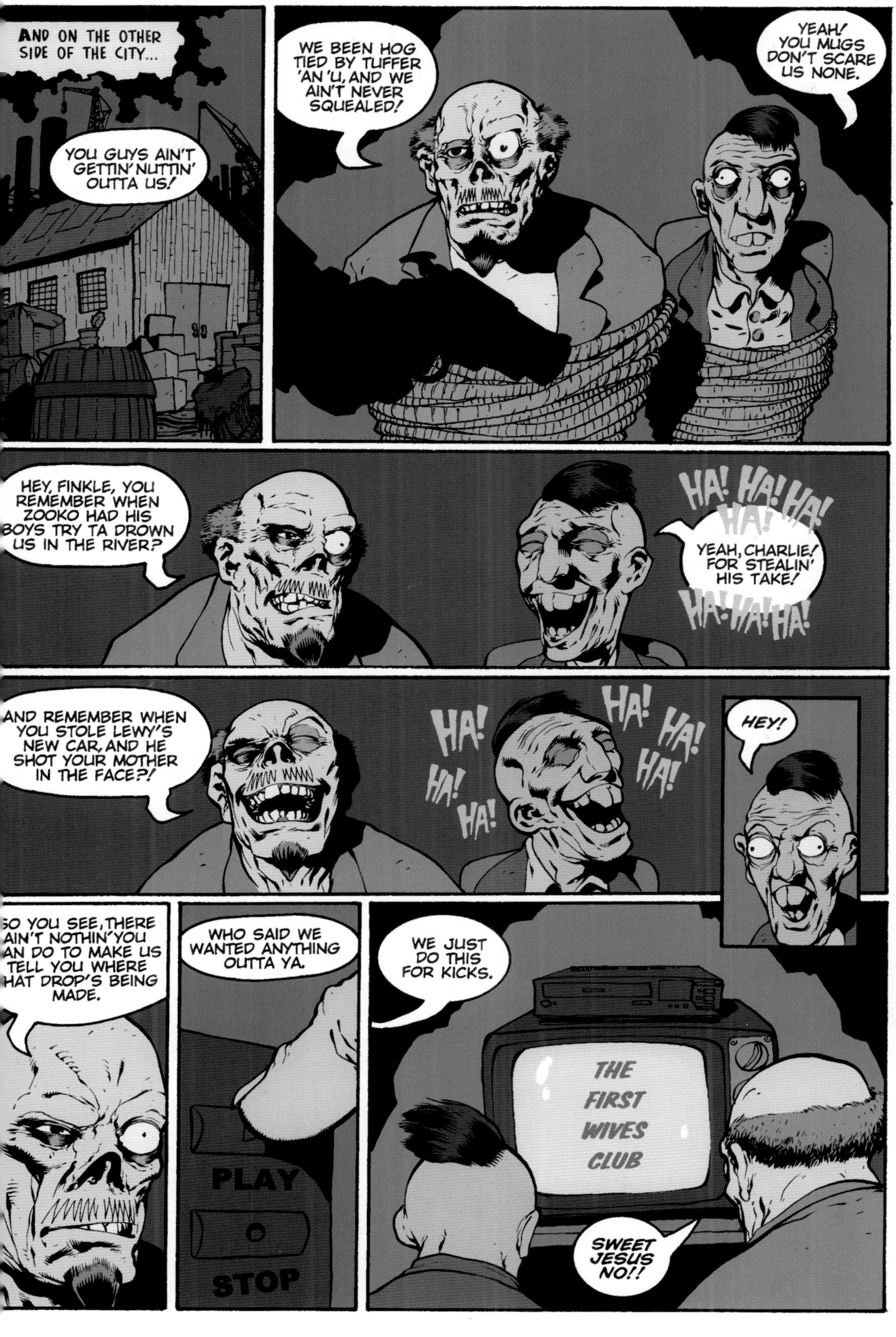
AND ON THE OTHER SIDE OF THE CITY...
YOU GUYS AIN'T GETTIN' NUTTIN' OUTTA US!
WE BEEN HOG TIED BY TUFFER 'AN 'U, AND WE AIN'T NEVER SQUEALED!
YEAH! YOU MUGS DON'T SCARE US NONE.
HEY, FINKLE, YOU REMEMBER WHEN ZOOKO HAD HIS BOYS TRY TA DROWN US IN THE RIVER?
HA! HA! HA! HA!
YEAH, CHARLIE! FOR STEALIN' HIS TAKE!
HA! HA! HA!
AND REMEMBER WHEN YOU STOLE LEWY'S NEW CAR, AND HE SHOT YOUR MOTHER IN THE FACE?!
HA! HA! HA!
HA! HA! HA!
HEY!
SO YOU SEE, THERE AIN'T NOTHIN' YOU CAN DO TO MAKE US TELL YOU WHERE THAT DROP'S BEING MADE.
WHO SAID WE WANTED ANYTHING OUTTA YA.
PLAY
STOP
WE JUST DO THIS FOR KICKS.
THE FIRST WIVES CLUB
SWEET JESUS NO!!

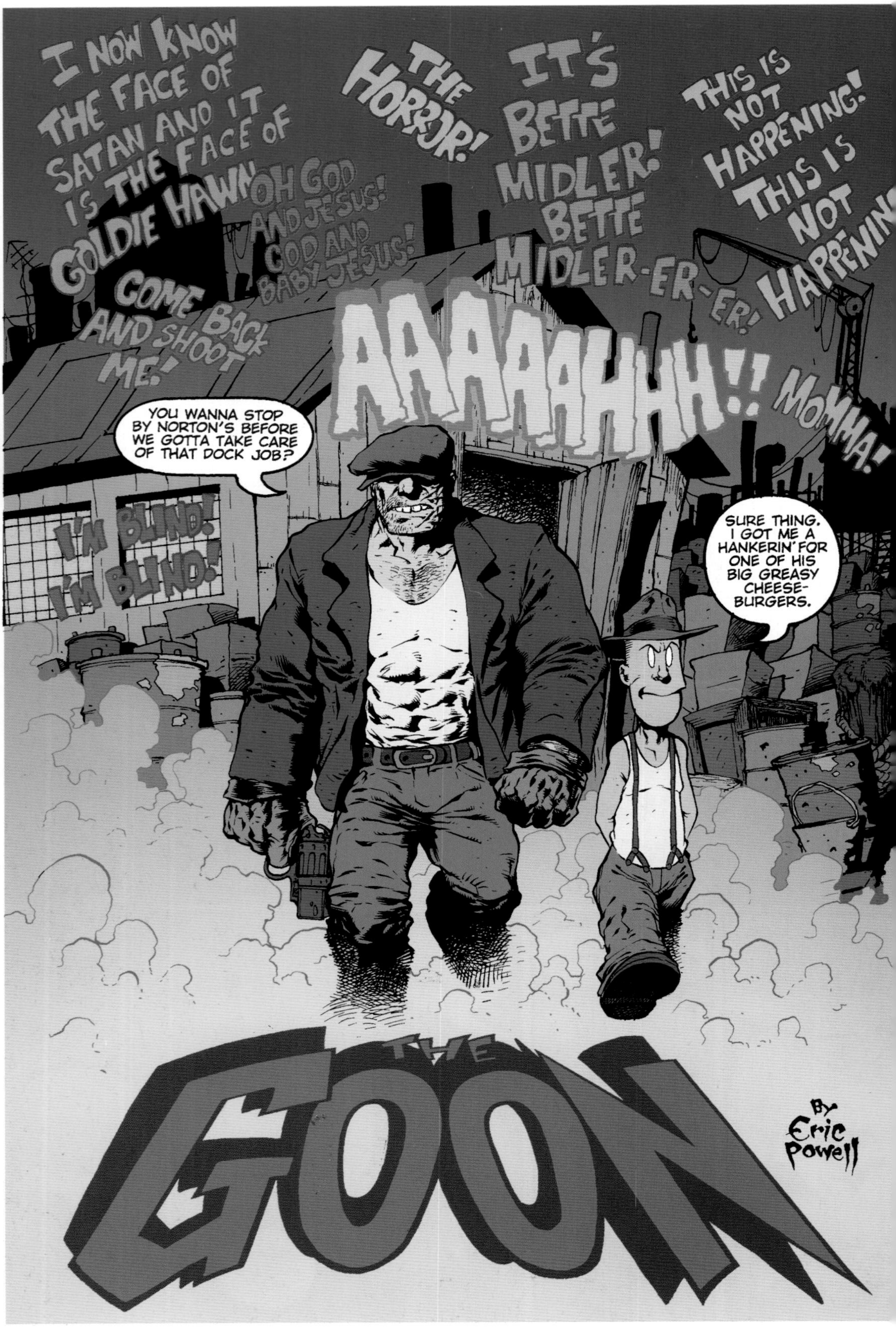
I NOW KNOW THE FACE OF SATAN AND IT IS THE FACE OF GOLDIE HAWN
THE HORROR!
IT'S BETTE MIDLER! BETTE MIDLER-ER-ER!
THIS IS NOT HAPPENING! THIS IS NOT HAPPENIN
OH GOD AND JESUS! GOD AND BABY JESUS!
COME BACK AND SHOOT ME!
AAAAAHHH!!
MOMMA!
YOU WANNA STOP BY NORTON'S BEFORE WE GOTTA TAKE CARE OF THAT DOCK JOB?
I'M BLIND! I'M BLIND!
SURE THING. I GOT ME A HANKERIN' FOR ONE OF HIS BIG GREASY CHEESE-BURGERS.
THE GOON
By Eric Powell

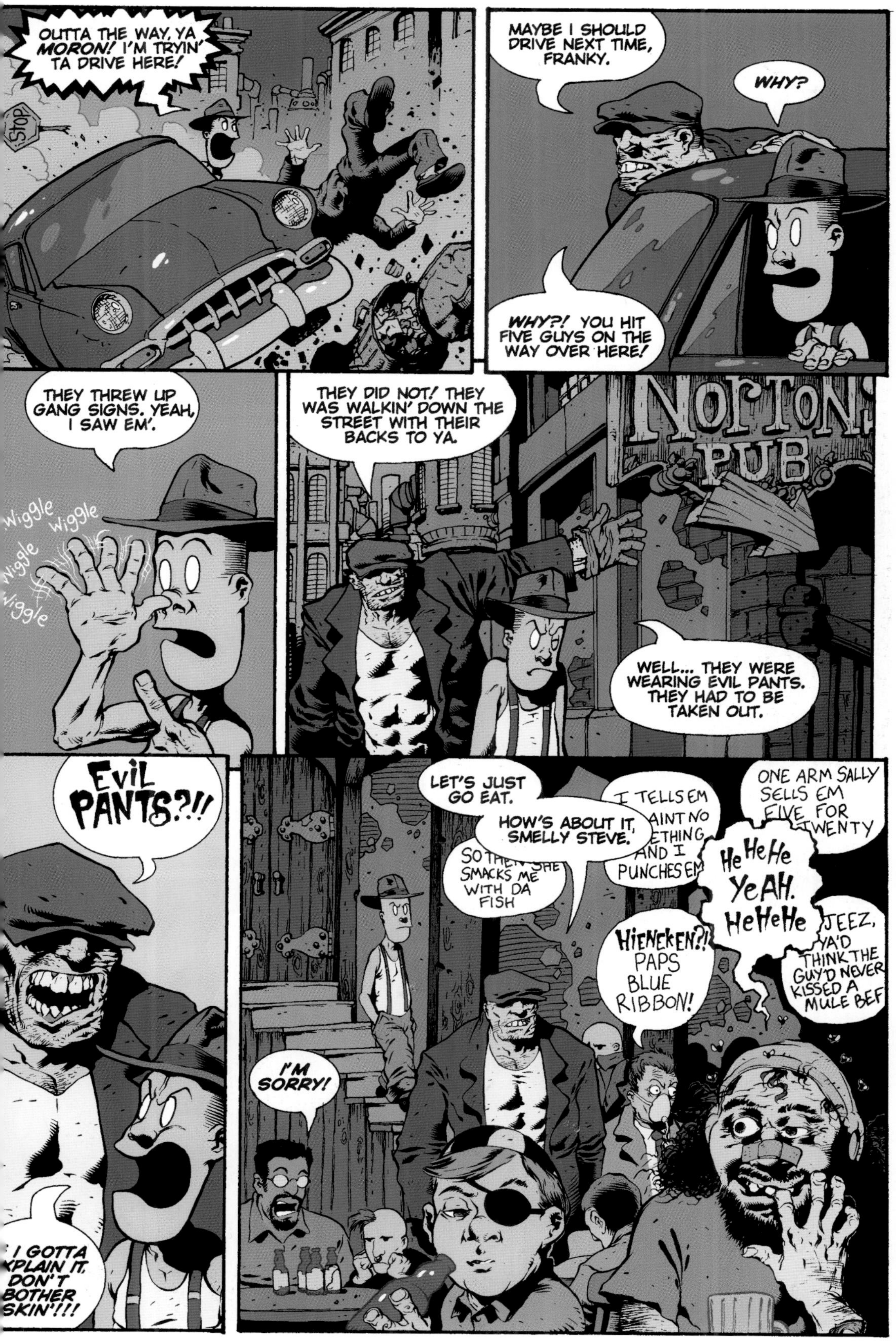
OUTTA THE WAY, YA MORON! I'M TRYIN' TA DRIVE HERE!
STOP
MAYBE I SHOULD DRIVE NEXT TIME, FRANKY.
WHY?
WHY?! YOU HIT FIVE GUYS ON THE WAY OVER HERE!
THEY THREW UP GANG SIGNS. YEAH, I SAW EM'.
wiggle wiggle wiggle wiggle
THEY DID NOT! THEY WAS WALKIN' DOWN THE STREET WITH THEIR BACKS TO YA.
NORTON'S PUB
WELL... THEY WERE WEARING EVIL PANTS. THEY HAD TO BE TAKEN OUT.
EVIL PANTS?!!
I GOTTA XPLAIN IT, DON'T BOTHER SKIN'!!!!
LET'S JUST GO EAT.
HOW'S ABOUT IT, SMELLY STEVE.
SO THEN SHE SMACKS ME WITH DA FISH
I TELLS EM AINT NO ETHING AND I PUNCHES EM
ONE ARM SALLY SELLS EM FIVE FOR TWENTY
He HeHe YeAH. HeHeHe
JEEZ, YA'D THINK THE GUY'D NEVER KISSED A MULE BEF
HIENEKEN?! PAPS BLUE RIBBON!
I'M SORRY!

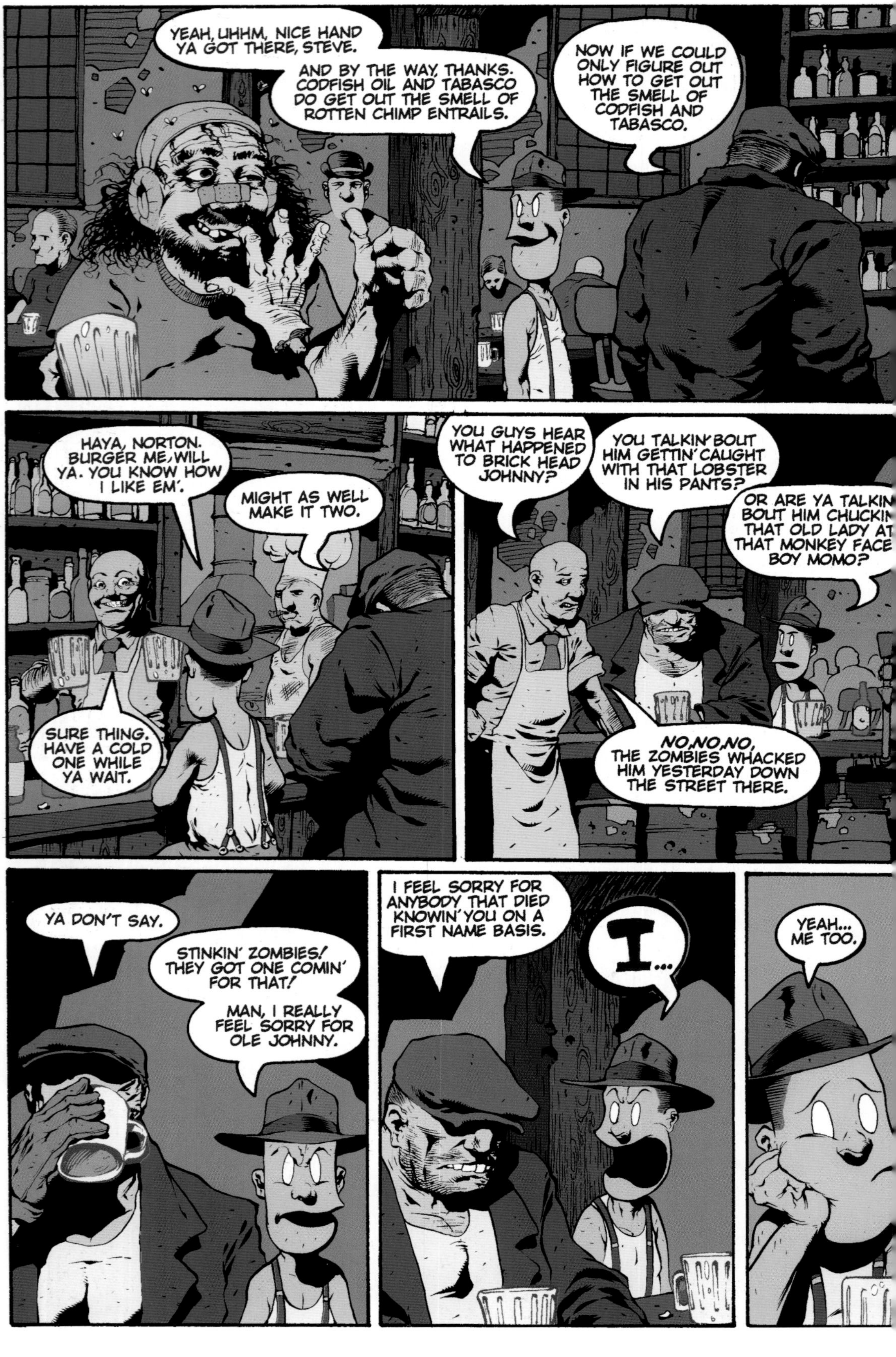
YEAH, UHHM, NICE HAND YA GOT THERE, STEVE.
AND BY THE WAY, THANKS. CODFISH OIL AND TABASCO DO GET OUT THE SMELL OF ROTTEN CHIMP ENTRAILS.
NOW IF WE COULD ONLY FIGURE OUT HOW TO GET OUT THE SMELL OF CODFISH AND TABASCO.
HAYA, NORTON. BURGER ME, WILL YA. YOU KNOW HOW I LIKE EM'.
MIGHT AS WELL MAKE IT TWO.
SURE THING. HAVE A COLD ONE WHILE YA WAIT.
YOU GUYS HEAR WHAT HAPPENED TO BRICK HEAD JOHNNY?
YOU TALKIN' BOUT HIM GETTIN' CAUGHT WITH THAT LOBSTER IN HIS PANTS?
OR ARE YA TALKIN BOUT HIM CHUCKIN THAT OLD LADY AT THAT MONKEY FACE BOY MOMO?
NO,NO,NO, THE ZOMBIES WHACKED HIM YESTERDAY DOWN THE STREET THERE.
YA DON'T SAY.
STINKIN' ZOMBIES! THEY GOT ONE COMIN' FOR THAT!
MAN, I REALLY FEEL SORRY FOR OLE JOHNNY.
I FEEL SORRY FOR ANYBODY THAT DIED KNOWIN' YOU ON A FIRST NAME BASIS.
I...
YEAH... ME TOO.

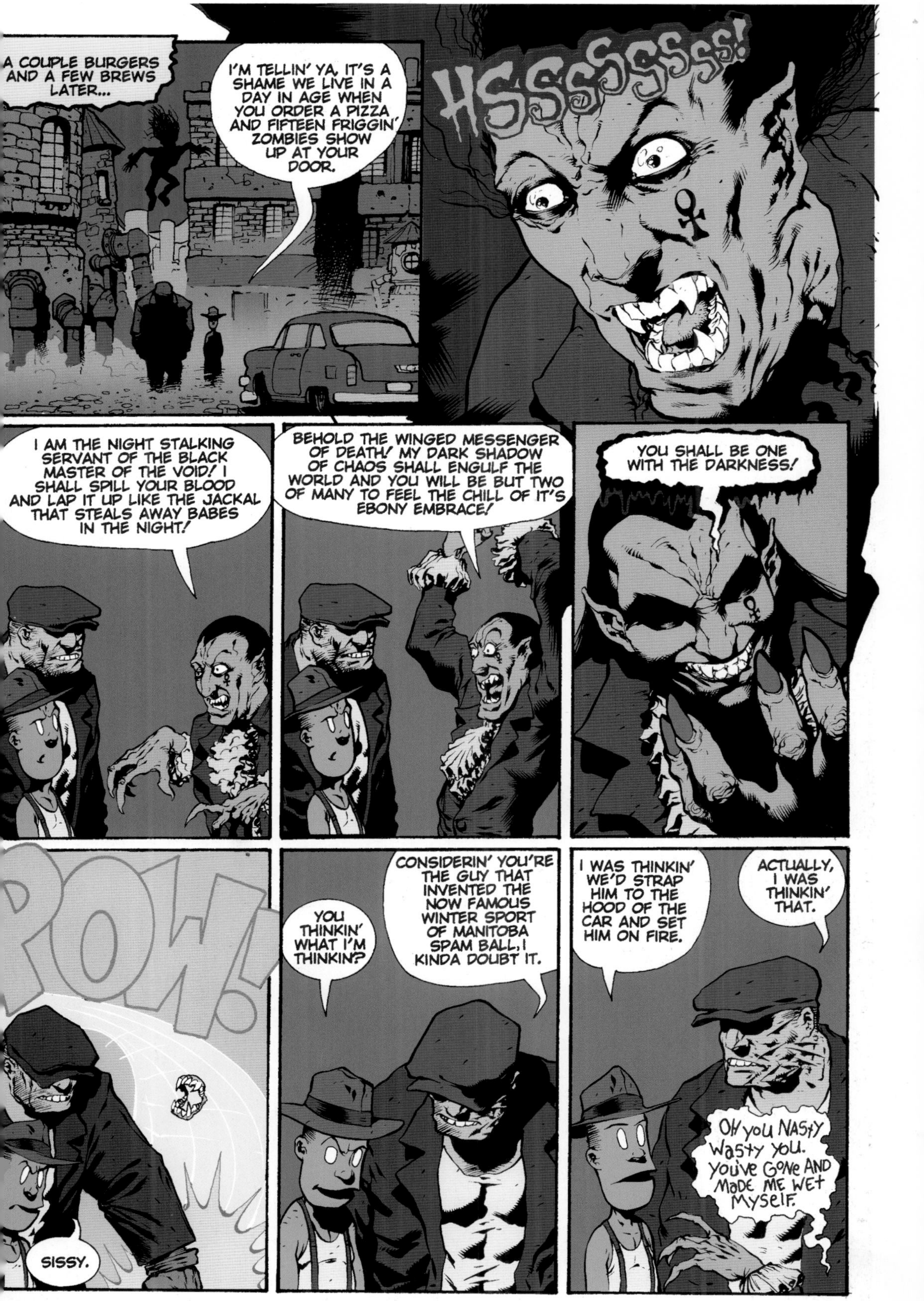
A COUPLE BURGERS AND A FEW BREWS LATER...
I'M TELLIN' YA, IT'S A SHAME WE LIVE IN A DAY IN AGE WHEN YOU ORDER A PIZZA AND FIFTEEN FRIGGIN' ZOMBIES SHOW UP AT YOUR DOOR.
HSSSSSSSS!
I AM THE NIGHT STALKING SERVANT OF THE BLACK MASTER OF THE VOID! I SHALL SPILL YOUR BLOOD AND LAP IT UP LIKE THE JACKAL THAT STEALS AWAY BABES IN THE NIGHT!
BEHOLD THE WINGED MESSENGER OF DEATH! MY DARK SHADOW OF CHAOS SHALL ENGULF THE WORLD AND YOU WILL BE BUT TWO OF MANY TO FEEL THE CHILL OF IT'S EBONY EMBRACE!
YOU SHALL BE ONE WITH THE DARKNESS!
POW!
SISSY.
YOU THINKIN' WHAT I'M THINKIN?
CONSIDERIN' YOU'RE THE GUY THAT INVENTED THE NOW FAMOUS WINTER SPORT OF MANITOBA SPAM BALL, I KINDA DOUBT IT.
I WAS THINKIN' WE'D STRAP HIM TO THE HOOD OF THE CAR AND SET HIM ON FIRE.
ACTUALLY, I WAS THINKIN' THAT.
OH YOU NASTY WASTY YOU. YOU'VE GONE AND MADE ME WET MYSELF.

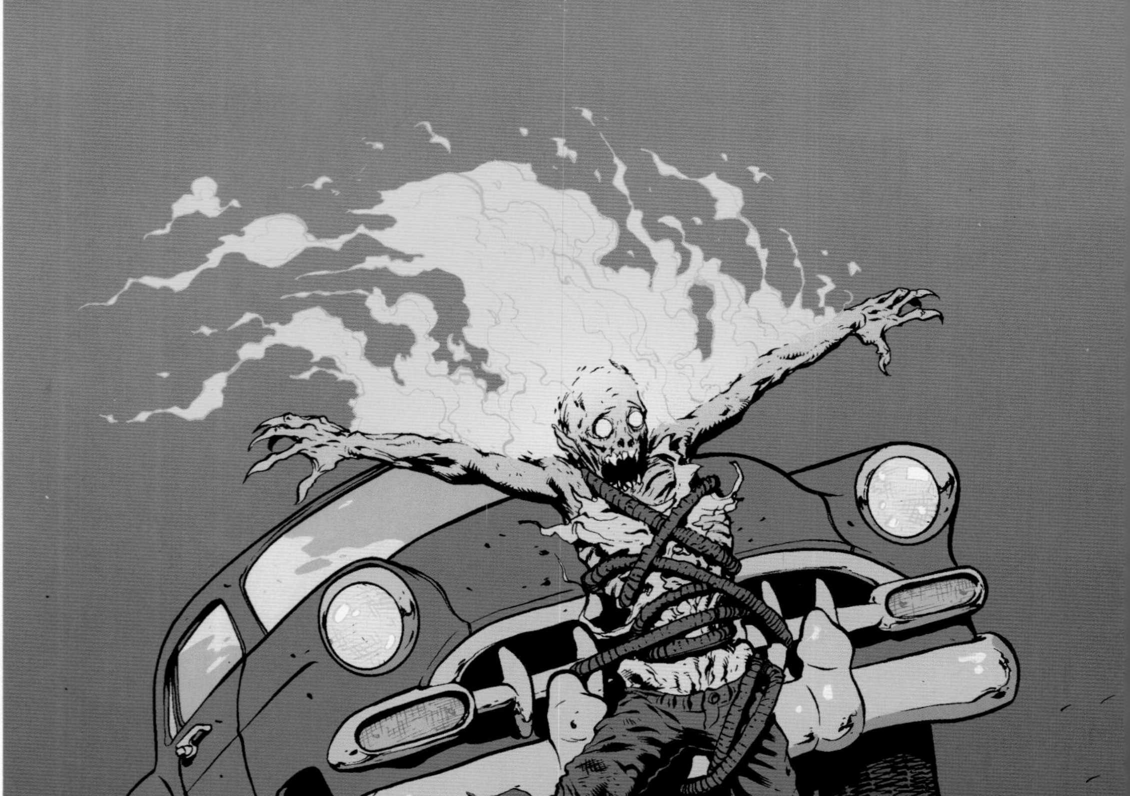

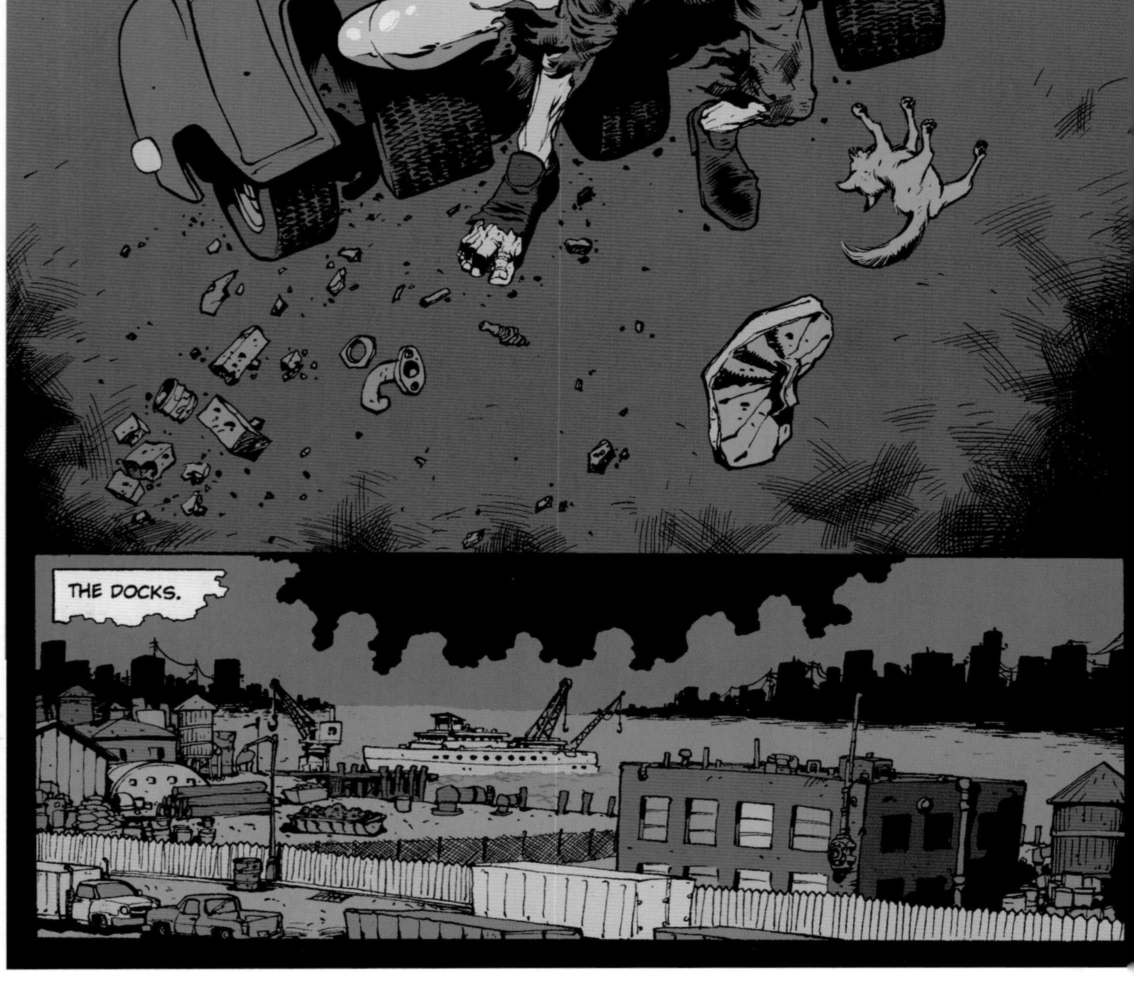
THE DOCKS.

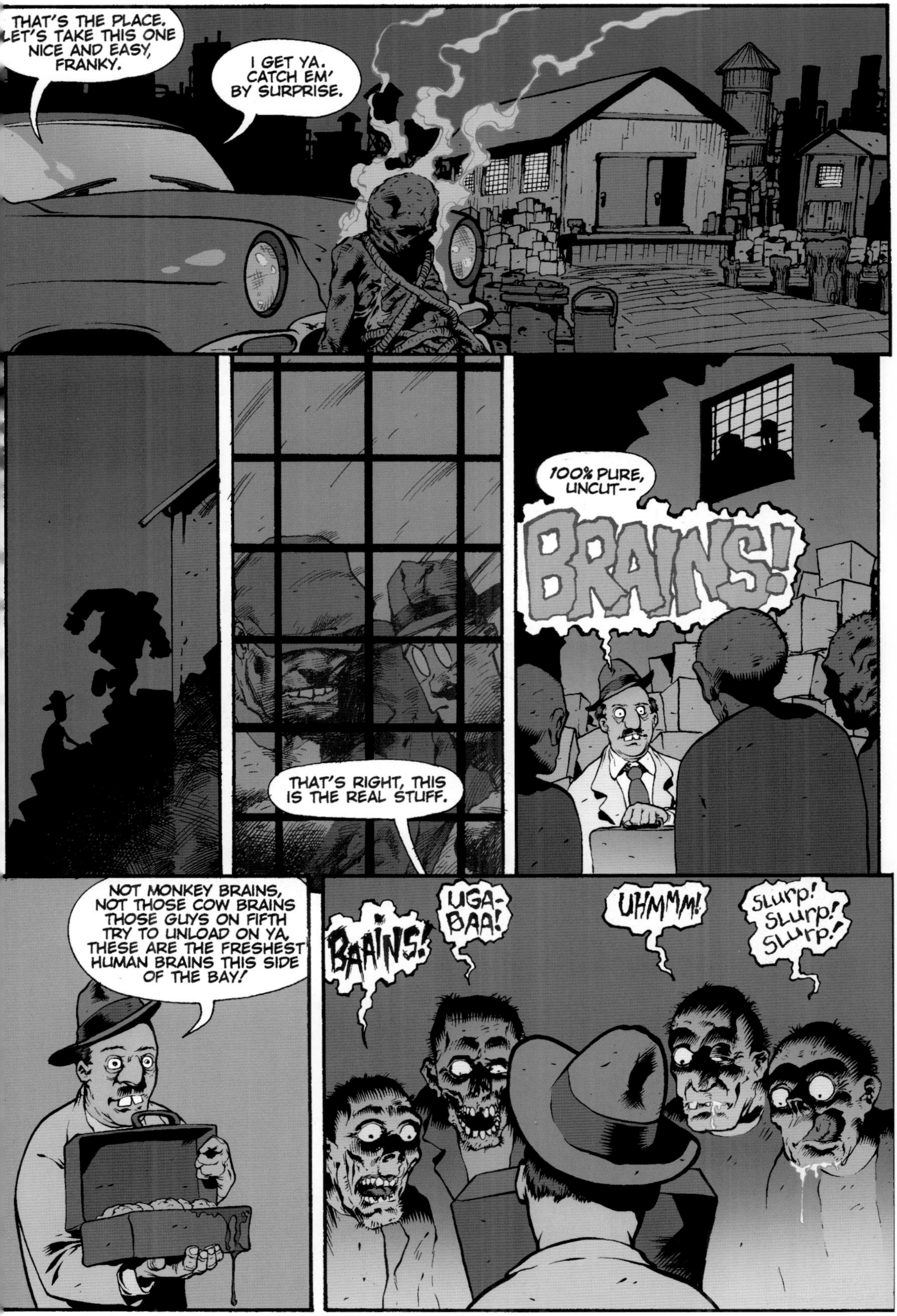
THAT'S THE PLACE. LET'S TAKE THIS ONE NICE AND EASY, FRANKY.
I GET YA. CATCH EM' BY SURPRISE.
100% PURE, UNCUT--
BRAINS!
THAT'S RIGHT, THIS IS THE REAL STUFF.
NOT MONKEY BRAINS, NOT THOSE COW BRAINS THOSE GUYS ON FIFTH TRY TO UNLOAD ON YA, THESE ARE THE FRESHEST HUMAN BRAINS THIS SIDE OF THE BAY!
BAAINS!
UGA-BAA!
UHMMM!
Slurp! Slurp! Slurp!

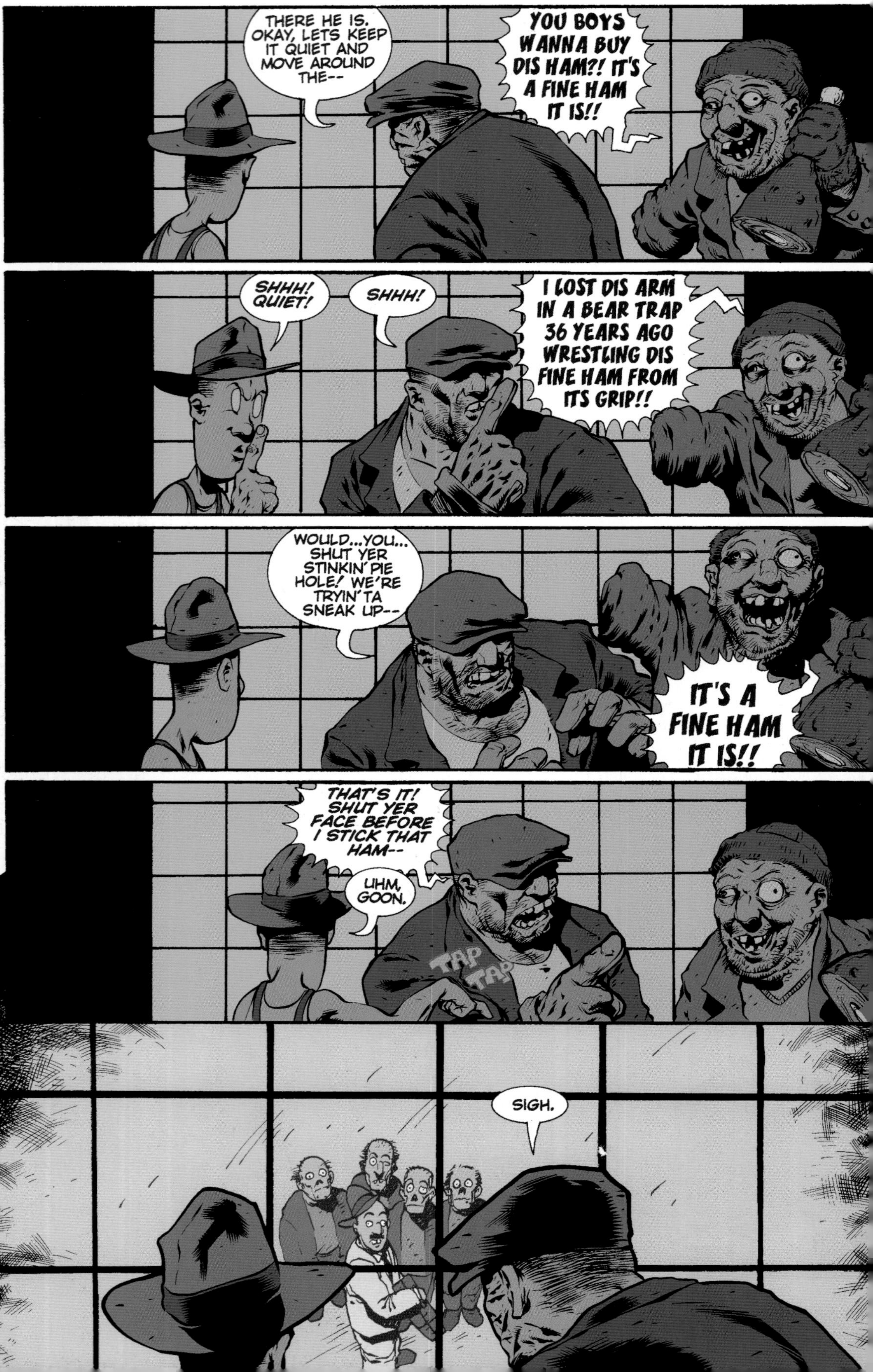
THERE HE IS. OKAY, LETS KEEP IT QUIET AND MOVE AROUND THE--
YOU BOYS WANNA BUY DIS HAM?! IT'S A FINE HAM IT IS!!
SHHH! QUIET!
SHHH!
I LOST DIS ARM IN A BEAR TRAP 36 YEARS AGO WRESTLING DIS FINE HAM FROM ITS GRIP!!
WOULD...YOU... SHUT YER STINKIN' PIE HOLE! WE'RE TRYIN' TA SNEAK UP--
IT'S A FINE HAM IT IS!!
THAT'S IT! SHUT YER FACE BEFORE I STICK THAT HAM--
UHM, GOON.
TAP TAP
SIGH.

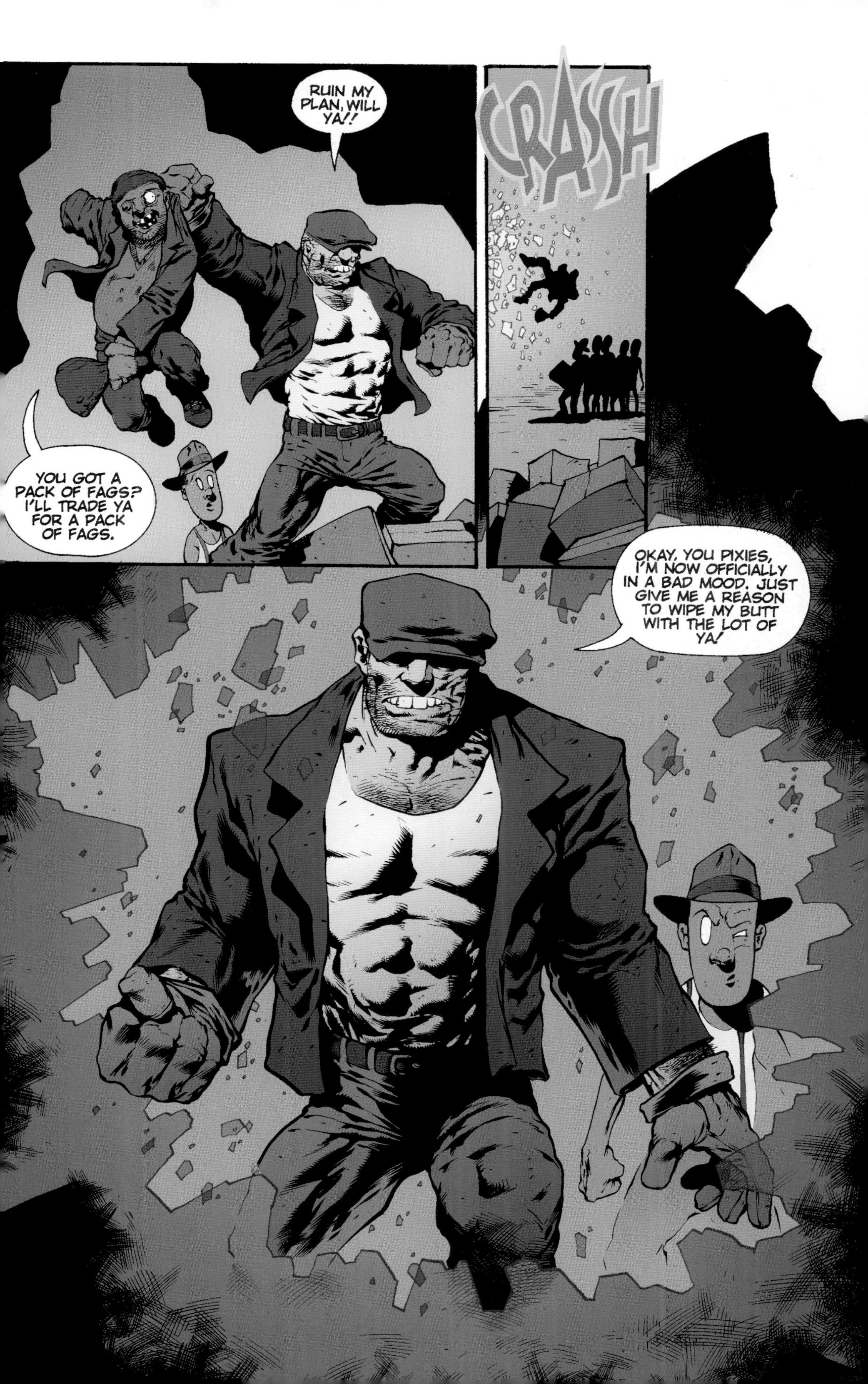
RUIN MY PLAN, WILL YA!!
YOU GOT A PACK OF FAGS? I'LL TRADE YA FOR A PACK OF FAGS.
CRASH
OKAY, YOU PIXIES, I'M NOW OFFICIALLY IN A BAD MOOD. JUST GIVE ME A REASON TO WIPE MY BUTT WITH THE LOT OF YA!

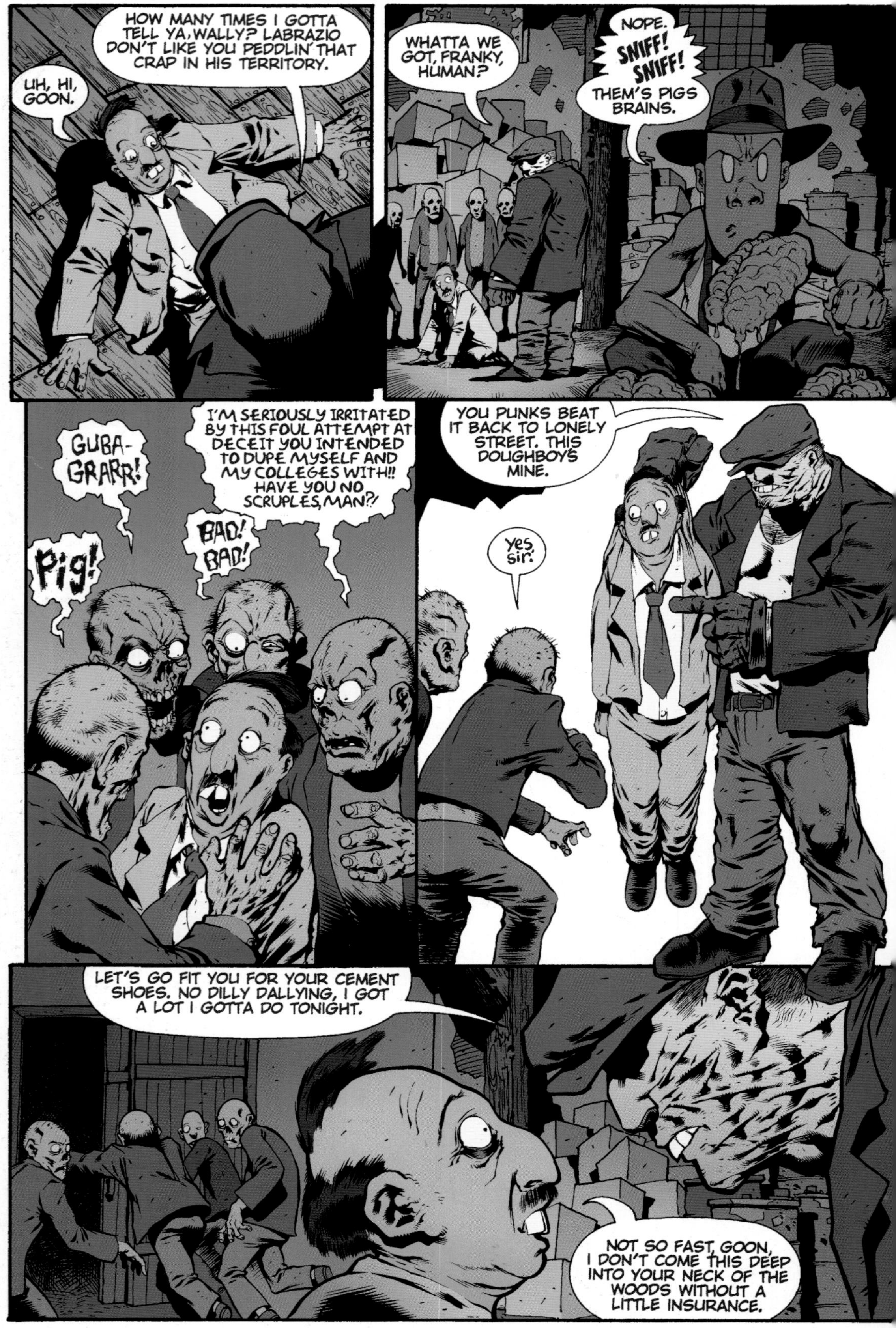

HOW MANY TIMES I GOTTA TELL YA, WALLY? LABRAZIO DON'T LIKE YOU PEDDLIN' THAT CRAP IN HIS TERRITORY.
UH, HI, GOON.
WHATTA WE GOT, FRANKY, HUMAN?
NOPE.
SNIFF! SNIFF!
THEM'S PIGS BRAINS.
GUBA-GRARR!
I'M SERIOUSLY IRRITATED BY THIS FOUL ATTEMPT AT DECEIT YOU INTENDED TO DUPE MYSELF AND MY COLLEGES WITH!! HAVE YOU NO SCRUPLES, MAN?!
PIG!
BAD! BAD!
YOU PUNKS BEAT IT BACK TO LONELY STREET. THIS DOUGHBOY'S MINE.
YES SIR.
LET'S GO FIT YOU FOR YOUR CEMENT SHOES. NO DILLY DALLYING, I GOT A LOT I GOTTA DO TONIGHT.
NOT SO FAST, GOON, I DON'T COME THIS DEEP INTO YOUR NECK OF THE WOODS WITHOUT A LITTLE INSURANCE.

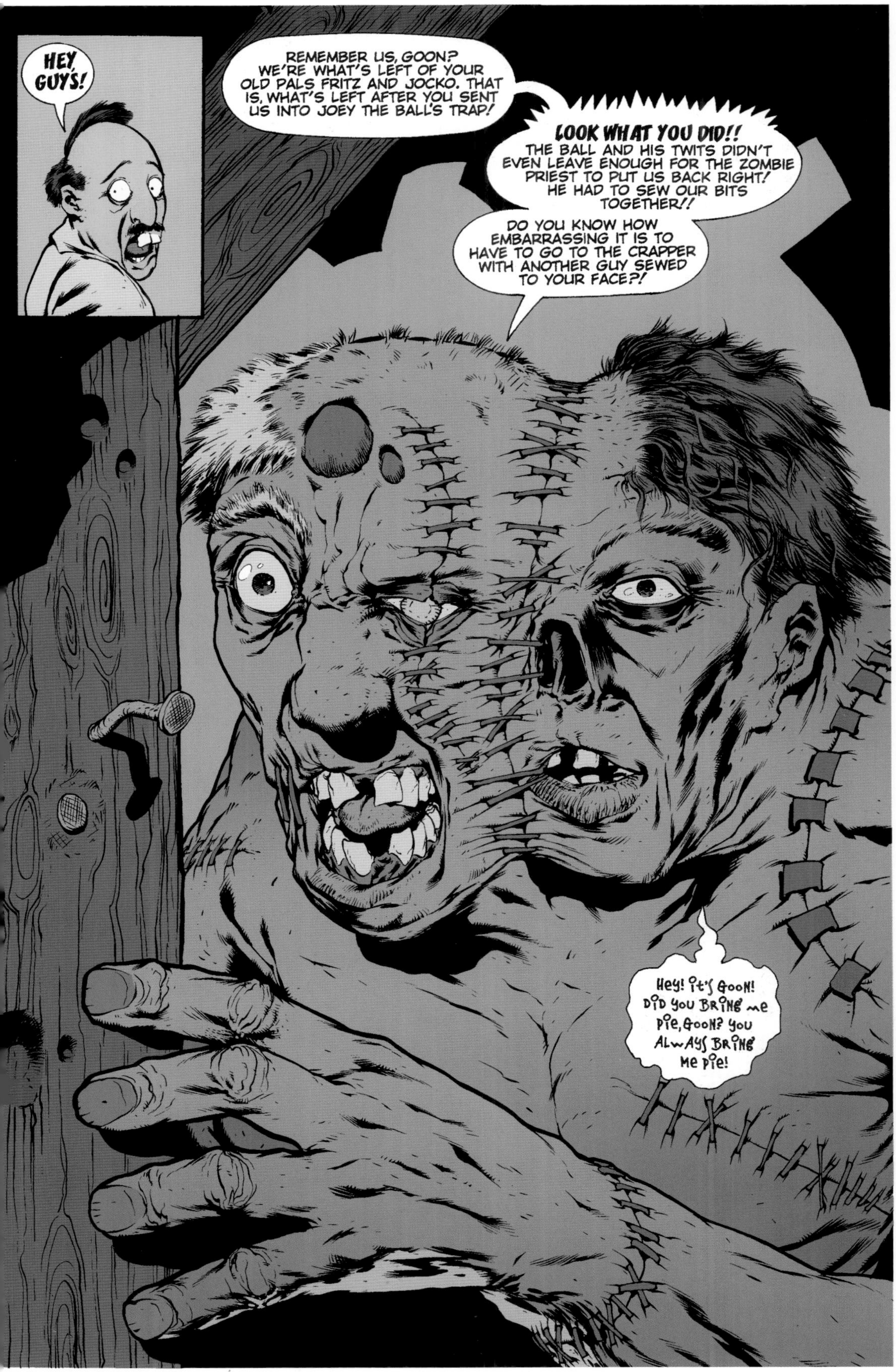
HEY, GUYS!
REMEMBER US, GOON? WE'RE WHAT'S LEFT OF YOUR OLD PALS FRITZ AND JOCKO. THAT IS, WHAT'S LEFT AFTER YOU SENT US INTO JOEY THE BALL'S TRAP!
LOOK WHAT YOU DID!! THE BALL AND HIS TWITS DIDN'T EVEN LEAVE ENOUGH FOR THE ZOMBIE PRIEST TO PUT US BACK RIGHT! HE HAD TO SEW OUR BITS TOGETHER!!
DO YOU KNOW HOW EMBARRASSING IT IS TO HAVE TO GO TO THE CRAPPER WITH ANOTHER GUY SEWED TO YOUR FACE?!
Hey! It's Goon! Did you bring me pie, Goon? You always bring me pie!

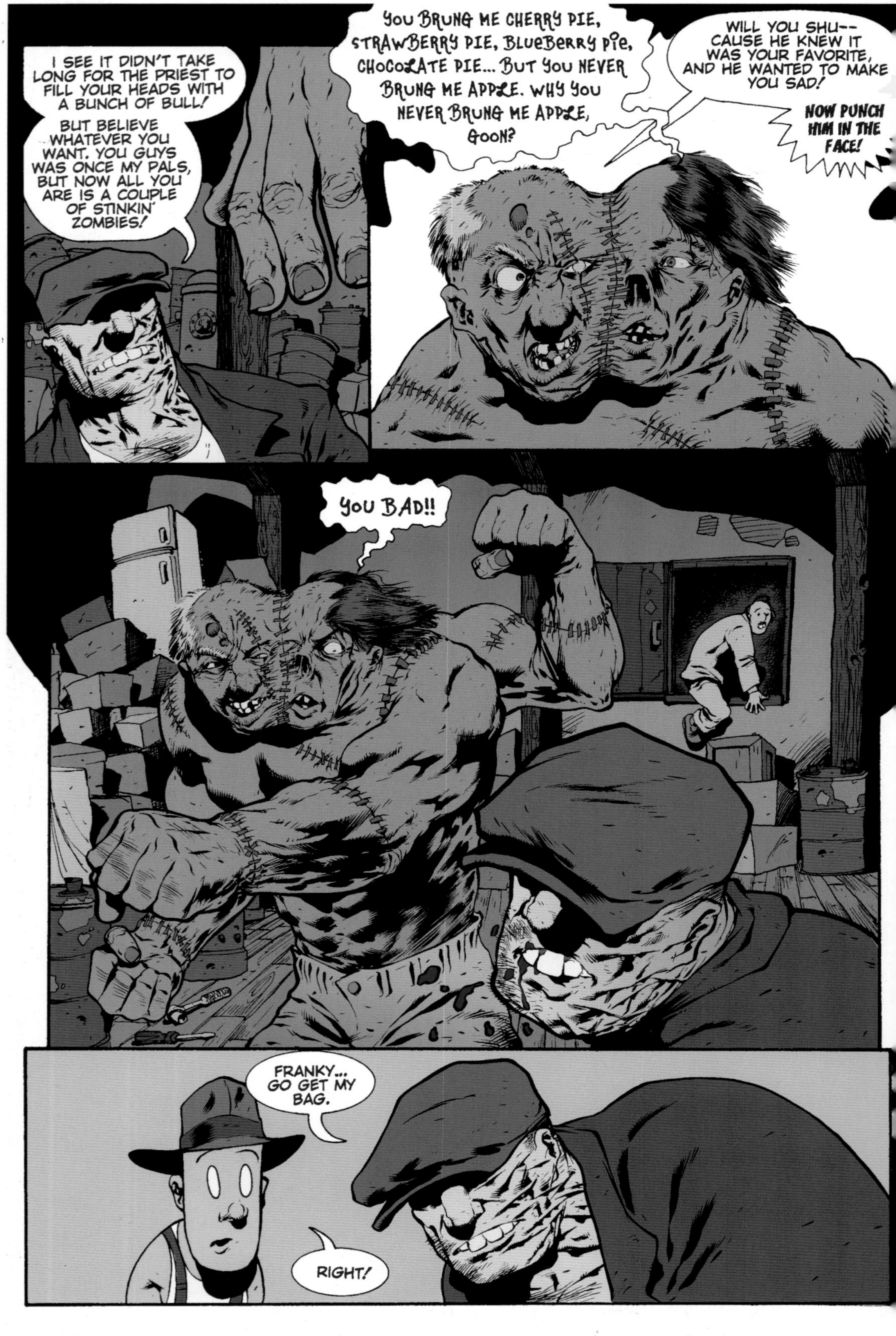
I SEE IT DIDN'T TAKE LONG FOR THE PRIEST TO FILL YOUR HEADS WITH A BUNCH OF BULL!
BUT BELIEVE WHATEVER YOU WANT. YOU GUYS WAS ONCE MY PALS, BUT NOW ALL YOU ARE IS A COUPLE OF STINKIN' ZOMBIES!
YOU BRUNG ME CHERRY PIE, STRAWBERRY PIE, BLUEBERRY PIE, CHOCOLATE PIE... BUT YOU NEVER BRUNG ME APPLE. WHY YOU NEVER BRUNG ME APPLE, GOON?
WILL YOU SHU-- CAUSE HE KNEW IT WAS YOUR FAVORITE, AND HE WANTED TO MAKE YOU SAD!
NOW PUNCH HIM IN THE FACE!
YOU BAD!!
FRANKY... GO GET MY BAG.
RIGHT!

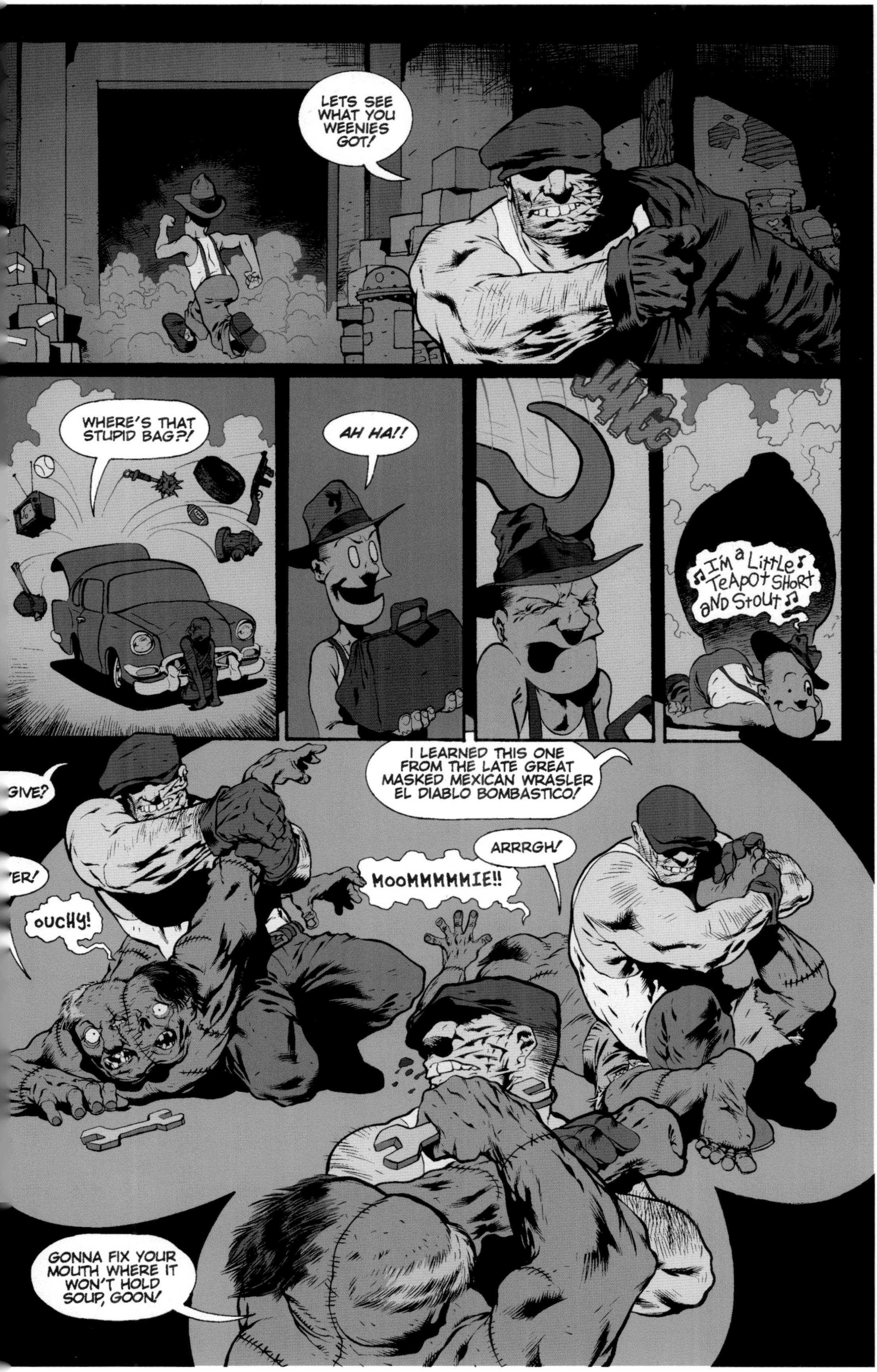
LETS SEE WHAT YOU WEENIES GOT!
WHERE'S THAT STUPID BAG?!
AH HA!!
I'M a Little TeApot SHORt and Stout
GIVE?
ER!
OUCHY!
I LEARNED THIS ONE FROM THE LATE GREAT MASKED MEXICAN WRASLER EL DIABLO BOMBASTICO!
MOOMMMMMIE!!
ARRRGH!
GONNA FIX YOUR MOUTH WHERE IT WON'T HOLD SOUP, GOON!

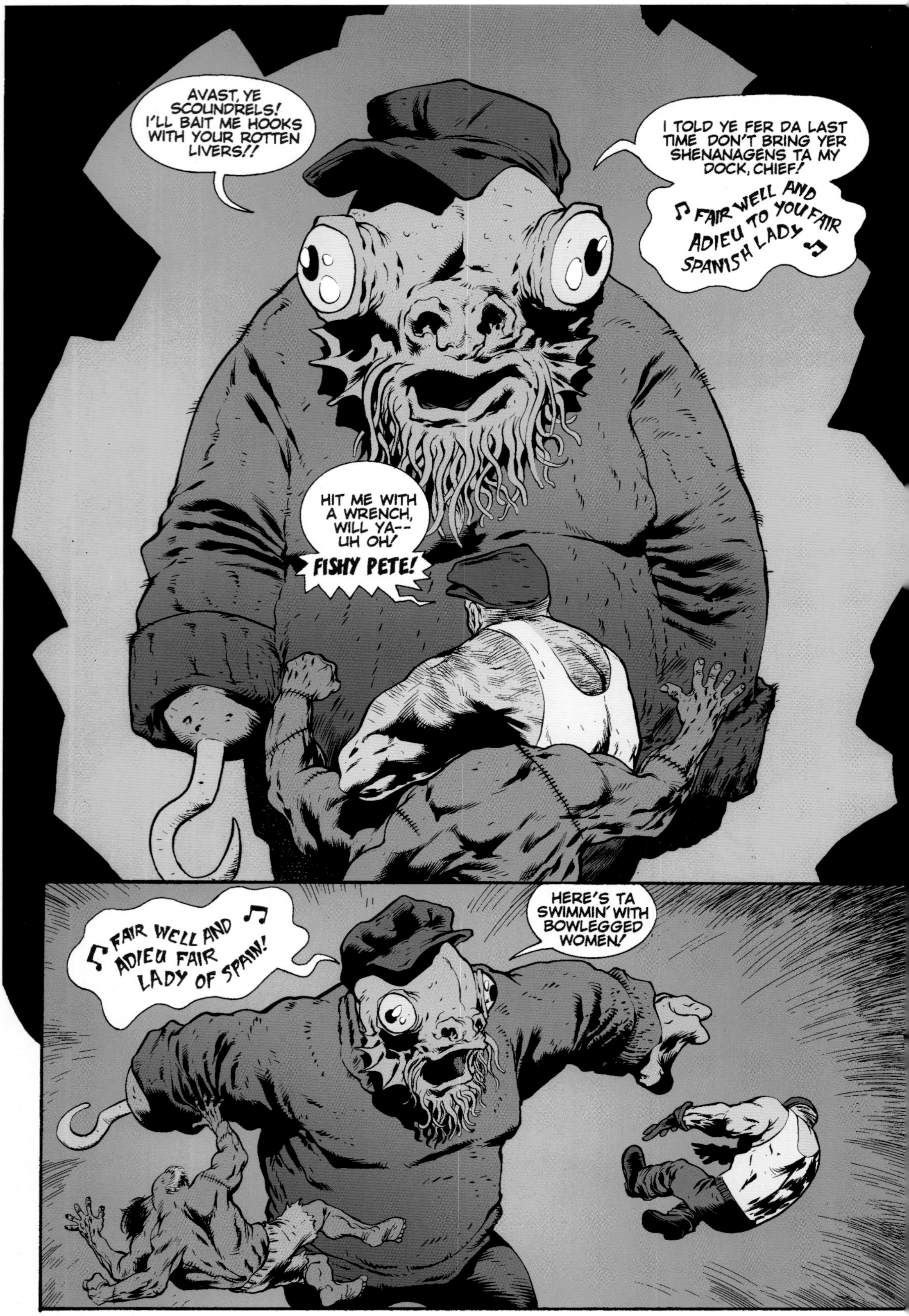
AVAST, YE SCOUNDRELS! I'LL BAIT ME HOOKS WITH YOUR ROTTEN LIVERS!!
I TOLD YE FER DA LAST TIME DON'T BRING YER SHENANAGENS TA MY DOCK, CHIEF!
♪ FAIR WELL AND ADIEU TO YOU FAIR SPANISH LADY ♪
HIT ME WITH A WRENCH, WILL YA-- UH OH!
FISHY PETE!
♪ FAIR WELL AND ADIEU FAIR LADY OF SPAIN! ♪
HERE'S TA SWIMMIN' WITH BOWLEGGED WOMEN!

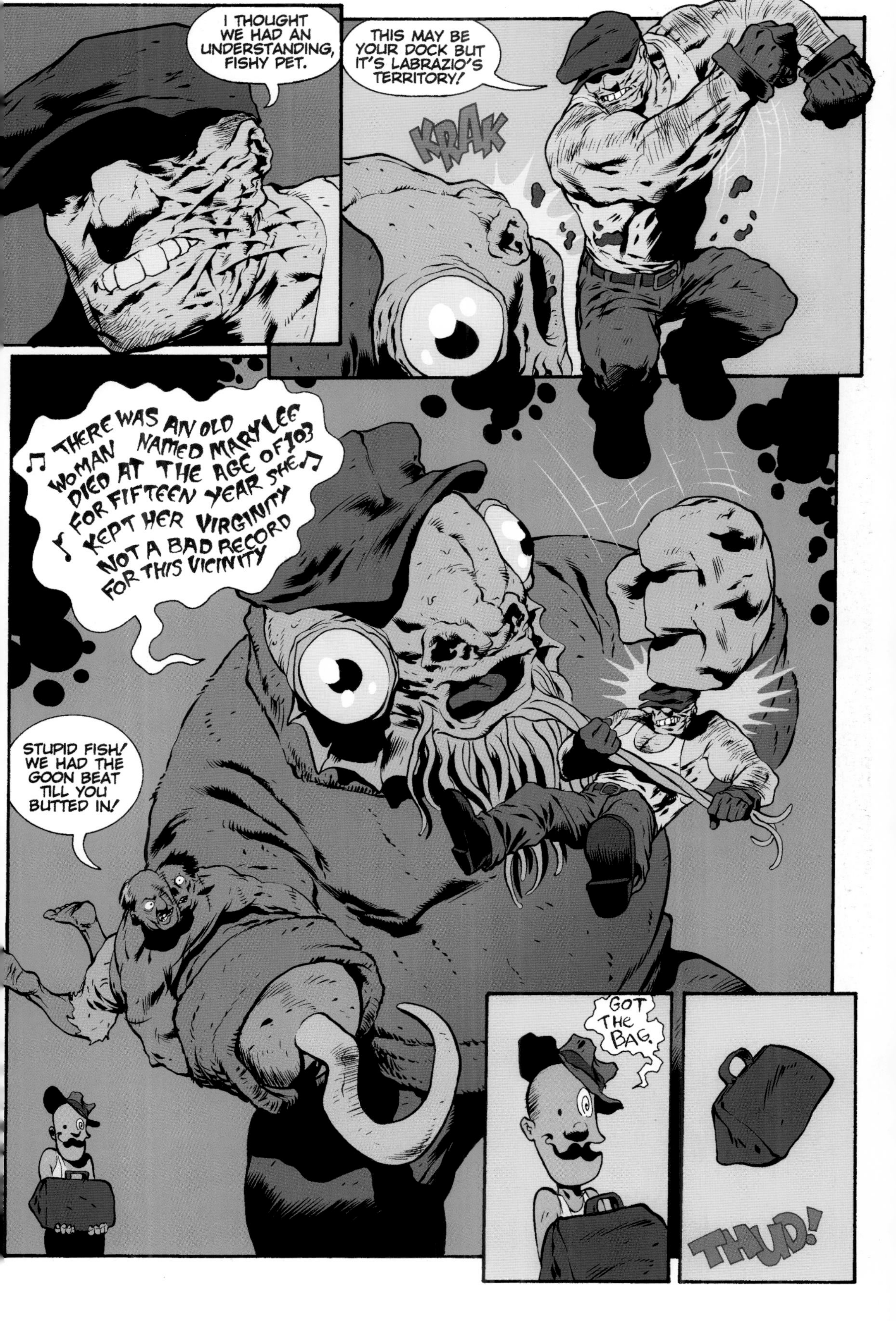
I THOUGHT WE HAD AN UNDERSTANDING, FISHY PET.
THIS MAY BE YOUR DOCK BUT IT'S LABRAZIO'S TERRITORY!
KRAK
♫ THERE WAS AN OLD WOMAN NAMED MARYLEE DIED AT THE AGE OF 103 ♫ FOR FIFTEEN YEAR SHE ♫ KEPT HER VIRGINITY NOT A BAD RECORD FOR THIS VICINITY
STUPID FISH! WE HAD THE GOON BEAT TILL YOU BUTTED IN!
GOT THE BAG.
THUD!

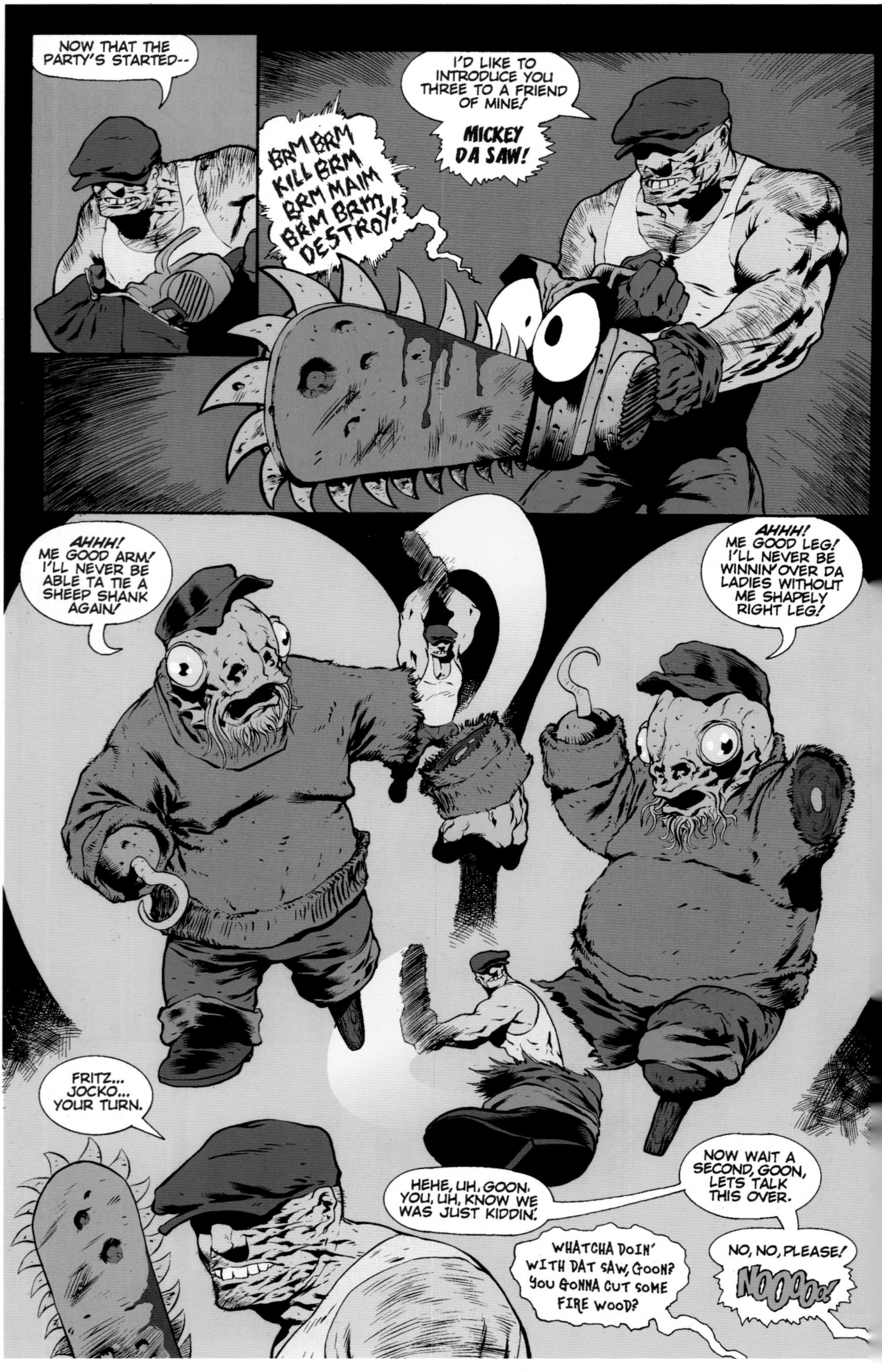
NOW THAT THE PARTY'S STARTED--
I'D LIKE TO INTRODUCE YOU THREE TO A FRIEND OF MINE!
MICKEY DA SAW!
BRM BRM KILL BRM BRM MAIM BRM BRM DESTROY!
AHHH! ME GOOD ARM! I'LL NEVER BE ABLE TA TIE A SHEEP SHANK AGAIN!
AHHH! ME GOOD LEG! I'LL NEVER BE WINNIN' OVER DA LADIES WITHOUT ME SHAPELY RIGHT LEG!
FRITZ... JOCKO... YOUR TURN.
HEHE, UH, GOON. YOU, UH, KNOW WE WAS JUST KIDDIN'.
NOW WAIT A SECOND, GOON, LETS TALK THIS OVER.
WHATCHA DOIN' WITH DAT SAW, GOON? YOU GONNA CUT SOME FIRE WOOD?
NO, NO, PLEASE!
NOOOOo!

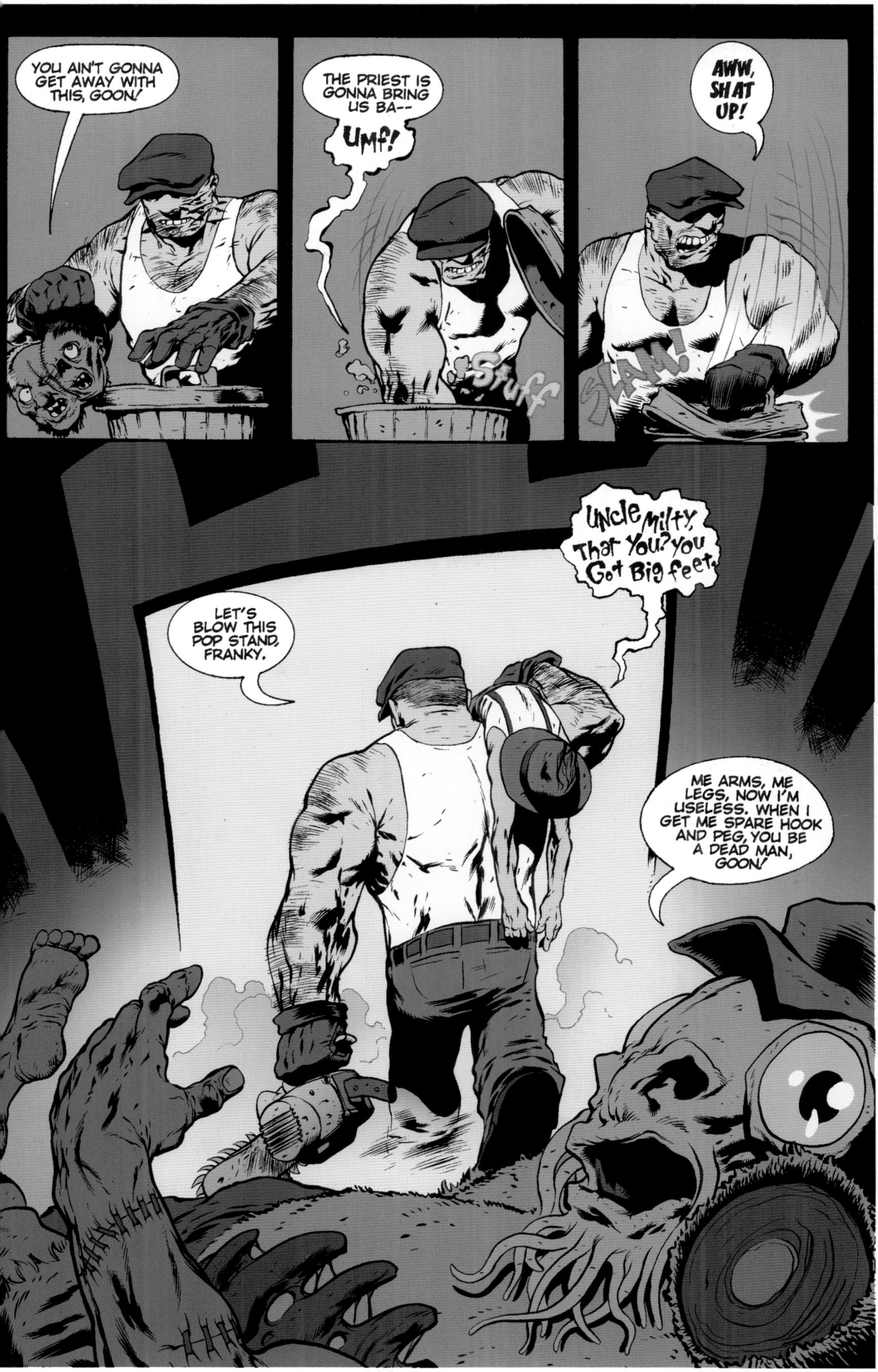
YOU AIN'T GONNA GET AWAY WITH THIS, GOON!
THE PRIEST IS GONNA BRING US BA--
UMF!
STUFF
AWW, SHAT UP!
SLAM!
UNCLE MILTY, THAT YOU? YOU GOT BIG FEET.
LET'S BLOW THIS POP STAND, FRANKY.
ME ARMS, ME LEGS, NOW I'M USELESS. WHEN I GET ME SPARE HOOK AND PEG, YOU BE A DEAD MAN, GOON!

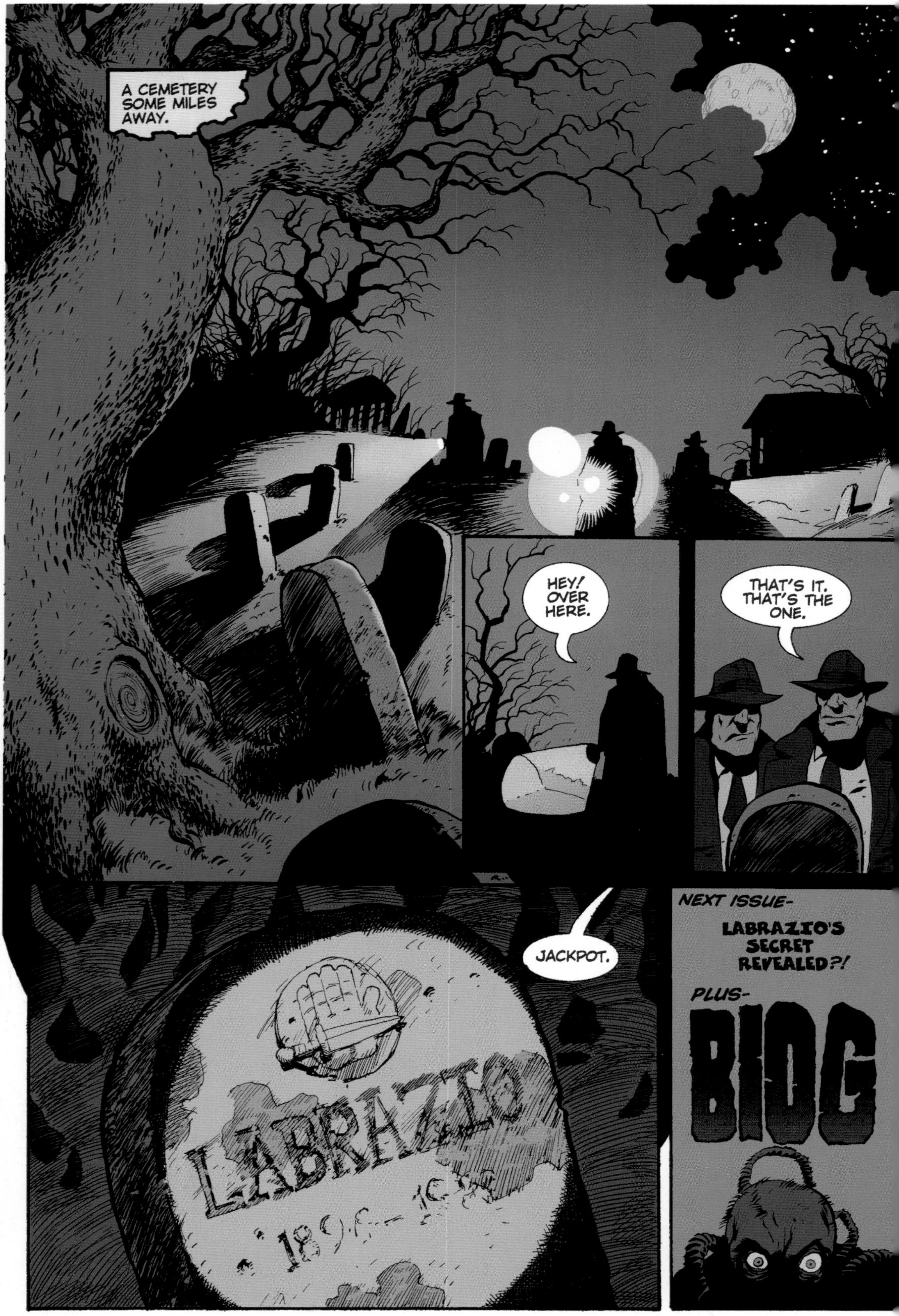
A CEMETERY SOME MILES AWAY.
HEY! OVER HERE.
THAT'S IT. THAT'S THE ONE.
JACKPOT.
LABRAZIO
NEXT ISSUE-
LABRAZIO'S SECRET REVEALED?!
PLUS-
BIOG

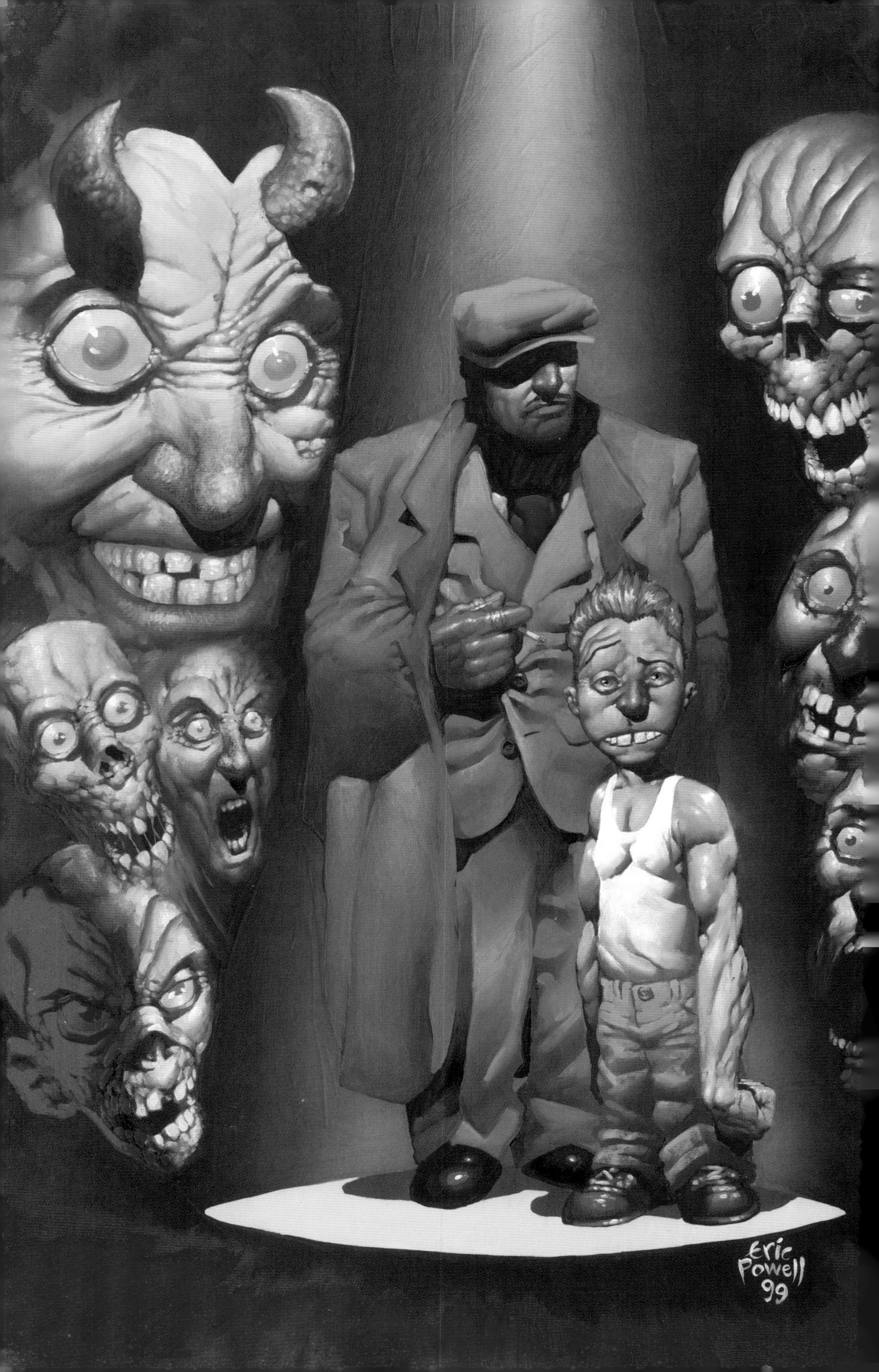
Eric
Powell
99

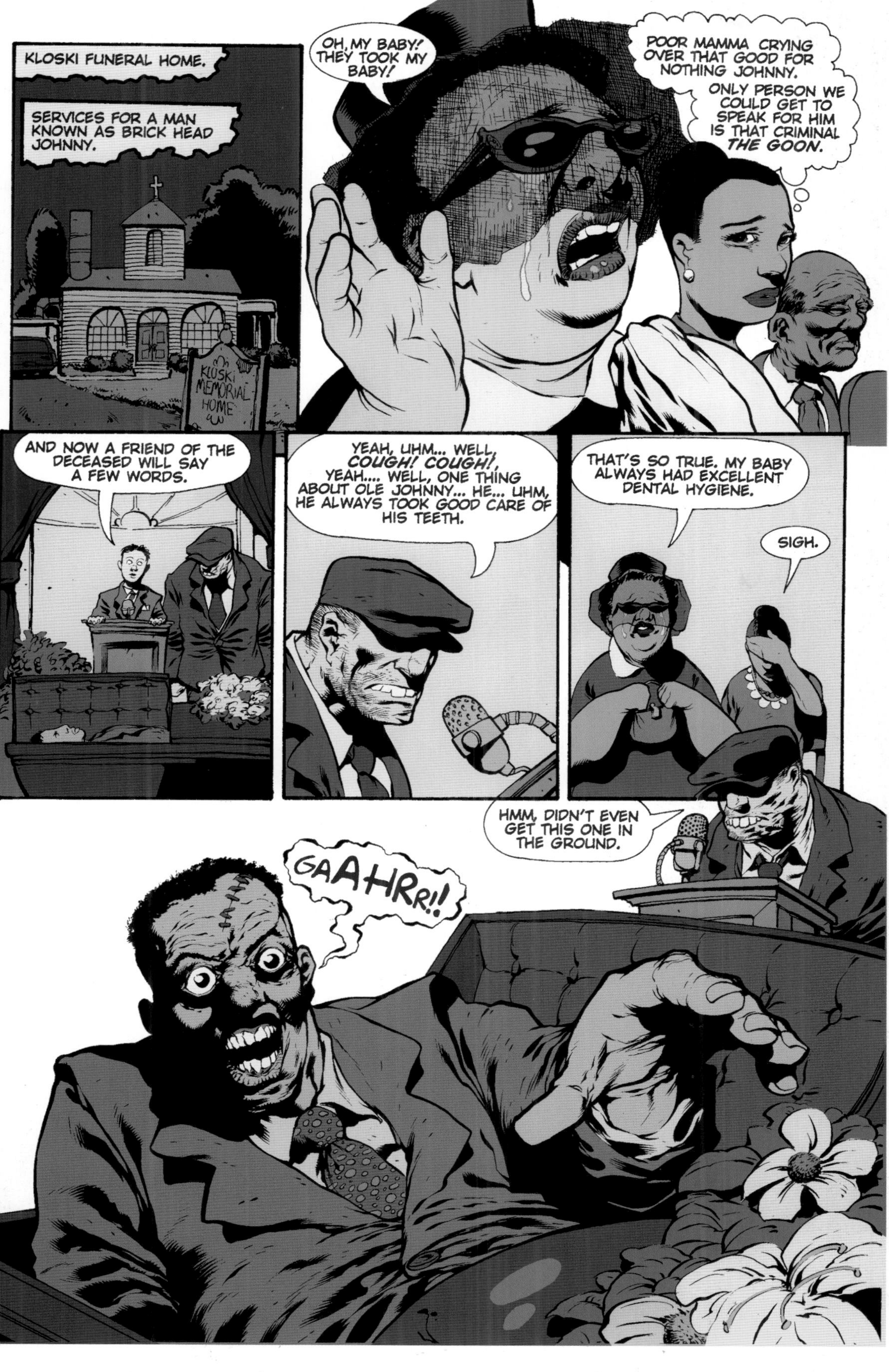
KLOSKI FUNERAL HOME.
SERVICES FOR A MAN KNOWN AS BRICK HEAD JOHNNY.
KLUSKI MEMORIAL HOME
OH, MY BABY! THEY TOOK MY BABY!
POOR MAMMA CRYING OVER THAT GOOD FOR NOTHING JOHNNY.
ONLY PERSON WE COULD GET TO SPEAK FOR HIM IS THAT CRIMINAL THE GOON.
AND NOW A FRIEND OF THE DECEASED WILL SAY A FEW WORDS.
YEAH, UHM... WELL, COUGH! COUGH!, YEAH.... WELL, ONE THING ABOUT OLE JOHNNY... HE... UHM, HE ALWAYS TOOK GOOD CARE OF HIS TEETH.
THAT'S SO TRUE. MY BABY ALWAYS HAD EXCELLENT DENTAL HYGIENE.
SIGH.
HMM, DIDN'T EVEN GET THIS ONE IN THE GROUND.
GAAHRR!!

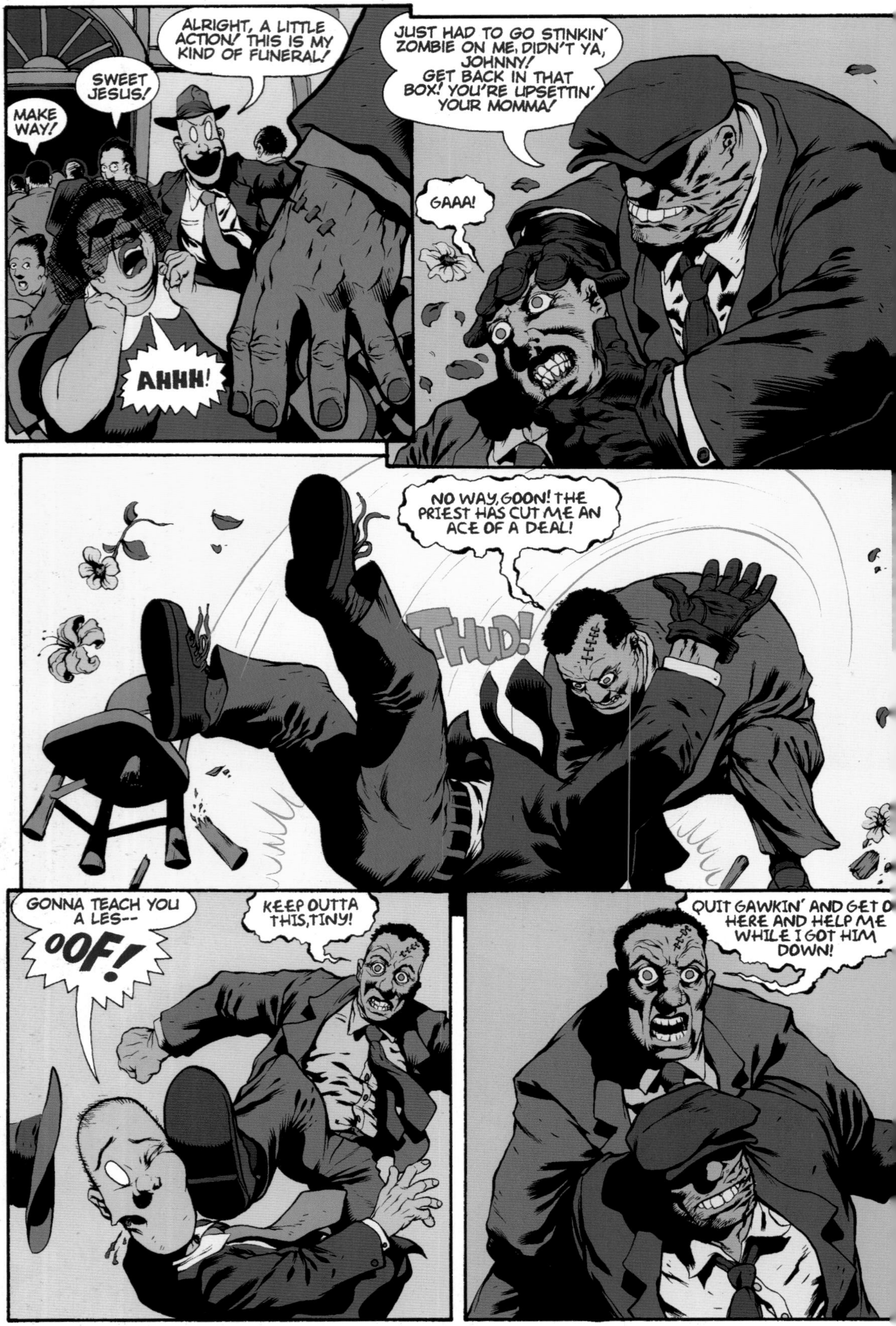
MAKE WAY!
SWEET JESUS!
ALRIGHT, A LITTLE ACTION! THIS IS MY KIND OF FUNERAL!
AHHH!
JUST HAD TO GO STINKIN' ZOMBIE ON ME, DIDN'T YA, JOHNNY! GET BACK IN THAT BOX! YOU'RE UPSETTIN' YOUR MOMMA!
GAAA!
NO WAY, GOON! THE PRIEST HAS CUT ME AN ACE OF A DEAL!
THUD!
GONNA TEACH YOU A LES--
OOF!
KEEP OUTTA THIS, TINY!
QUIT GAWKIN' AND GET O
HERE AND HELP ME WHILE I GOT HIM DOWN!

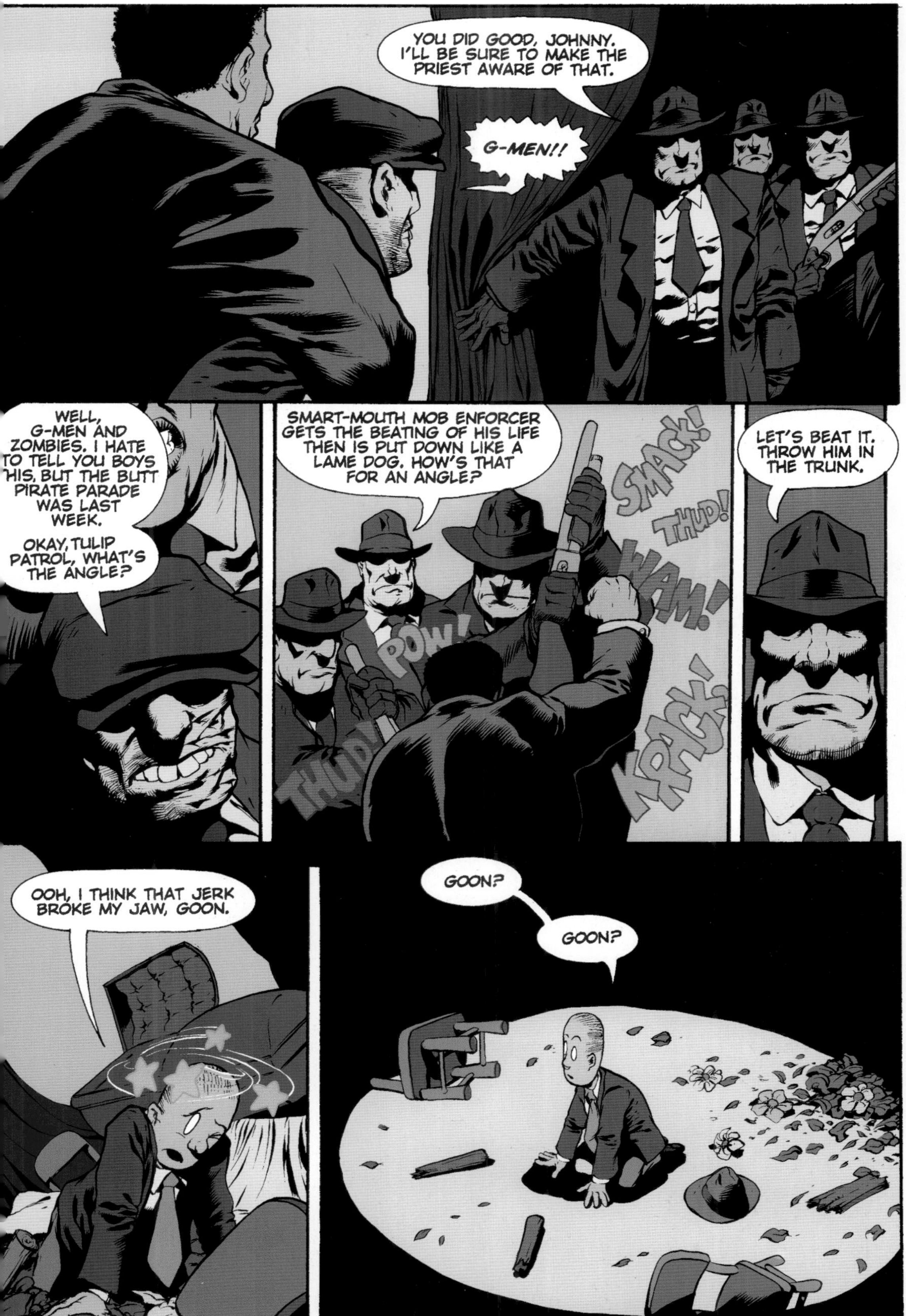
YOU DID GOOD, JOHNNY. I'LL BE SURE TO MAKE THE PRIEST AWARE OF THAT.
G-MEN!!
WELL, G-MEN AND ZOMBIES. I HATE TO TELL YOU BOYS THIS, BUT THE BUTT PIRATE PARADE WAS LAST WEEK.
OKAY, TULIP PATROL, WHAT'S THE ANGLE?
SMART-MOUTH MOB ENFORCER GETS THE BEATING OF HIS LIFE THEN IS PUT DOWN LIKE A LAME DOG. HOW'S THAT FOR AN ANGLE?
SMACK!
THUD!
WAM!
POW!
THUD!
KRACK!
LET'S BEAT IT. THROW HIM IN THE TRUNK.
OOH, I THINK THAT JERK BROKE MY JAW, GOON.
GOON?
GOON?

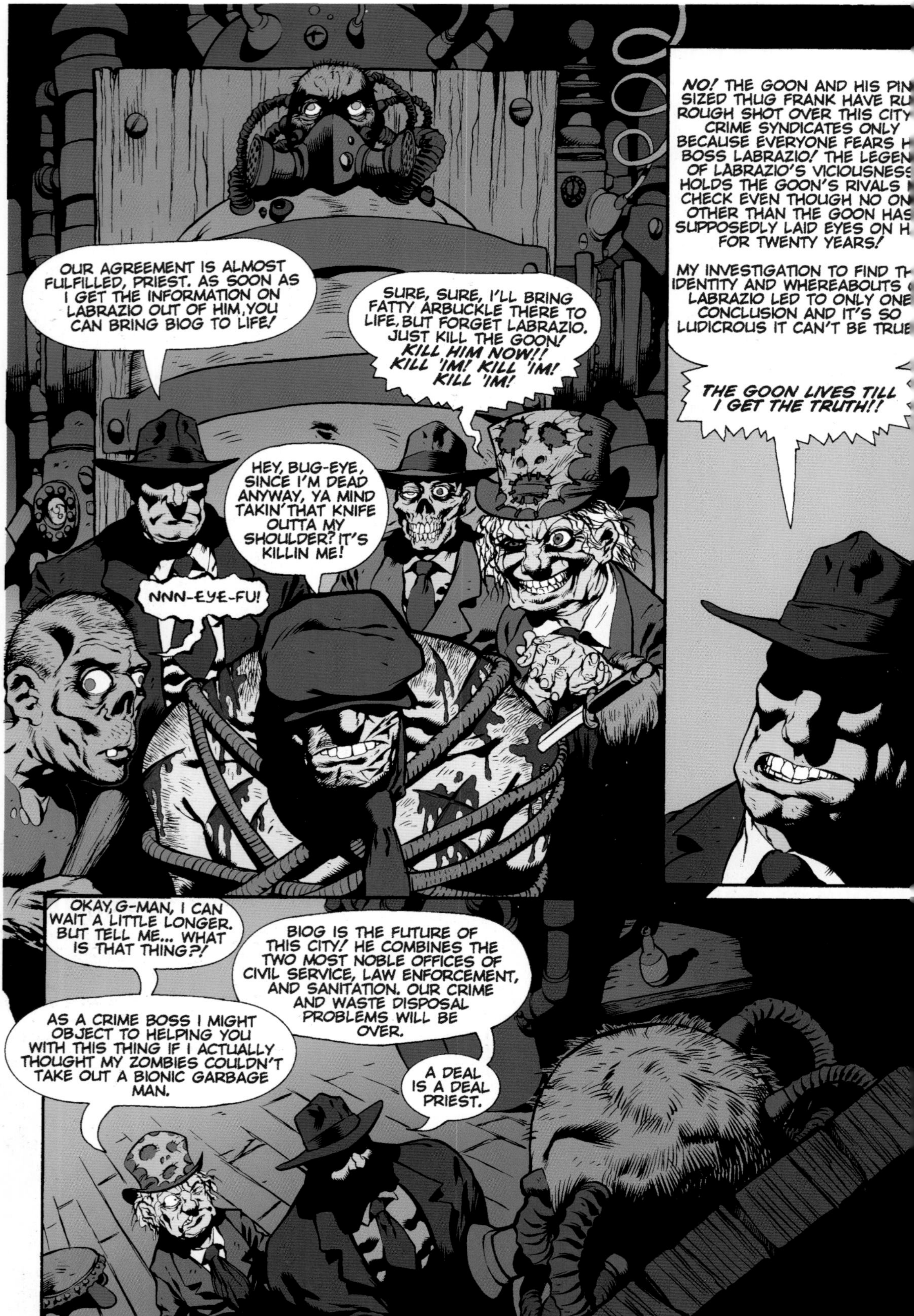
OUR AGREEMENT IS ALMOST FULFILLED, PRIEST. AS SOON AS I GET THE INFORMATION ON LABRAZIO OUT OF HIM, YOU CAN BRING BIOG TO LIFE!
SURE, SURE, I'LL BRING FATTY ARBUCKLE THERE TO LIFE, BUT FORGET LABRAZIO. JUST KILL THE GOON! KILL HIM NOW!! KILL 'IM! KILL 'IM! KILL 'IM!
NO! THE GOON AND HIS PIN SIZED THUG FRANK HAVE RU ROUGH SHOT OVER THIS CITY CRIME SYNDICATES ONLY BECAUSE EVERYONE FEARS H BOSS LABRAZIO! THE LEGEN OF LABRAZIO'S VICIOUSNESS HOLDS THE GOON'S RIVALS I CHECK EVEN THOUGH NO ON OTHER THAN THE GOON HAS SUPPOSEDLY LAID EYES ON H FOR TWENTY YEARS!
MY INVESTIGATION TO FIND TH IDENTITY AND WHEREABOUTS LABRAZIO LED TO ONLY ONE CONCLUSION AND IT'S SO LUDICROUS IT CAN'T BE TRUE
THE GOON LIVES TILL I GET THE TRUTH!!
HEY, BUG-EYE, SINCE I'M DEAD ANYWAY, YA MIND TAKIN' THAT KNIFE OUTTA MY SHOULDER? IT'S KILLIN ME!
NNN-EYE-FU!
OKAY, G-MAN, I CAN WAIT A LITTLE LONGER. BUT TELL ME... WHAT IS THAT THING?!
BIOG IS THE FUTURE OF THIS CITY! HE COMBINES THE TWO MOST NOBLE OFFICES OF CIVIL SERVICE, LAW ENFORCEMENT, AND SANITATION. OUR CRIME AND WASTE DISPOSAL PROBLEMS WILL BE OVER.
AS A CRIME BOSS I MIGHT OBJECT TO HELPING YOU WITH THIS THING IF I ACTUALLY THOUGHT MY ZOMBIES COULDN'T TAKE OUT A BIONIC GARBAGE MAN.
A DEAL IS A DEAL PRIEST.

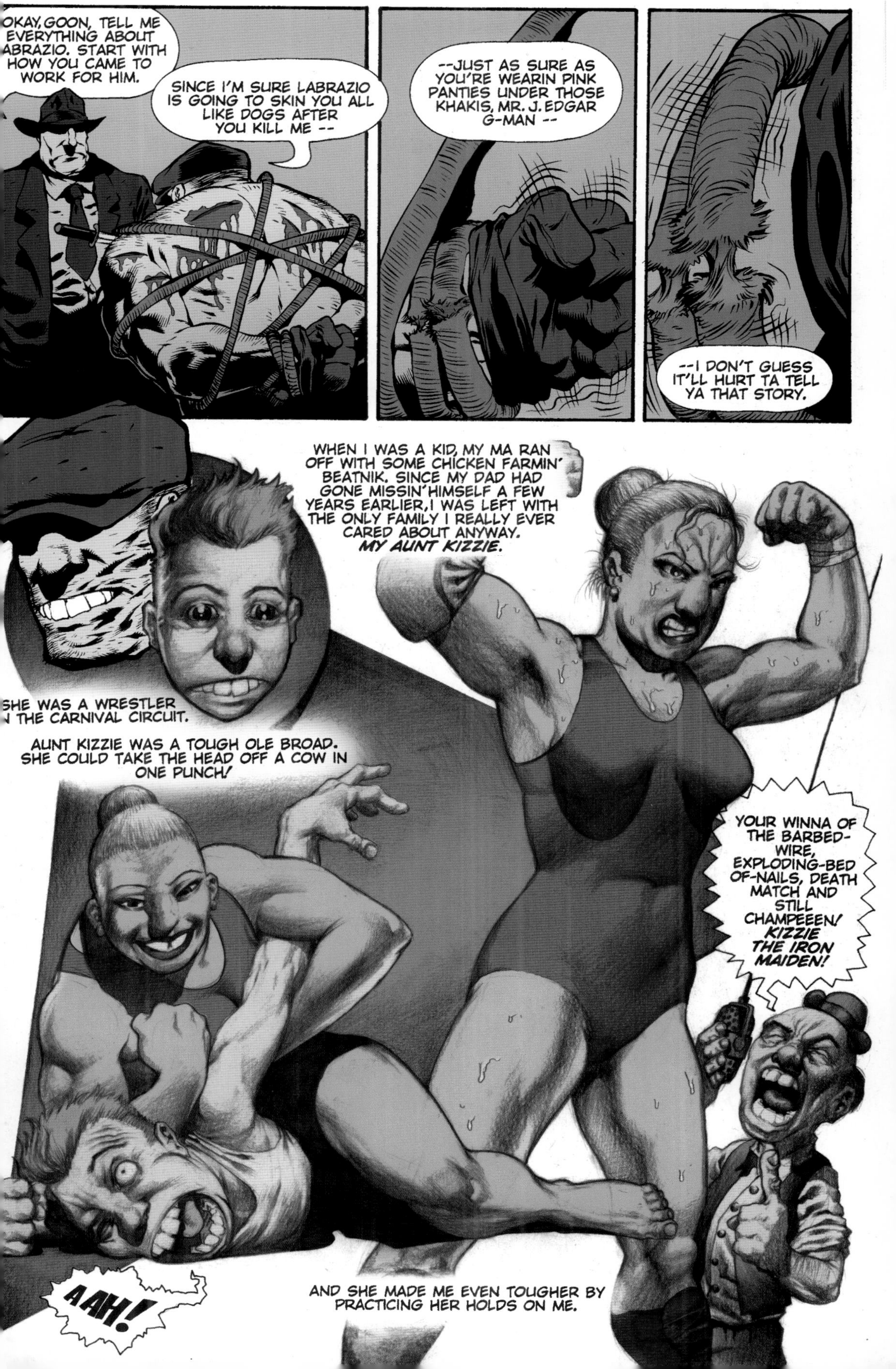
OKAY, GOON, TELL ME EVERYTHING ABOUT LABRAZIO. START WITH HOW YOU CAME TO WORK FOR HIM.
SINCE I'M SURE LABRAZIO IS GOING TO SKIN YOU ALL LIKE DOGS AFTER YOU KILL ME --
--JUST AS SURE AS YOU'RE WEARIN PINK PANTIES UNDER THOSE KHAKIS, MR. J. EDGAR G-MAN --
--I DON'T GUESS IT'LL HURT TA TELL YA THAT STORY.
WHEN I WAS A KID, MY MA RAN OFF WITH SOME CHICKEN FARMIN' BEATNIK. SINCE MY DAD HAD GONE MISSIN' HIMSELF A FEW YEARS EARLIER, I WAS LEFT WITH THE ONLY FAMILY I REALLY EVER CARED ABOUT ANYWAY. MY AUNT KIZZIE.
SHE WAS A WRESTLER ON THE CARNIVAL CIRCUIT.
AUNT KIZZIE WAS A TOUGH OLE BROAD. SHE COULD TAKE THE HEAD OFF A COW IN ONE PUNCH!
YOUR WINNA OF THE BARBED-WIRE, EXPLODING-BED OF-NAILS, DEATH MATCH AND STILL CHAMPEEEN! KIZZIE THE IRON MAIDEN!
AAH!
AND SHE MADE ME EVEN TOUGHER BY PRACTICING HER HOLDS ON ME.

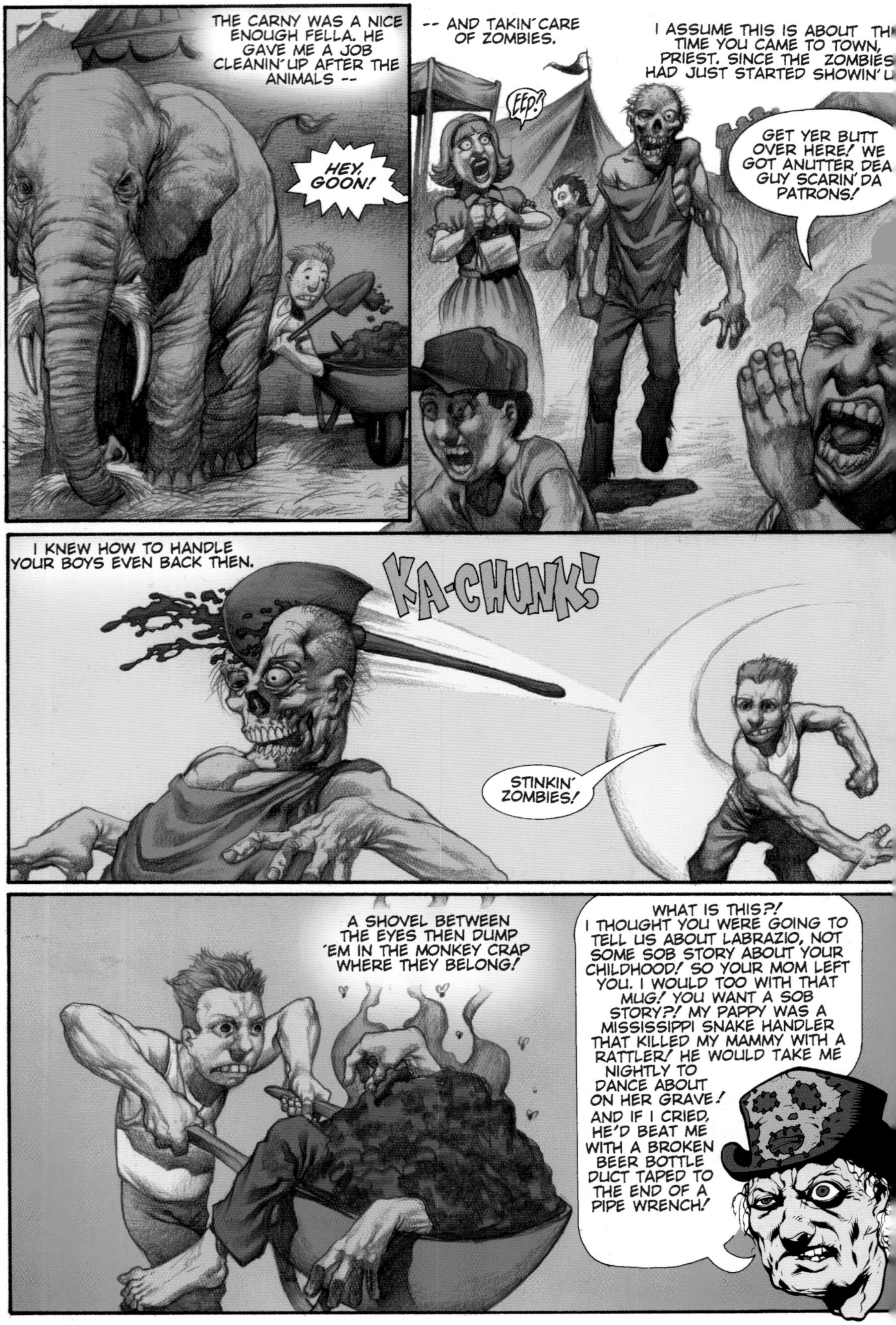

THE CARNY WAS A NICE ENOUGH FELLA. HE GAVE ME A JOB CLEANIN' UP AFTER THE ANIMALS --
HEY, GOON!
-- AND TAKIN' CARE OF ZOMBIES.
I ASSUME THIS IS ABOUT TH TIME YOU CAME TO TOWN, PRIEST. SINCE THE ZOMBIES HAD JUST STARTED SHOWIN' U
EEP!
GET YER BUTT OVER HERE! WE GOT ANUTTER DEA GUY SCARIN' DA PATRONS!
I KNEW HOW TO HANDLE YOUR BOYS EVEN BACK THEN.
KA-CHUNK!
STINKIN' ZOMBIES!
A SHOVEL BETWEEN THE EYES THEN DUMP 'EM IN THE MONKEY CRAP WHERE THEY BELONG!
WHAT IS THIS?! I THOUGHT YOU WERE GOING TO TELL US ABOUT LABRAZIO, NOT SOME SOB STORY ABOUT YOUR CHILDHOOD! SO YOUR MOM LEFT YOU. I WOULD TOO WITH THAT MUG! YOU WANT A SOB STORY?! MY PAPPY WAS A MISSISSIPPI SNAKE HANDLER THAT KILLED MY MAMMY WITH A RATTLER! HE WOULD TAKE ME NIGHTLY TO DANCE ABOUT ON HER GRAVE! AND IF I CRIED, HE'D BEAT ME WITH A BROKEN BEER BOTTLE DUCT TAPED TO THE END OF A PIPE WRENCH!

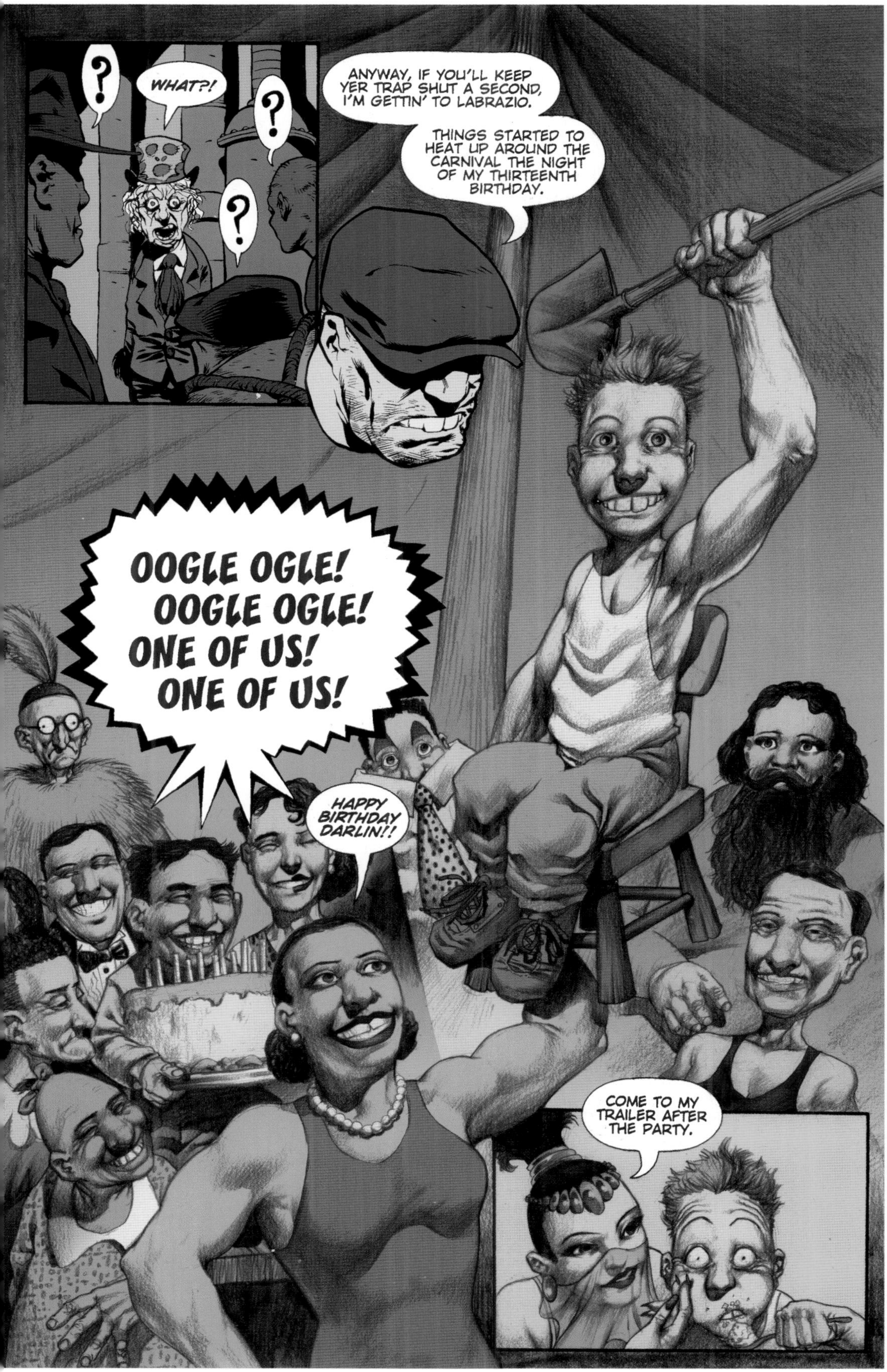
?
WHAT?!
?
?
ANYWAY, IF YOU'LL KEEP YER TRAP SHUT A SECOND, I'M GETTIN' TO LABRAZIO.
THINGS STARTED TO HEAT UP AROUND THE CARNIVAL THE NIGHT OF MY THIRTEENTH BIRTHDAY.
OOGLE OGLE! OOGLE OGLE! ONE OF US! ONE OF US!
HAPPY BIRTHDAY DARLIN!!
COME TO MY TRAILER AFTER THE PARTY.

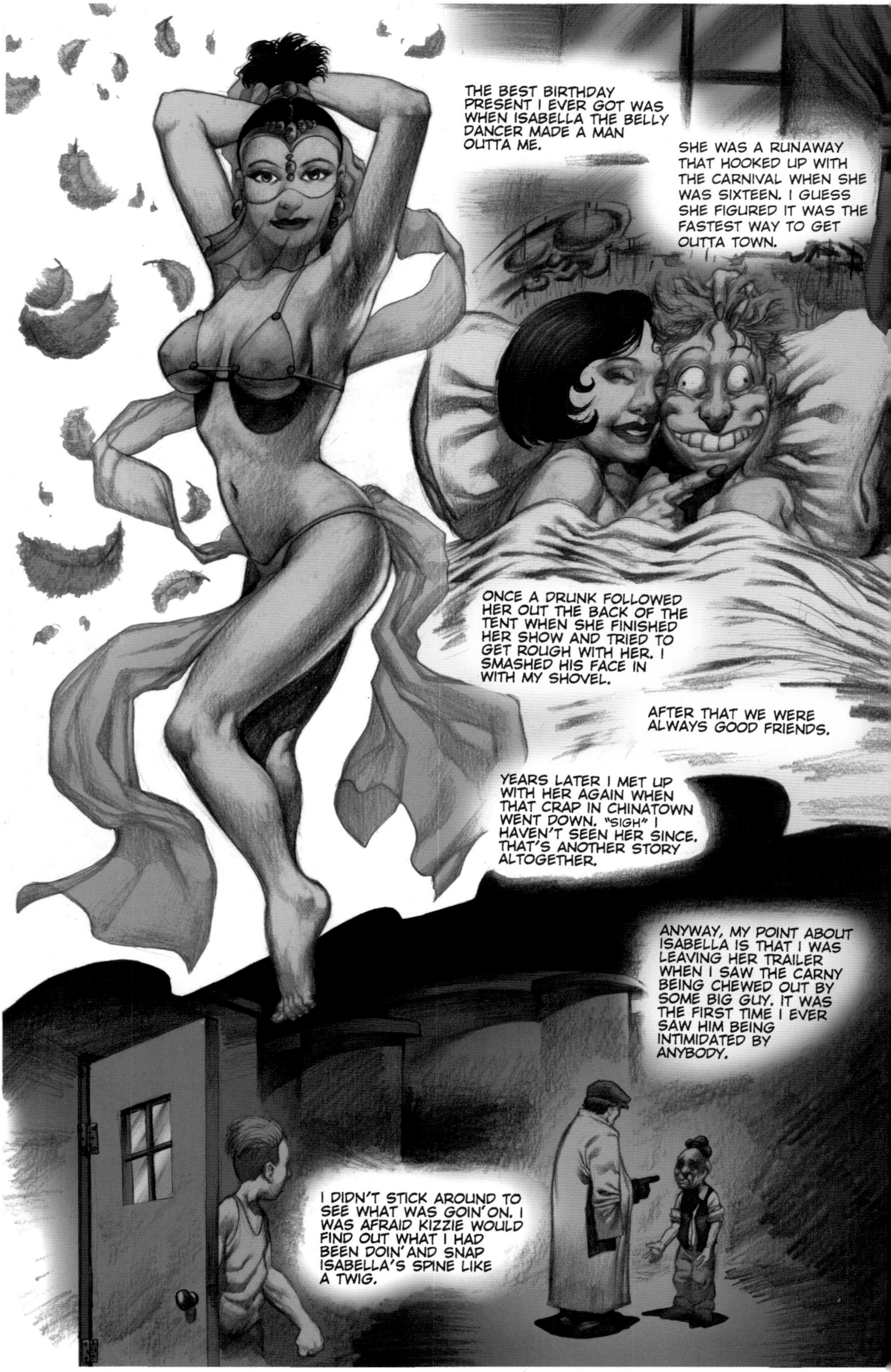
THE BEST BIRTHDAY PRESENT I EVER GOT WAS WHEN ISABELLA THE BELLY DANCER MADE A MAN OUTTA ME.
SHE WAS A RUNAWAY THAT HOOKED UP WITH THE CARNIVAL WHEN SHE WAS SIXTEEN. I GUESS SHE FIGURED IT WAS THE FASTEST WAY TO GET OUTTA TOWN.
ONCE A DRUNK FOLLOWED HER OUT THE BACK OF THE TENT WHEN SHE FINISHED HER SHOW AND TRIED TO GET ROUGH WITH HER. I SMASHED HIS FACE IN WITH MY SHOVEL.
AFTER THAT WE WERE ALWAYS GOOD FRIENDS.
YEARS LATER I MET UP WITH HER AGAIN WHEN THAT CRAP IN CHINATOWN WENT DOWN. "SIGH" I HAVEN'T SEEN HER SINCE. THAT'S ANOTHER STORY ALTOGETHER.
ANYWAY, MY POINT ABOUT ISABELLA IS THAT I WAS LEAVING HER TRAILER WHEN I SAW THE CARNY BEING CHEWED OUT BY SOME BIG GUY. IT WAS THE FIRST TIME I EVER SAW HIM BEING INTIMIDATED BY ANYBODY.
I DIDN'T STICK AROUND TO SEE WHAT WAS GOIN'ON. I WAS AFRAID KIZZIE WOULD FIND OUT WHAT I HAD BEEN DOIN'AND SNAP ISABELLA'S SPINE LIKE A TWIG.

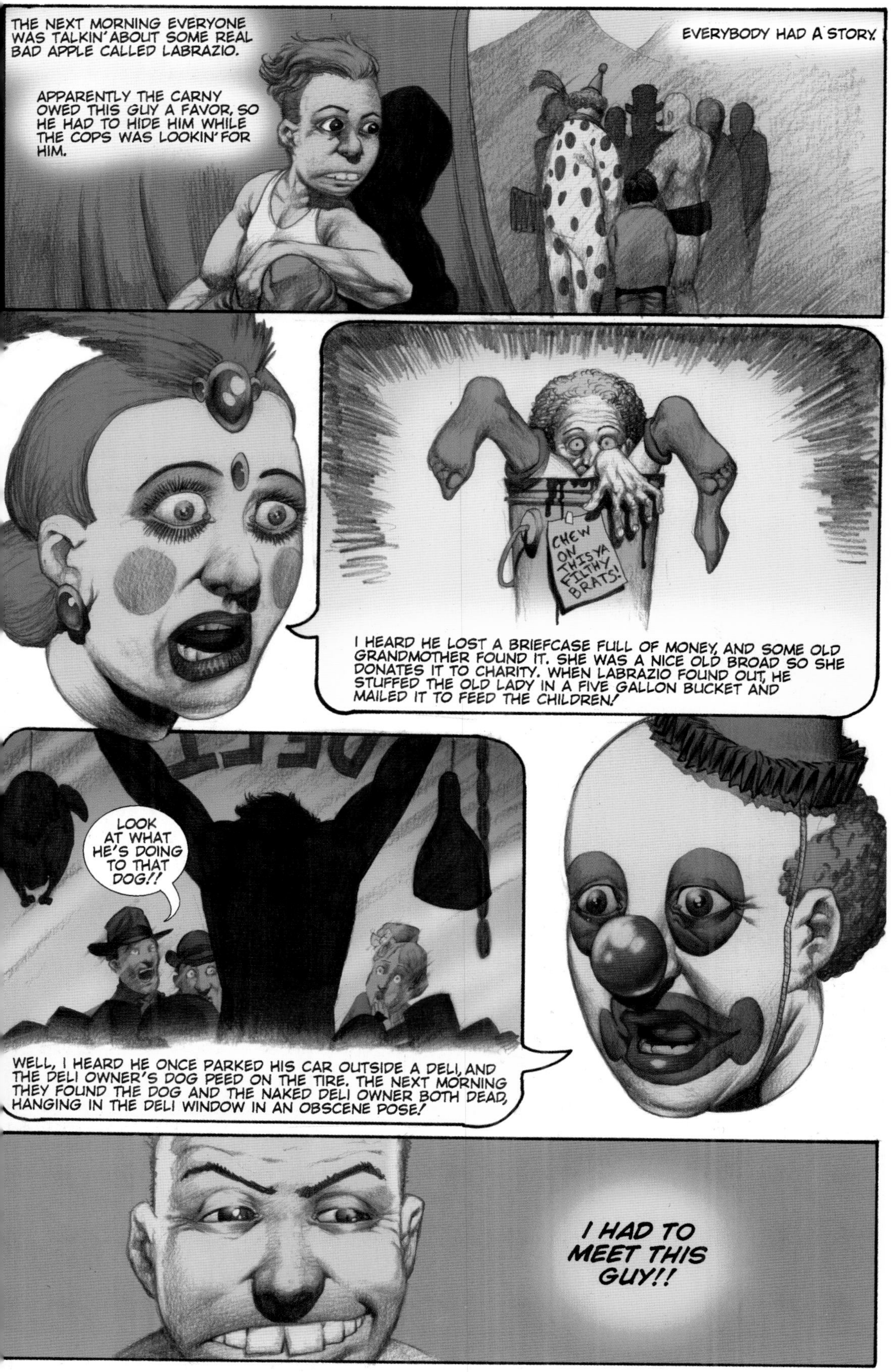
THE NEXT MORNING EVERYONE WAS TALKIN' ABOUT SOME REAL BAD APPLE CALLED LABRAZIO.
APPARENTLY THE CARNY OWED THIS GUY A FAVOR, SO HE HAD TO HIDE HIM WHILE THE COPS WAS LOOKIN' FOR HIM.
EVERYBODY HAD A STORY.
CHEW ON THIS YA FILTHY BRATS!
I HEARD HE LOST A BRIEFCASE FULL OF MONEY, AND SOME OLD GRANDMOTHER FOUND IT. SHE WAS A NICE OLD BROAD SO SHE DONATES IT TO CHARITY. WHEN LABRAZIO FOUND OUT, HE STUFFED THE OLD LADY IN A FIVE GALLON BUCKET AND MAILED IT TO FEED THE CHILDREN!
LOOK AT WHAT HE'S DOING TO THAT DOG!!
WELL, I HEARD HE ONCE PARKED HIS CAR OUTSIDE A DELI, AND THE DELI OWNER'S DOG PEED ON THE TIRE. THE NEXT MORNING THEY FOUND THE DOG AND THE NAKED DELI OWNER BOTH DEAD, HANGING IN THE DELI WINDOW IN AN OBSCENE POSE!
I HAD TO MEET THIS GUY!!

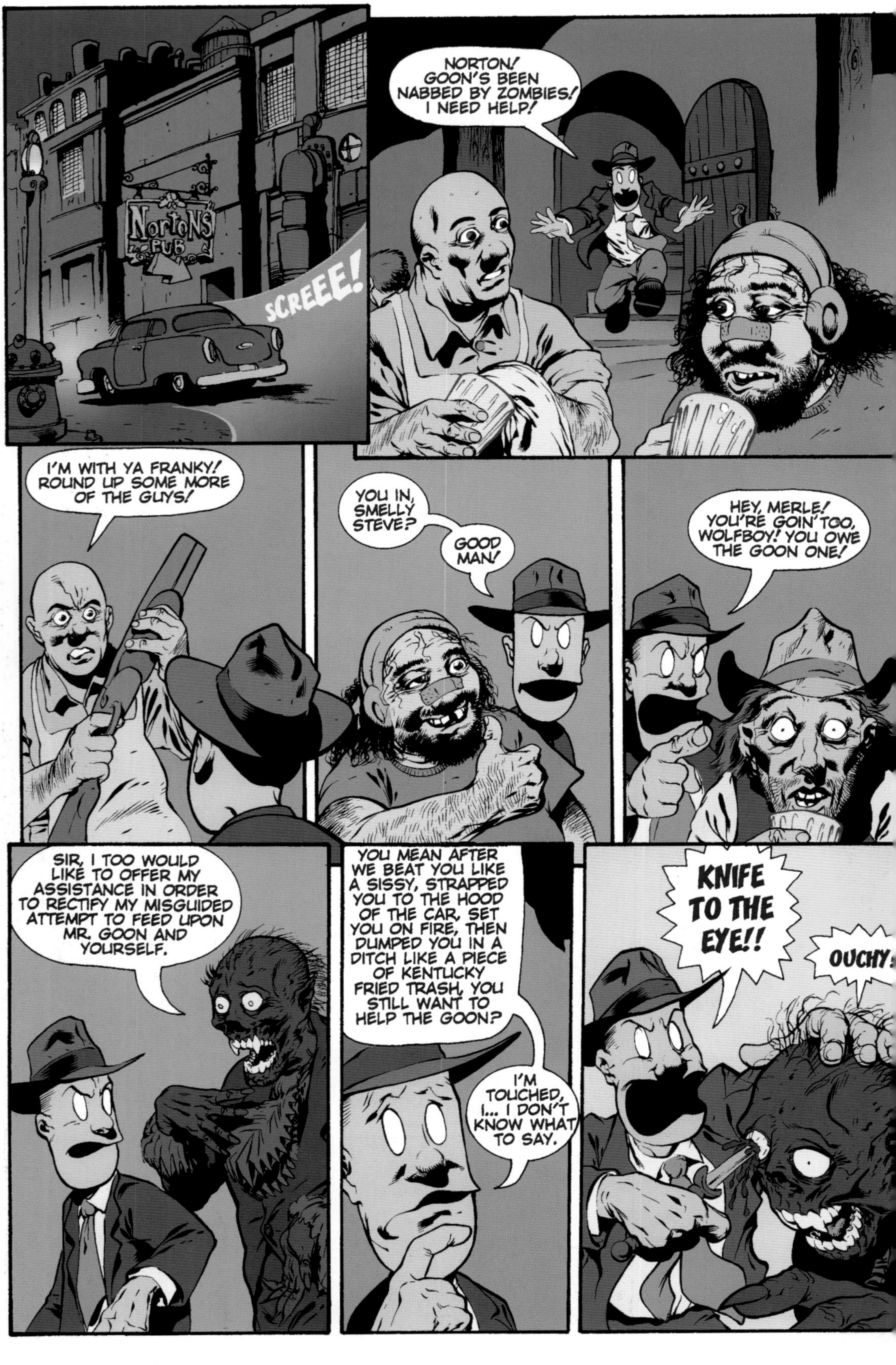

NORTON'S PUB
SCREEE!
NORTON! GOON'S BEEN NABBED BY ZOMBIES! I NEED HELP!
I'M WITH YA FRANKY! ROUND UP SOME MORE OF THE GUYS!
YOU IN, SMELLY STEVE?
GOOD MAN!
HEY, MERLE! YOU'RE GOIN' TOO, WOLFBOY! YOU OWE THE GOON ONE!
SIR, I TOO WOULD LIKE TO OFFER MY ASSISTANCE IN ORDER TO RECTIFY MY MISGUIDED ATTEMPT TO FEED UPON MR. GOON AND YOURSELF.
YOU MEAN AFTER WE BEAT YOU LIKE A SISSY, STRAPPED YOU TO THE HOOD OF THE CAR, SET YOU ON FIRE, THEN DUMPED YOU IN A DITCH LIKE A PIECE OF KENTUCKY FRIED TRASH, YOU STILL WANT TO HELP THE GOON?
I'M TOUCHED, I... I DON'T KNOW WHAT TO SAY.
KNIFE TO THE EYE!!
OUCHY!

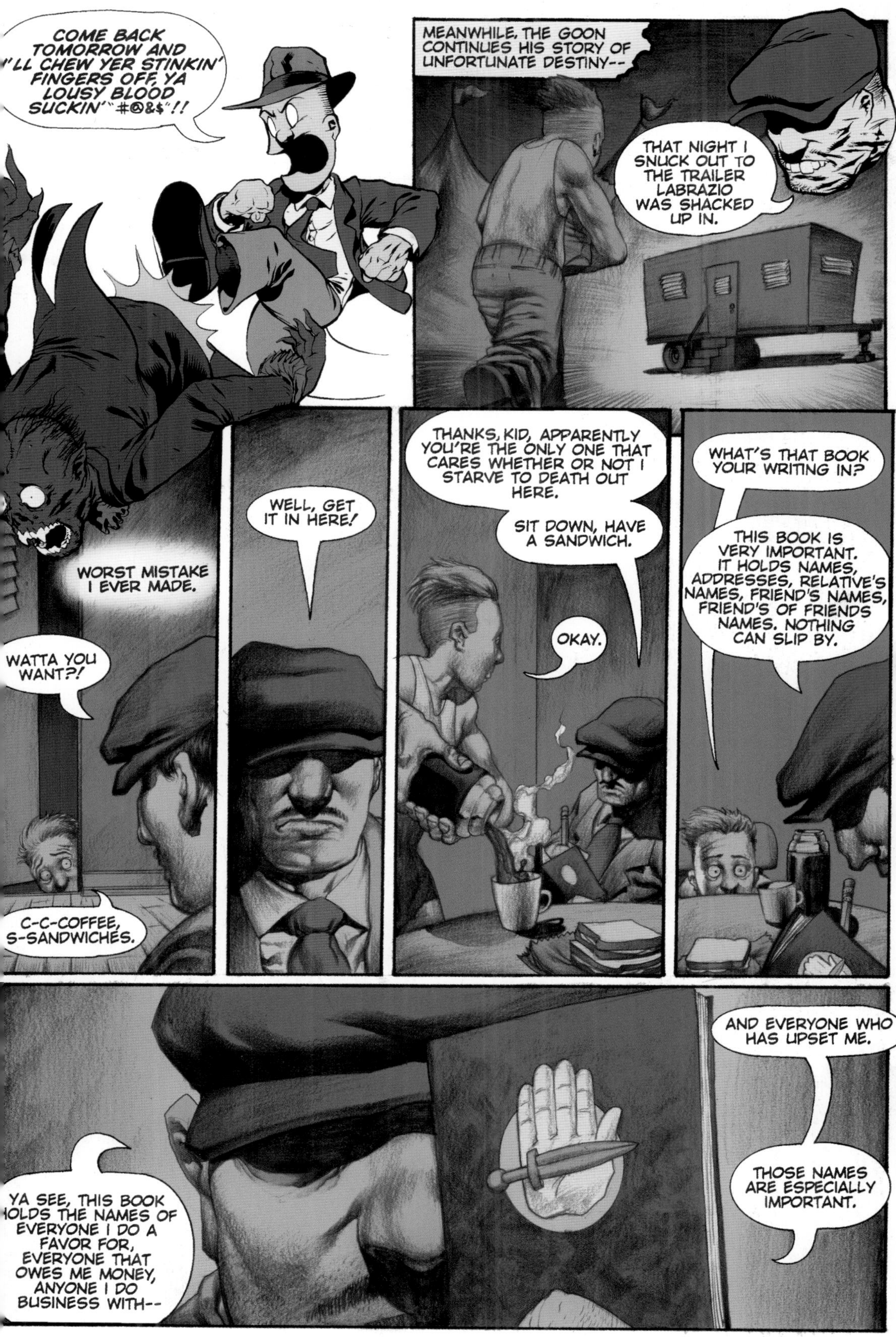
COME BACK TOMORROW AND I'LL CHEW YER STINKIN' FINGERS OFF, YA LOUSY BLOOD SUCKIN' "#@&$"!!
MEANWHILE, THE GOON CONTINUES HIS STORY OF UNFORTUNATE DESTINY--
THAT NIGHT I SNUCK OUT TO THE TRAILER LABRAZIO WAS SHACKED UP IN.
WORST MISTAKE I EVER MADE.
WATTA YOU WANT?!
C-C-COFFEE, S-SANDWICHES.
WELL, GET IT IN HERE!
THANKS, KID, APPARENTLY YOU'RE THE ONLY ONE THAT CARES WHETHER OR NOT I STARVE TO DEATH OUT HERE.
SIT DOWN, HAVE A SANDWICH.
OKAY.
WHAT'S THAT BOOK YOUR WRITING IN?
THIS BOOK IS VERY IMPORTANT. IT HOLDS NAMES, ADDRESSES, RELATIVE'S NAMES, FRIEND'S NAMES, FRIEND'S OF FRIENDS NAMES. NOTHING CAN SLIP BY.
YA SEE, THIS BOOK HOLDS THE NAMES OF EVERYONE I DO A FAVOR FOR, EVERYONE THAT OWES ME MONEY, ANYONE I DO BUSINESS WITH--
AND EVERYONE WHO HAS UPSET ME.
THOSE NAMES ARE ESPECIALLY IMPORTANT.

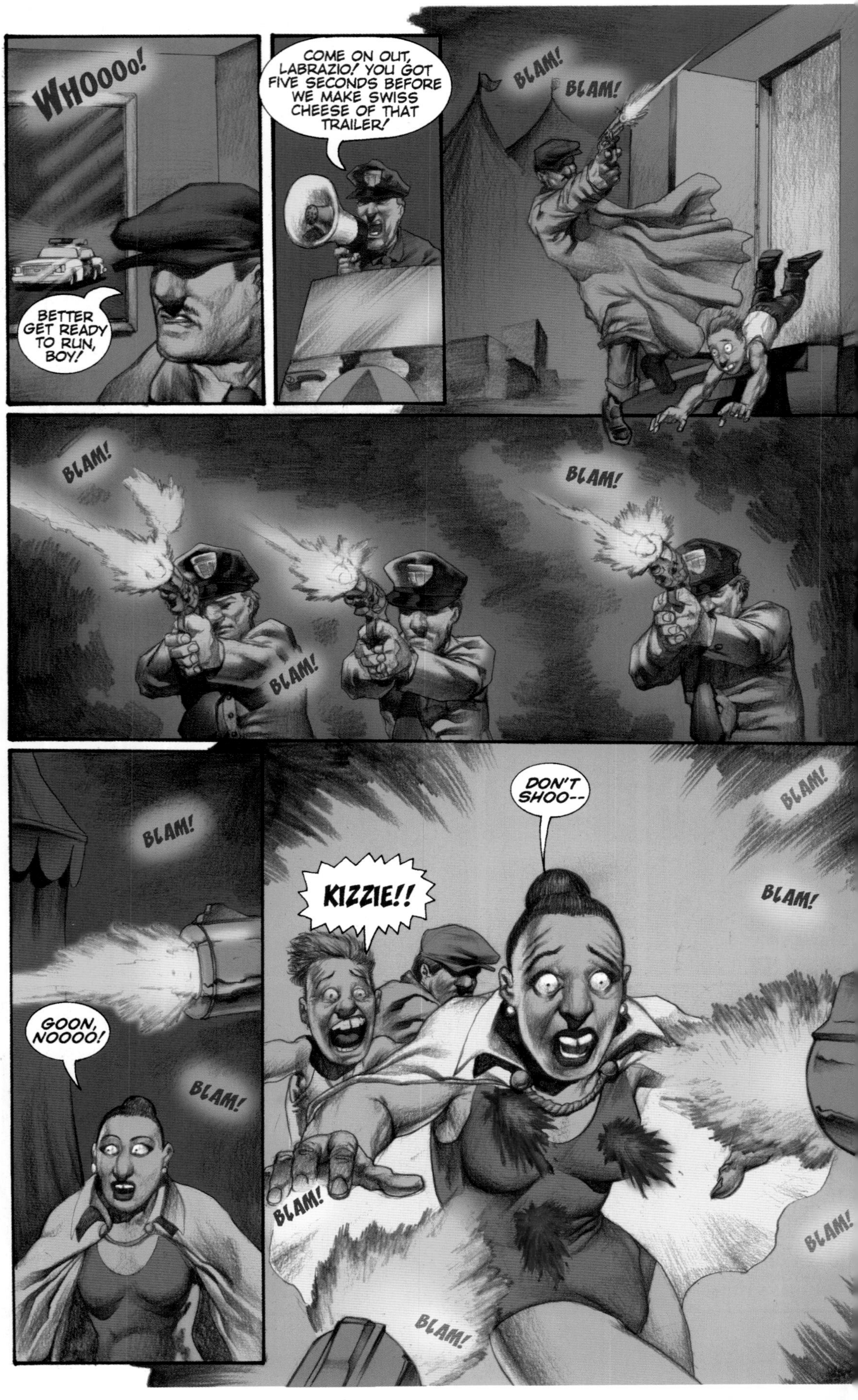
WHOOOo!
BETTER GET READY TO RUN, BOY!
COME ON OUT, LABRAZIO! YOU GOT FIVE SECONDS BEFORE WE MAKE SWISS CHEESE OF THAT TRAILER!
BLAM!
BLAM!
BLAM!
BLAM!
BLAM!
BLAM!
GOON, NOOOO!
BLAM!
DON'T SHOO--
BLAM!
KIZZIE!!
BLAM!
BLAM!
BLAM!
BLAM!

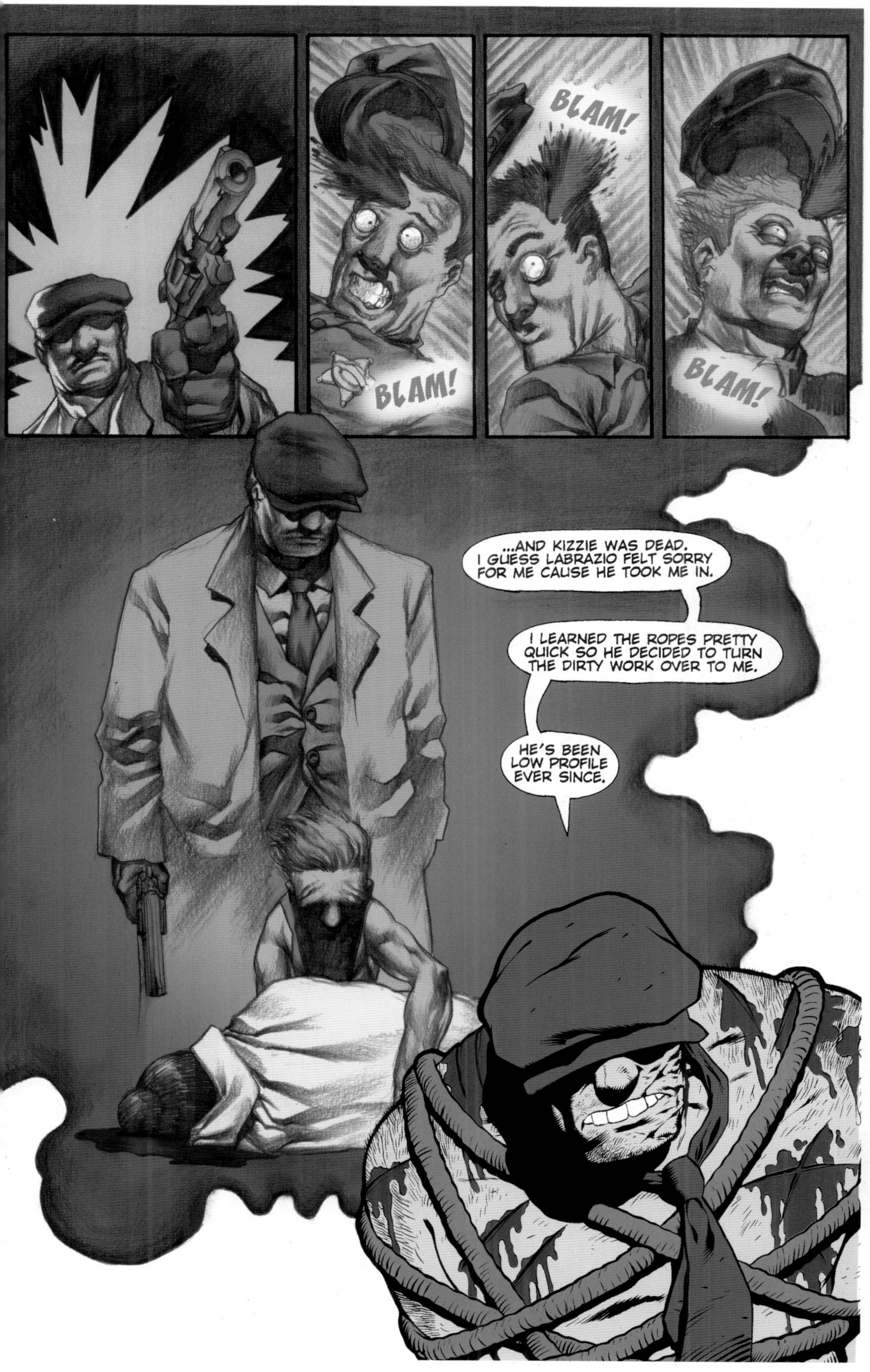
BLAM!
BLAM!
BLAM!
...AND KIZZIE WAS DEAD. I GUESS LABRAZIO FELT SORRY FOR ME CAUSE HE TOOK ME IN.
I LEARNED THE ROPES PRETTY QUICK SO HE DECIDED TO TURN THE DIRTY WORK OVER TO ME.
HE'S BEEN LOW PROFILE EVER SINCE.

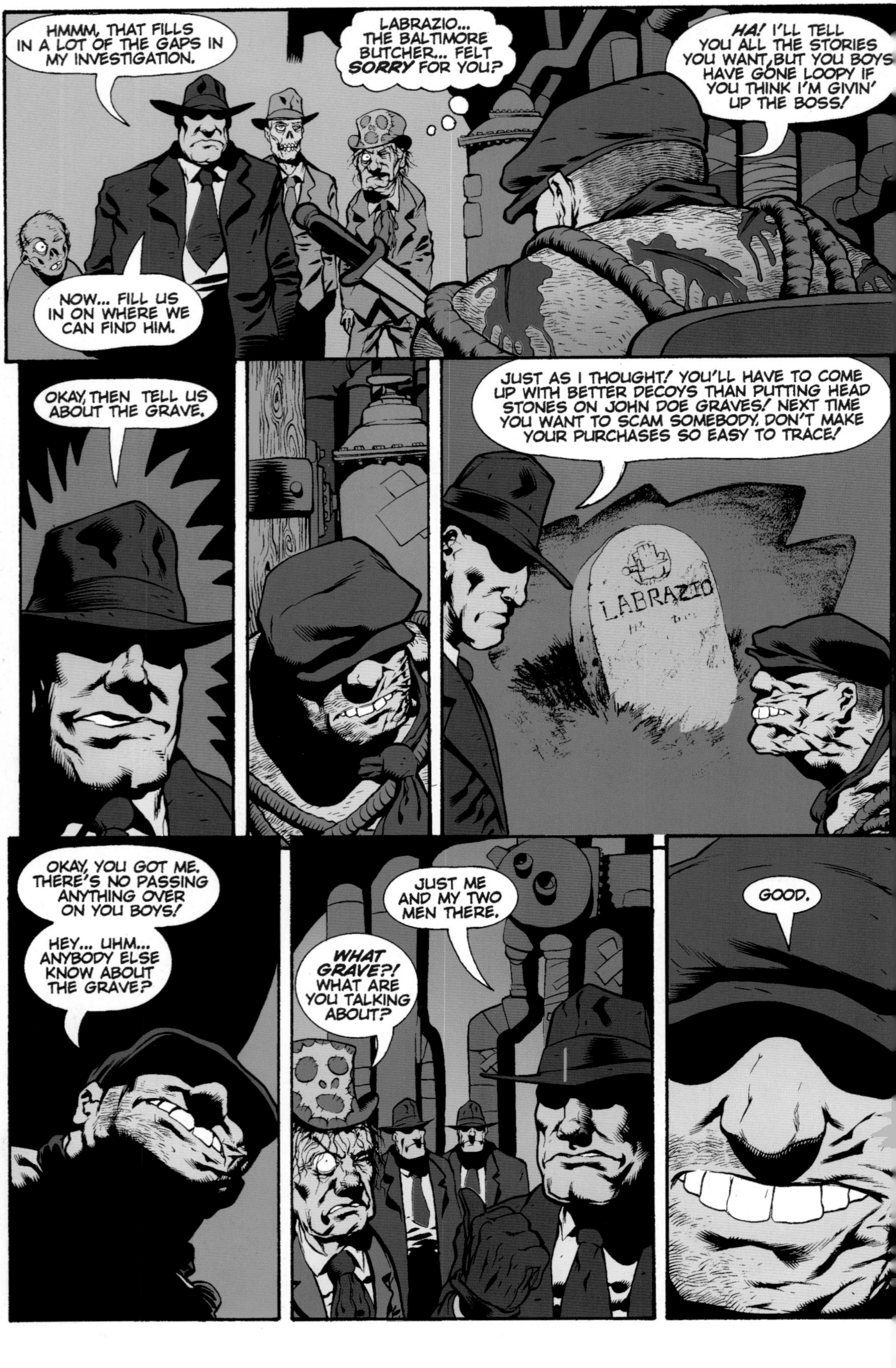

HMMM, THAT FILLS IN A LOT OF THE GAPS IN MY INVESTIGATION.
LABRAZIO... THE BALTIMORE BUTCHER... FELT SORRY FOR YOU?
HA! I'LL TELL YOU ALL THE STORIES YOU WANT, BUT YOU BOYS HAVE GONE LOOPY IF YOU THINK I'M GIVIN' UP THE BOSS!
NOW... FILL US IN ON WHERE WE CAN FIND HIM.
OKAY, THEN TELL US ABOUT THE GRAVE.
JUST AS I THOUGHT! YOU'LL HAVE TO COME UP WITH BETTER DECOYS THAN PUTTING HEAD STONES ON JOHN DOE GRAVES! NEXT TIME YOU WANT TO SCAM SOMEBODY, DON'T MAKE YOUR PURCHASES SO EASY TO TRACE!
LABRAZIO
OKAY, YOU GOT ME. THERE'S NO PASSING ANYTHING OVER ON YOU BOYS!
HEY... UHM... ANYBODY ELSE KNOW ABOUT THE GRAVE?
JUST ME AND MY TWO MEN THERE.
WHAT GRAVE?! WHAT ARE YOU TALKING ABOUT?
GOOD.

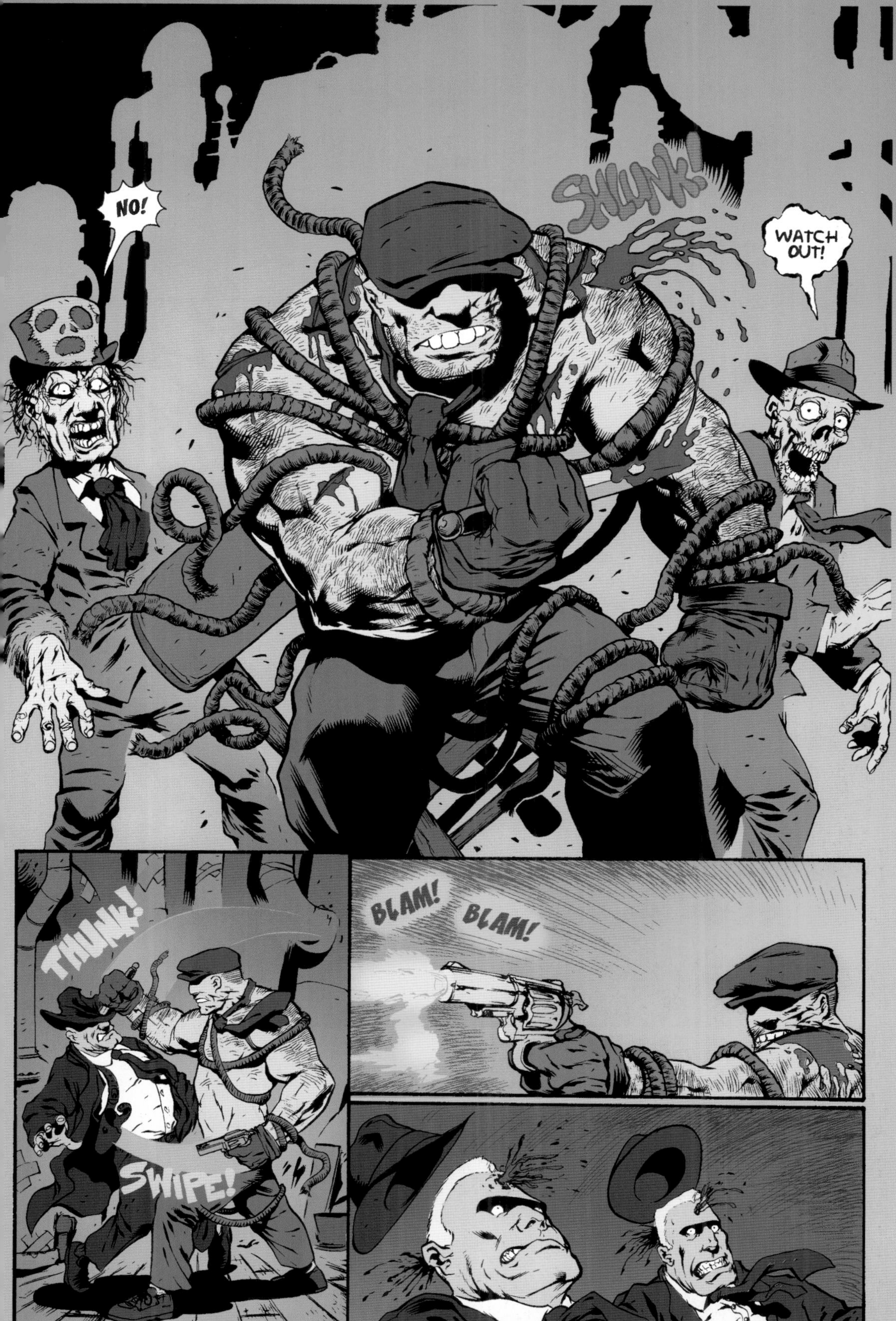
NO!
SHLUNK!
WATCH OUT!
THUNK!
SWIPE!
BLAM!
BLAM!

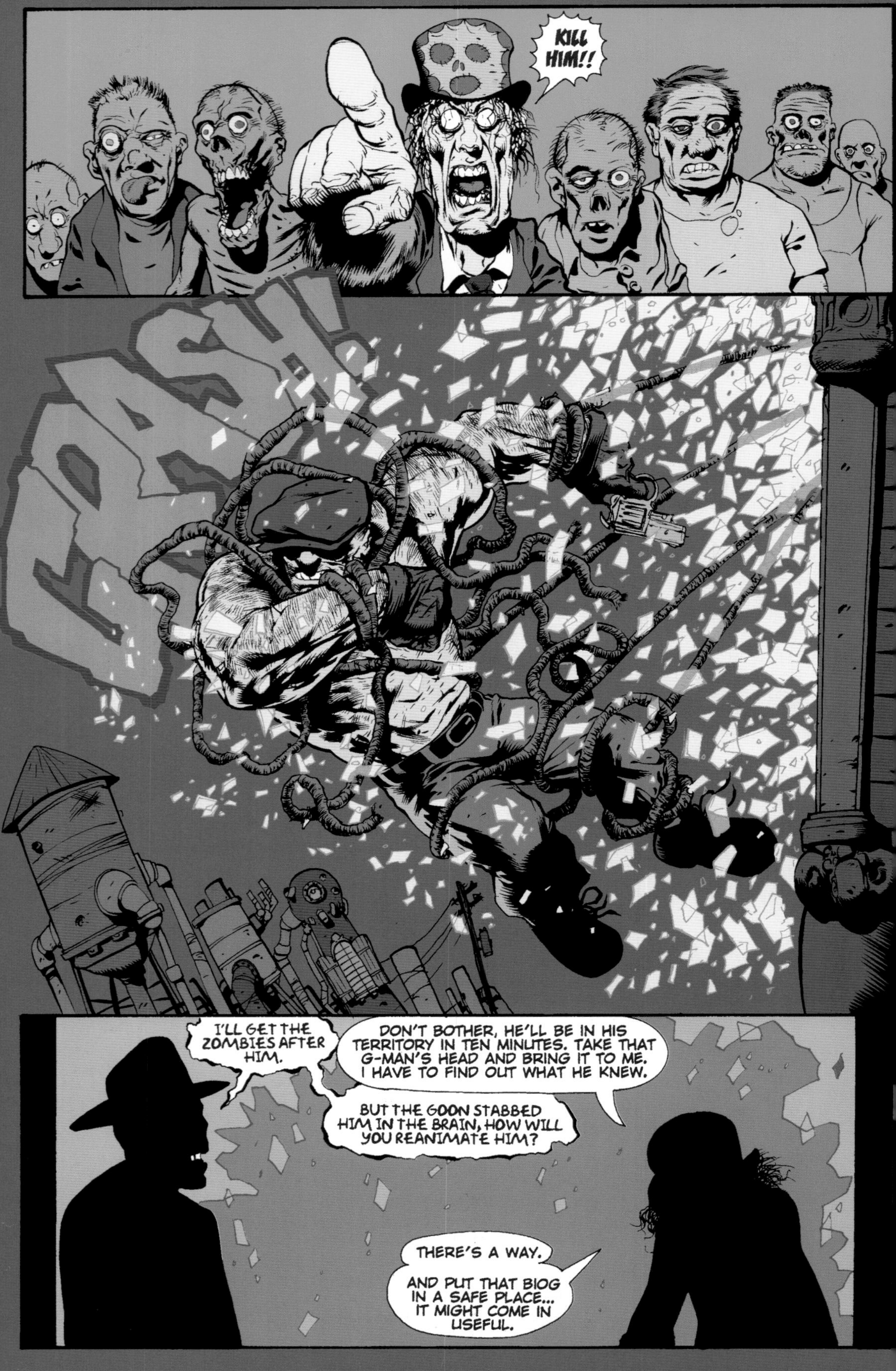
KILL HIM!!
CRASH!!
I'LL GET THE ZOMBIES AFTER HIM.
DON'T BOTHER, HE'LL BE IN HIS TERRITORY IN TEN MINUTES. TAKE THAT G-MAN'S HEAD AND BRING IT TO ME. I HAVE TO FIND OUT WHAT HE KNEW.
BUT THE GOON STABBED HIM IN THE BRAIN, HOW WILL YOU REANIMATE HIM?
THERE'S A WAY.
AND PUT THAT BIOG IN A SAFE PLACE... IT MIGHT COME IN USEFUL.

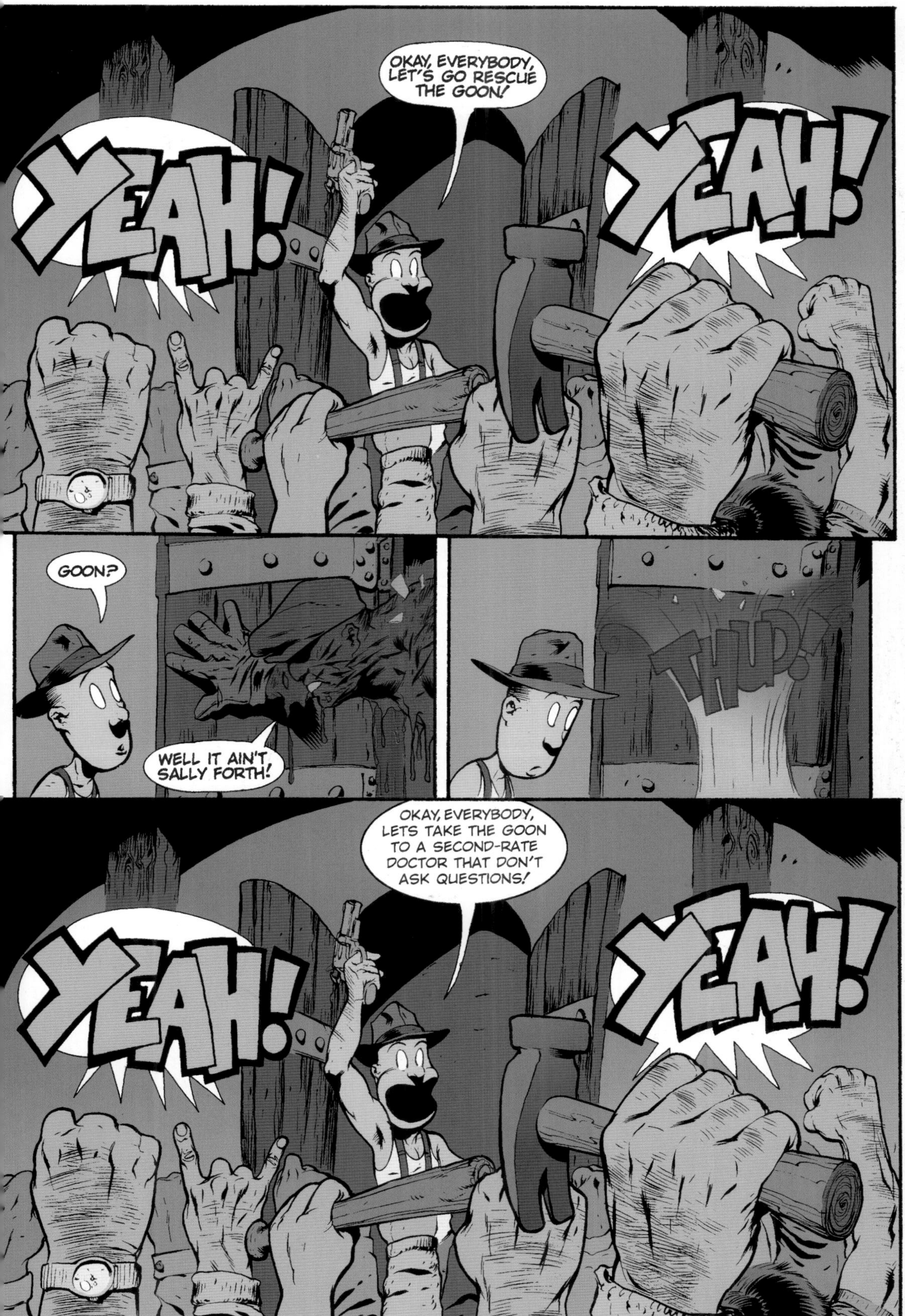
YEAH!
OKAY, EVERYBODY, LET'S GO RESCUE THE GOON!
YEAH!
GOON?
WELL IT AIN'T SALLY FORTH!
THUD!!
OKAY, EVERYBODY, LETS TAKE THE GOON TO A SECOND-RATE DOCTOR THAT DON'T ASK QUESTIONS!
YEAH!
YEAH!

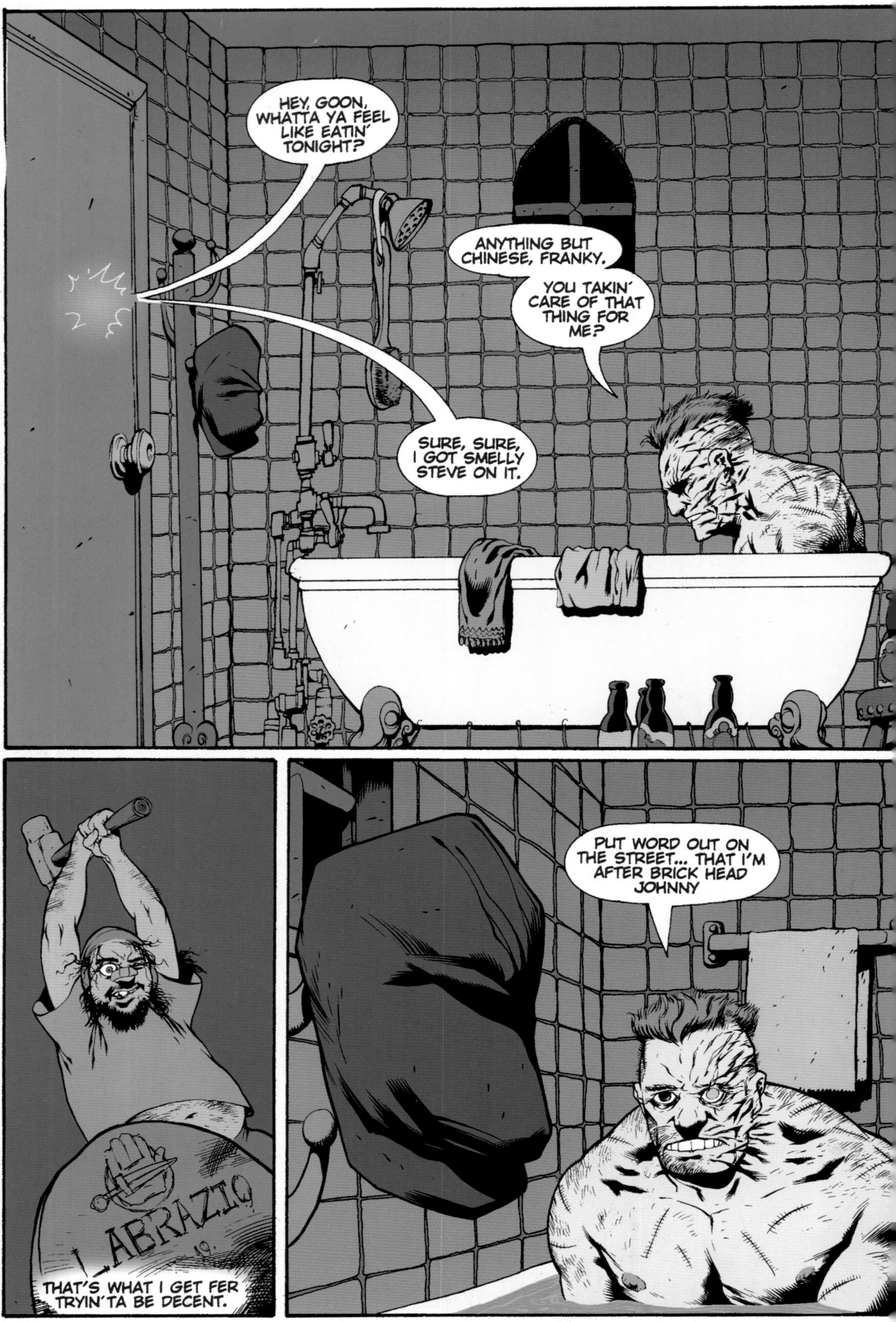
HEY, GOON, WHATTA YA FEEL LIKE EATIN' TONIGHT?
ANYTHING BUT CHINESE, FRANKY.
YOU TAKIN' CARE OF THAT THING FOR ME?
SURE, SURE, I GOT SMELLY STEVE ON IT.
ABRAZIO
THAT'S WHAT I GET FER TRYIN'TA BE DECENT.
PUT WORD OUT ON THE STREET... THAT I'M AFTER BRICK HEAD JOHNNY

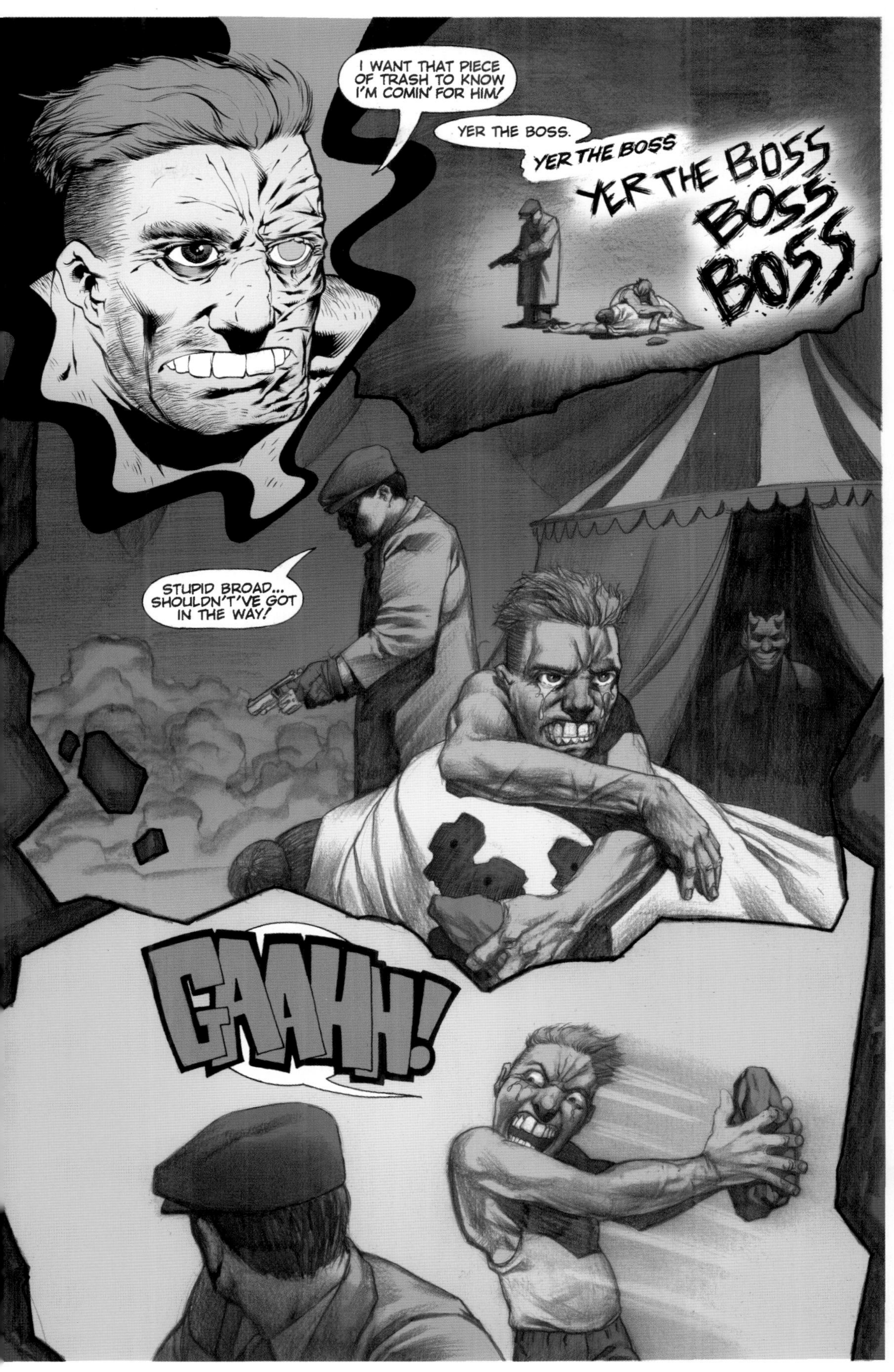
I WANT THAT PIECE OF TRASH TO KNOW I'M COMIN' FOR HIM!
YER THE BOSS.
YER THE BOSS
YER THE BOSS
BOSS
BOSS
STUPID BROAD... SHOULDN'T'VE GOT IN THE WAY!
GAAHH!

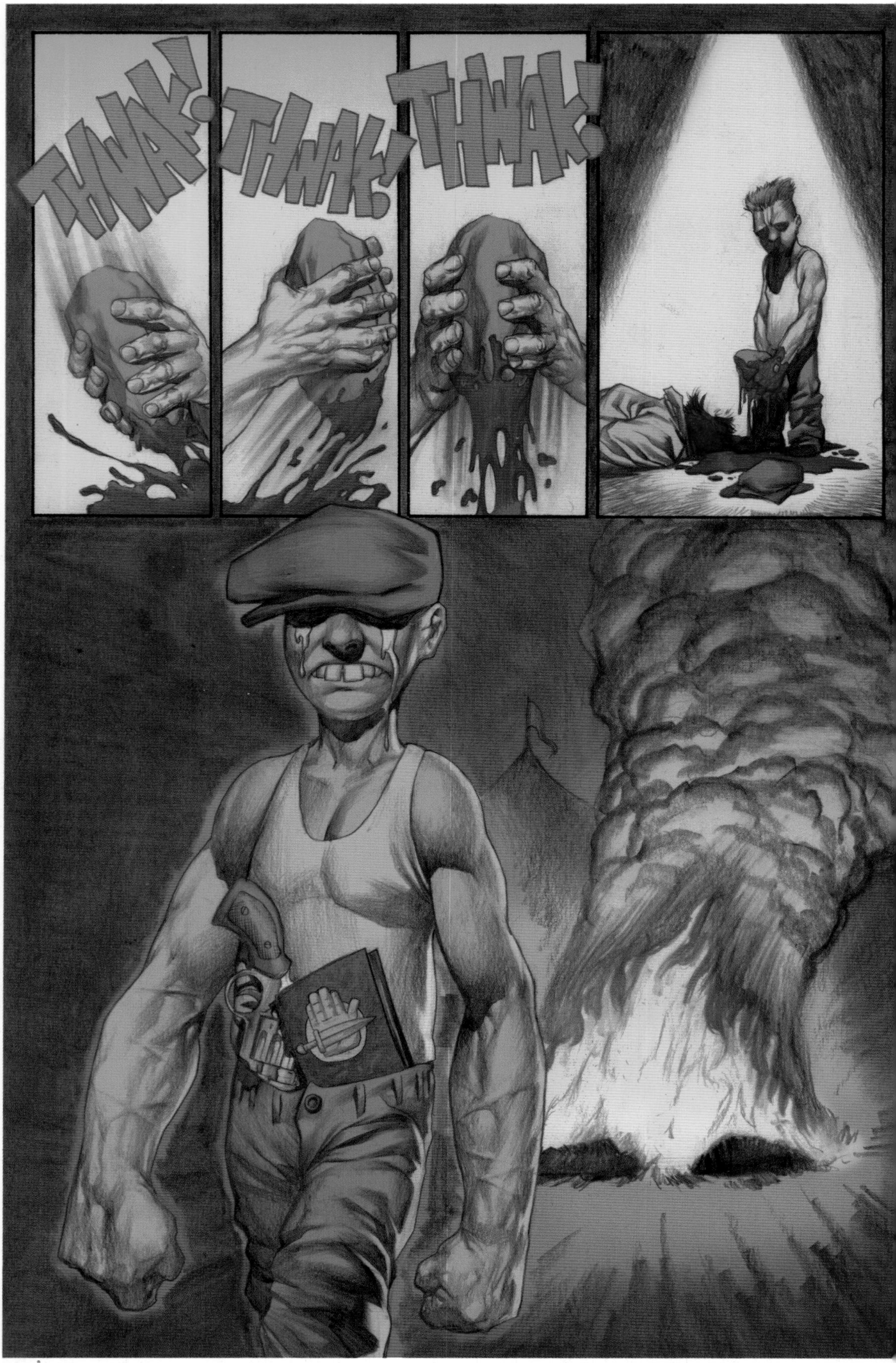
THWAK!
THWAK!
THWAK!

# THE GOON
## ROUGH STUFF

### STRIPS

originally presented on
thegoon.com

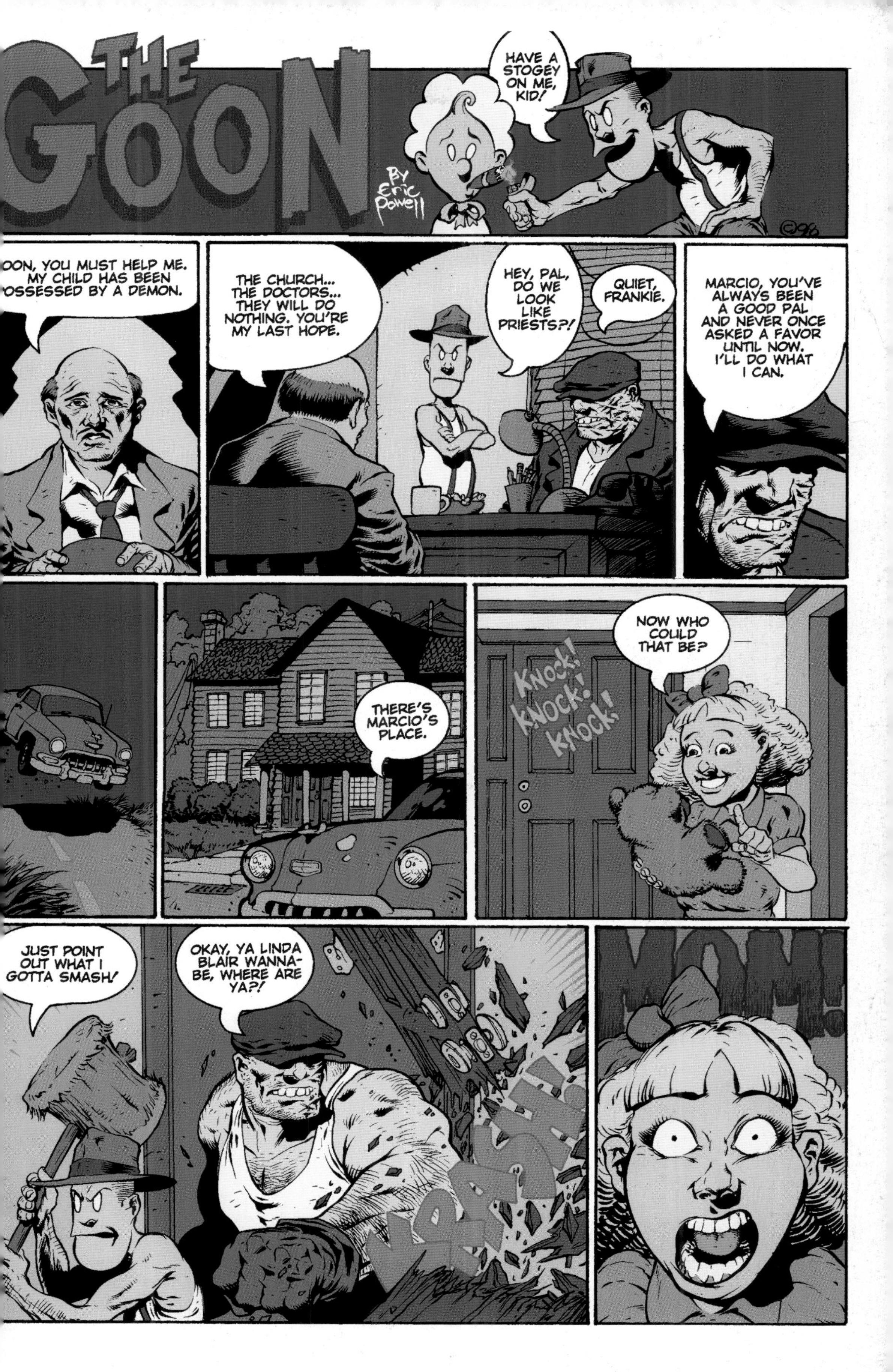
THE GOON
By Eric Powell
HAVE A STOGEY ON ME, KID!
©96
GOON, YOU MUST HELP ME. MY CHILD HAS BEEN POSSESSED BY A DEMON.
THE CHURCH... THE DOCTORS... THEY WILL DO NOTHING. YOU'RE MY LAST HOPE.
HEY, PAL, DO WE LOOK LIKE PRIESTS?!
QUIET, FRANKIE.
MARCIO, YOU'VE ALWAYS BEEN A GOOD PAL AND NEVER ONCE ASKED A FAVOR UNTIL NOW. I'LL DO WHAT I CAN.
THERE'S MARCIO'S PLACE.
KNOCK! KNOCK! KNOCK!
NOW WHO COULD THAT BE?
JUST POINT OUT WHAT I GOTTA SMASH!
OKAY, YA LINDA BLAIR WANNA-BE, WHERE ARE YA?!
KRASH!
MOM!

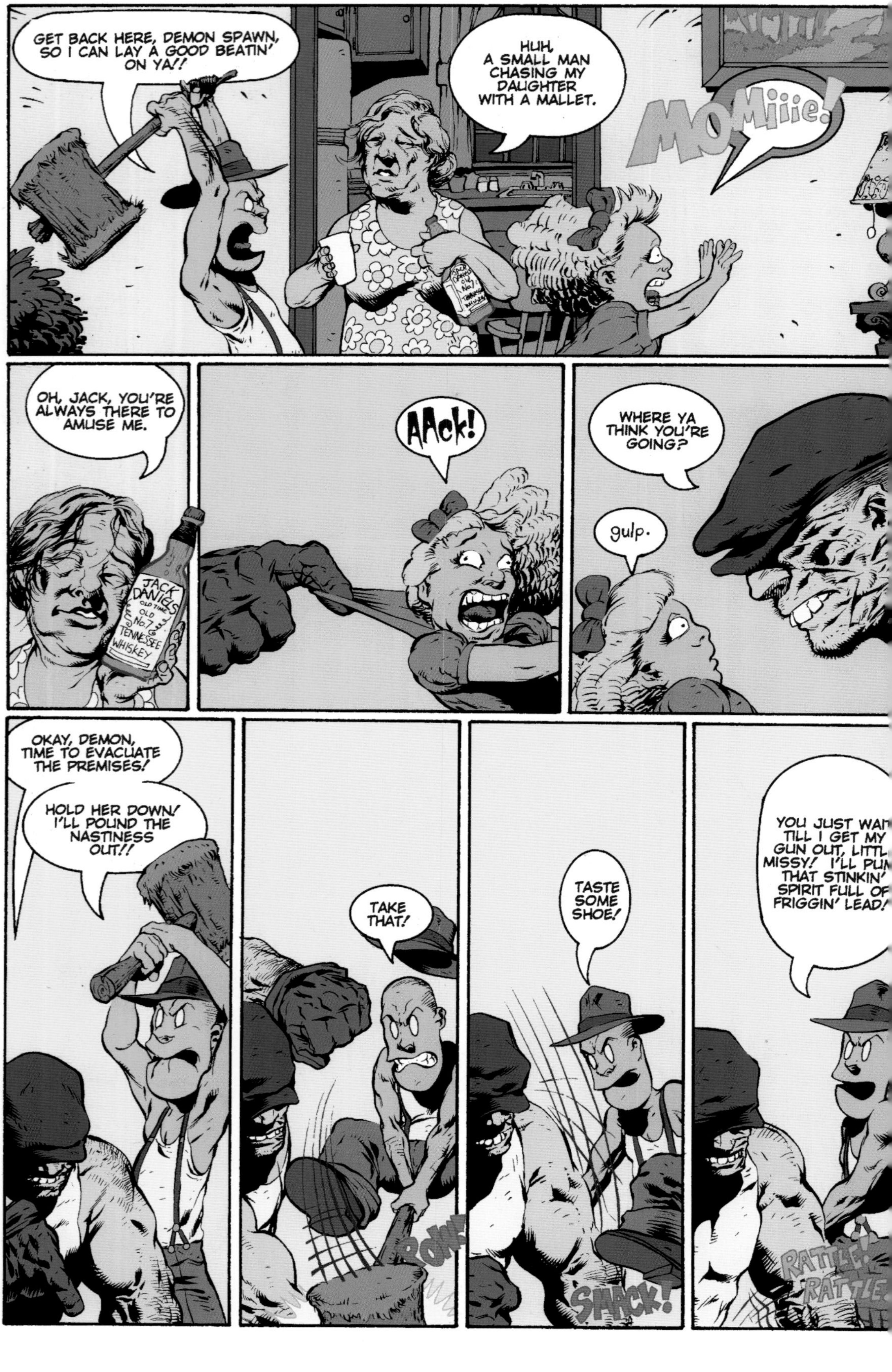
GET BACK HERE, DEMON SPAWN, SO I CAN LAY A GOOD BEATIN' ON YA!!
HUH, A SMALL MAN CHASING MY DAUGHTER WITH A MALLET.
MOMiiie!
OH, JACK, YOU'RE ALWAYS THERE TO AMUSE ME.
JACK DANIELS OLD TIME OLD No. 7 TENNESSEE WHISKEY
AAck!
WHERE YA THINK YOU'RE GOING?
gulp.
OKAY, DEMON, TIME TO EVACUATE THE PREMISES!
HOLD HER DOWN! I'LL POUND THE NASTINESS OUT!!
TAKE THAT!
TASTE SOME SHOE!
SMACK!
RATTLE! RATTLE!

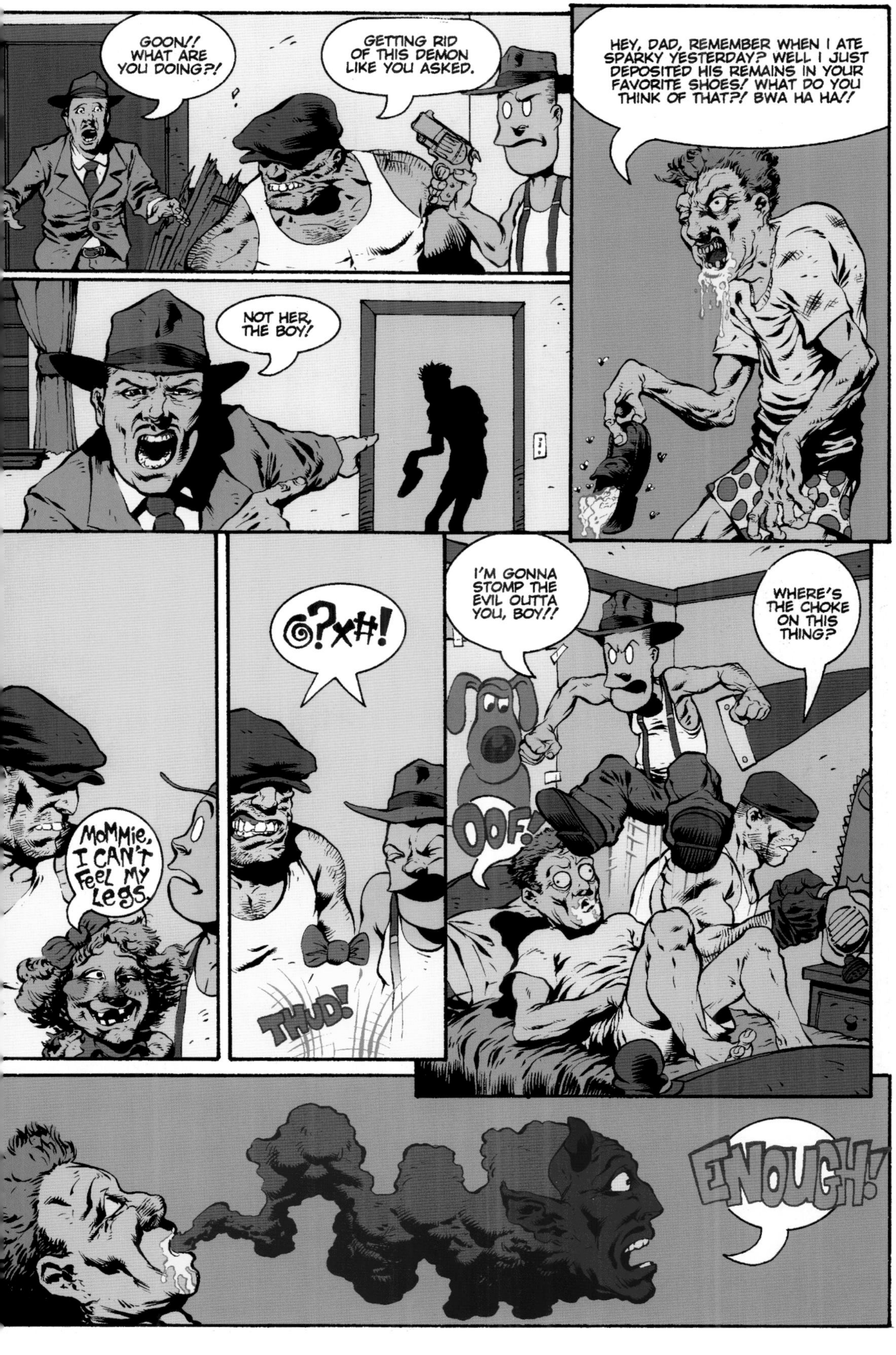
GOON!! WHAT ARE YOU DOING?!
GETTING RID OF THIS DEMON LIKE YOU ASKED.
HEY, DAD, REMEMBER WHEN I ATE SPARKY YESTERDAY? WELL I JUST DEPOSITED HIS REMAINS IN YOUR FAVORITE SHOES! WHAT DO YOU THINK OF THAT?! BWA HA HA!!
NOT HER, THE BOY!
MOMMIE, I CAN'T FEEL MY LEGS.
@?x#!
THUD!
I'M GONNA STOMP THE EVIL OUTTA YOU, BOY!!
WHERE'S THE CHOKE ON THIS THING?
OOF!
ENOUGH!

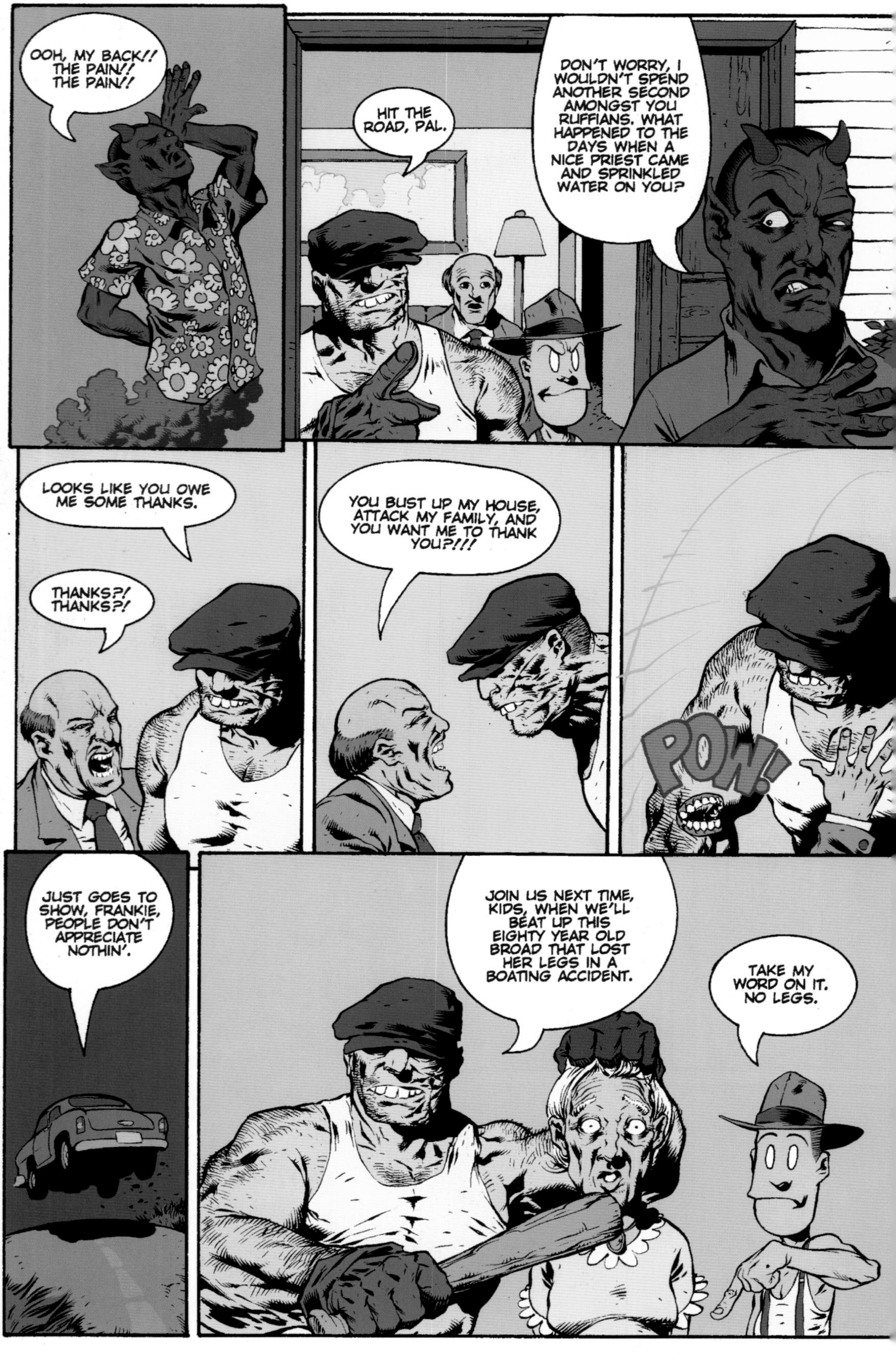
OOH, MY BACK!! THE PAIN!! THE PAIN!!
HIT THE ROAD, PAL.
DON'T WORRY, I WOULDN'T SPEND ANOTHER SECOND AMONGST YOU RUFFIANS. WHAT HAPPENED TO THE DAYS WHEN A NICE PRIEST CAME AND SPRINKLED WATER ON YOU?
LOOKS LIKE YOU OWE ME SOME THANKS.
THANKS?! THANKS?!
YOU BUST UP MY HOUSE, ATTACK MY FAMILY, AND YOU WANT ME TO THANK YOU?!!!
POW!
JUST GOES TO SHOW, FRANKIE, PEOPLE DON'T APPRECIATE NOTHIN'.
JOIN US NEXT TIME, KIDS, WHEN WE'LL BEAT UP THIS EIGHTY YEAR OLD BROAD THAT LOST HER LEGS IN A BOATING ACCIDENT.
TAKE MY WORD ON IT. NO LEGS.

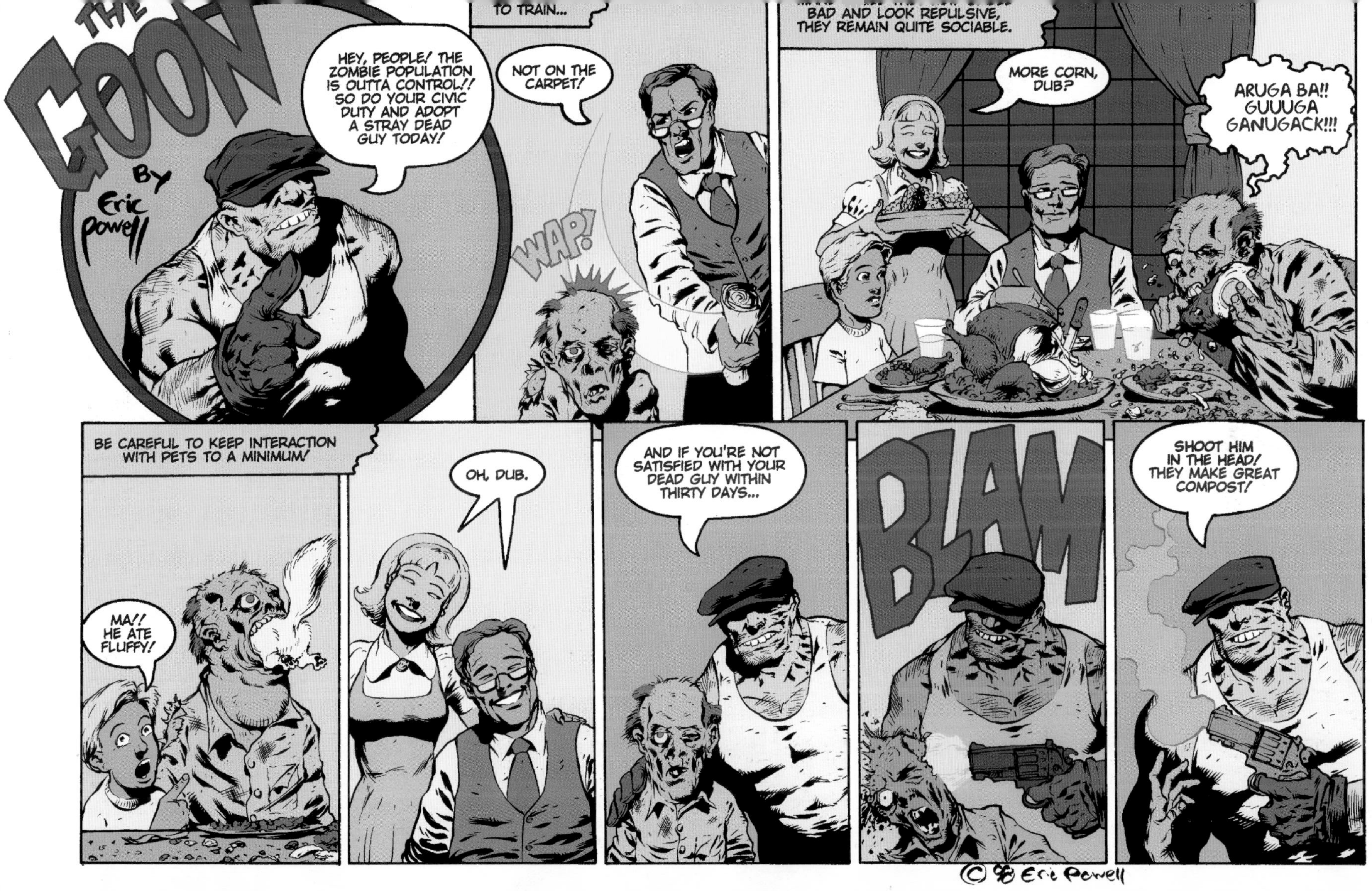
THE GOON
BY Eric Powell
HEY, PEOPLE! THE ZOMBIE POPULATION IS OUTTA CONTROL!! SO DO YOUR CIVIC DUTY AND ADOPT A STRAY DEAD GUY TODAY!
TO TRAIN...
NOT ON THE CARPET!
WAP!
BAD AND LOOK REPULSIVE, THEY REMAIN QUITE SOCIABLE.
MORE CORN, DUB?
ARUGA BA!! GUUUGA GANUGACK!!!
BE CAREFUL TO KEEP INTERACTION WITH PETS TO A MINIMUM!
MA!! HE ATE FLUFFY!
OH, DUB.
AND IF YOU'RE NOT SATISFIED WITH YOUR DEAD GUY WITHIN THIRTY DAYS...
BLAM
SHOOT HIM IN THE HEAD! THEY MAKE GREAT COMPOST!
© 98 Eric Powell

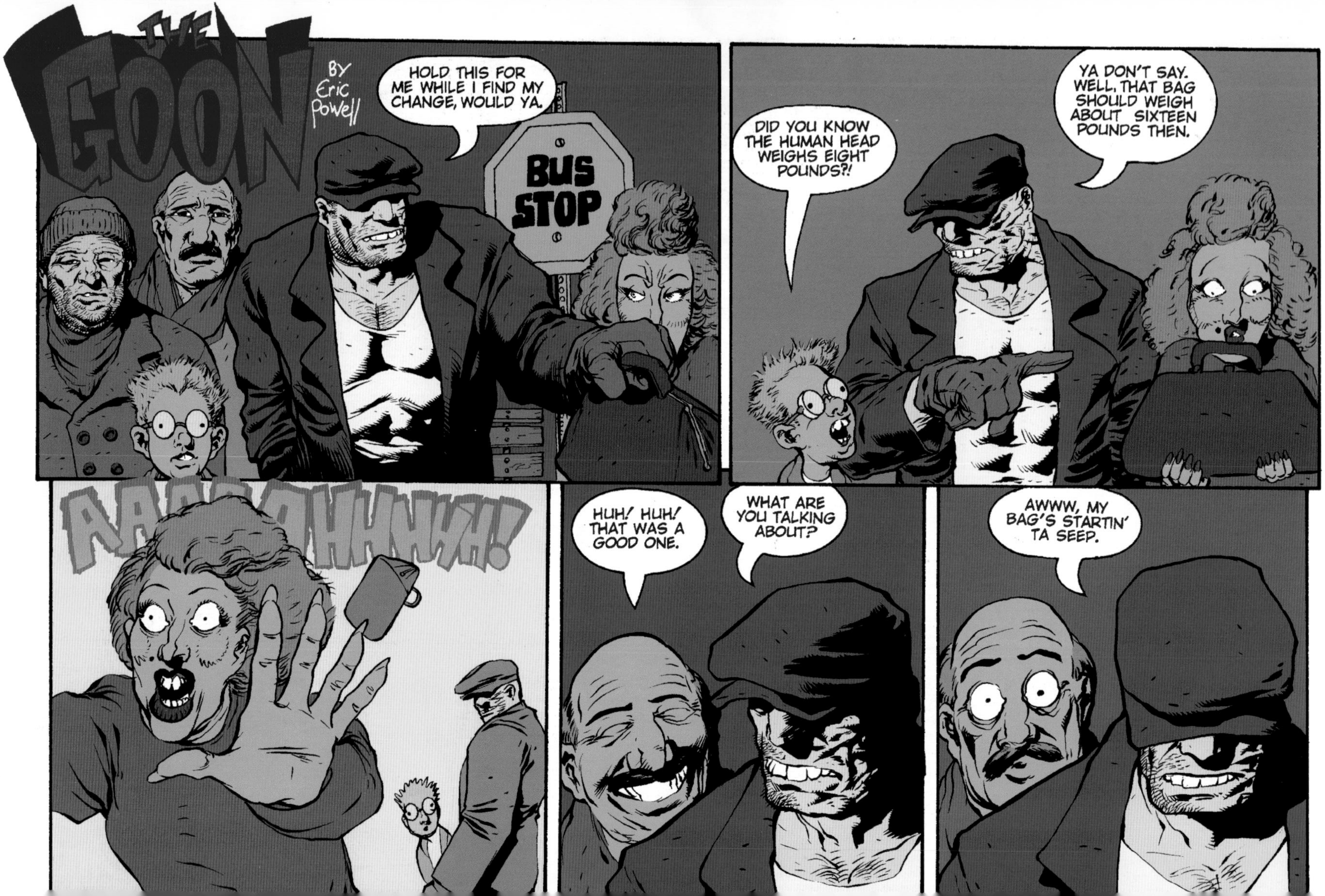
THE GOON
BY Eric Powell
HOLD THIS FOR ME WHILE I FIND MY CHANGE, WOULD YA.
BUS STOP
DID YOU KNOW THE HUMAN HEAD WEIGHS EIGHT POUNDS?!
YA DON'T SAY. WELL, THAT BAG SHOULD WEIGH ABOUT SIXTEEN POUNDS THEN.
HUH! HUH! THAT WAS A GOOD ONE.
WHAT ARE YOU TALKING ABOUT?
AWWW, MY BAG'S STARTIN' TA SEEP.

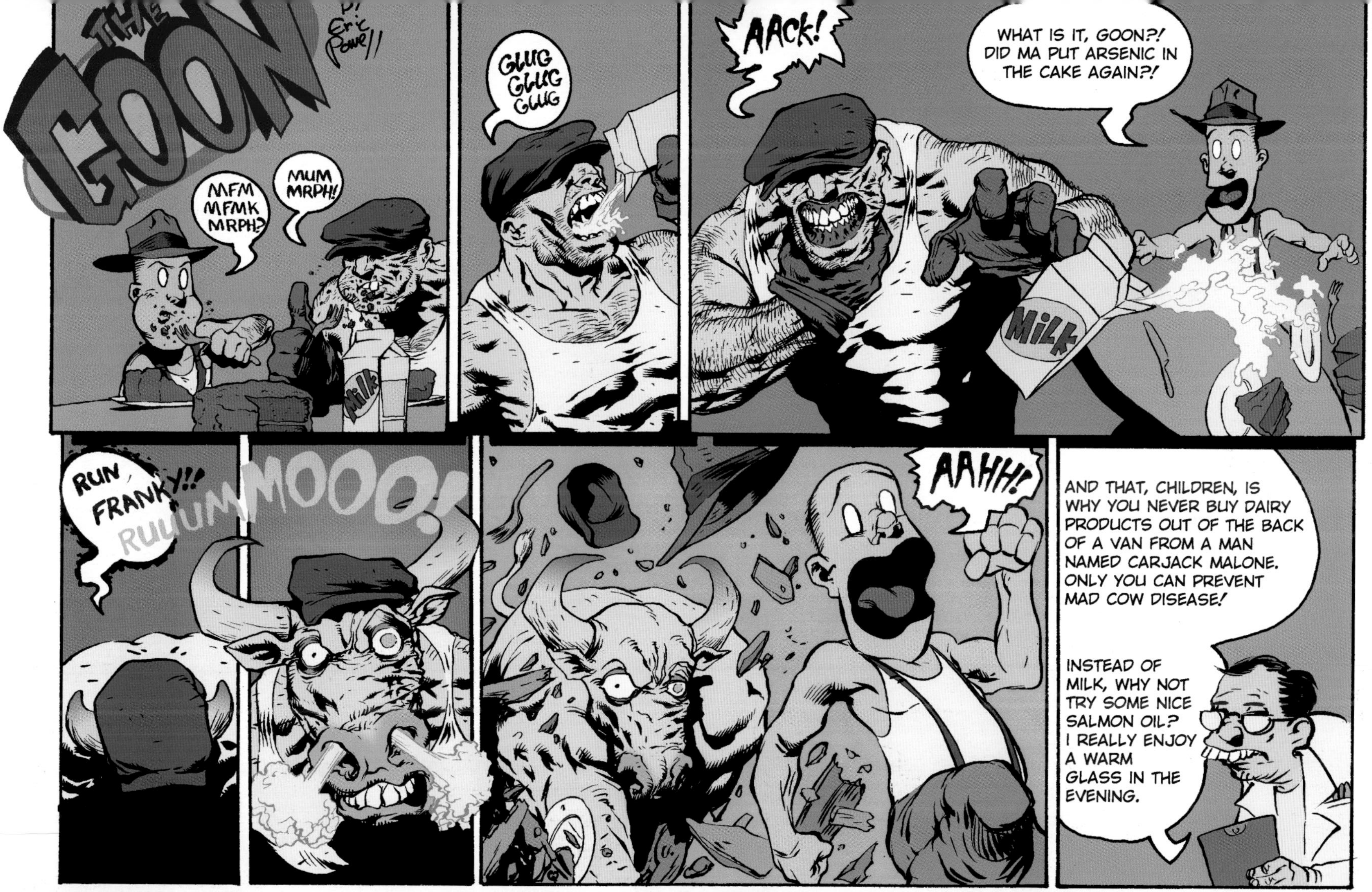
THE GOON
by Eric Powell!!
MFM MFMK MRPH?
MUM MRPH!
GLUG GLUG GLUG
AACK!
WHAT IS IT, GOON?! DID MA PUT ARSENIC IN THE CAKE AGAIN?!
MILK
RUN, FRANKY!!
RUUUMMOOO!
AAHH!
AND THAT, CHILDREN, IS WHY YOU NEVER BUY DAIRY PRODUCTS OUT OF THE BACK OF A VAN FROM A MAN NAMED CARJACK MALONE. ONLY YOU CAN PREVENT MAD COW DISEASE!
INSTEAD OF MILK, WHY NOT TRY SOME NICE SALMON OIL? I REALLY ENJOY A WARM GLASS IN THE EVENING.

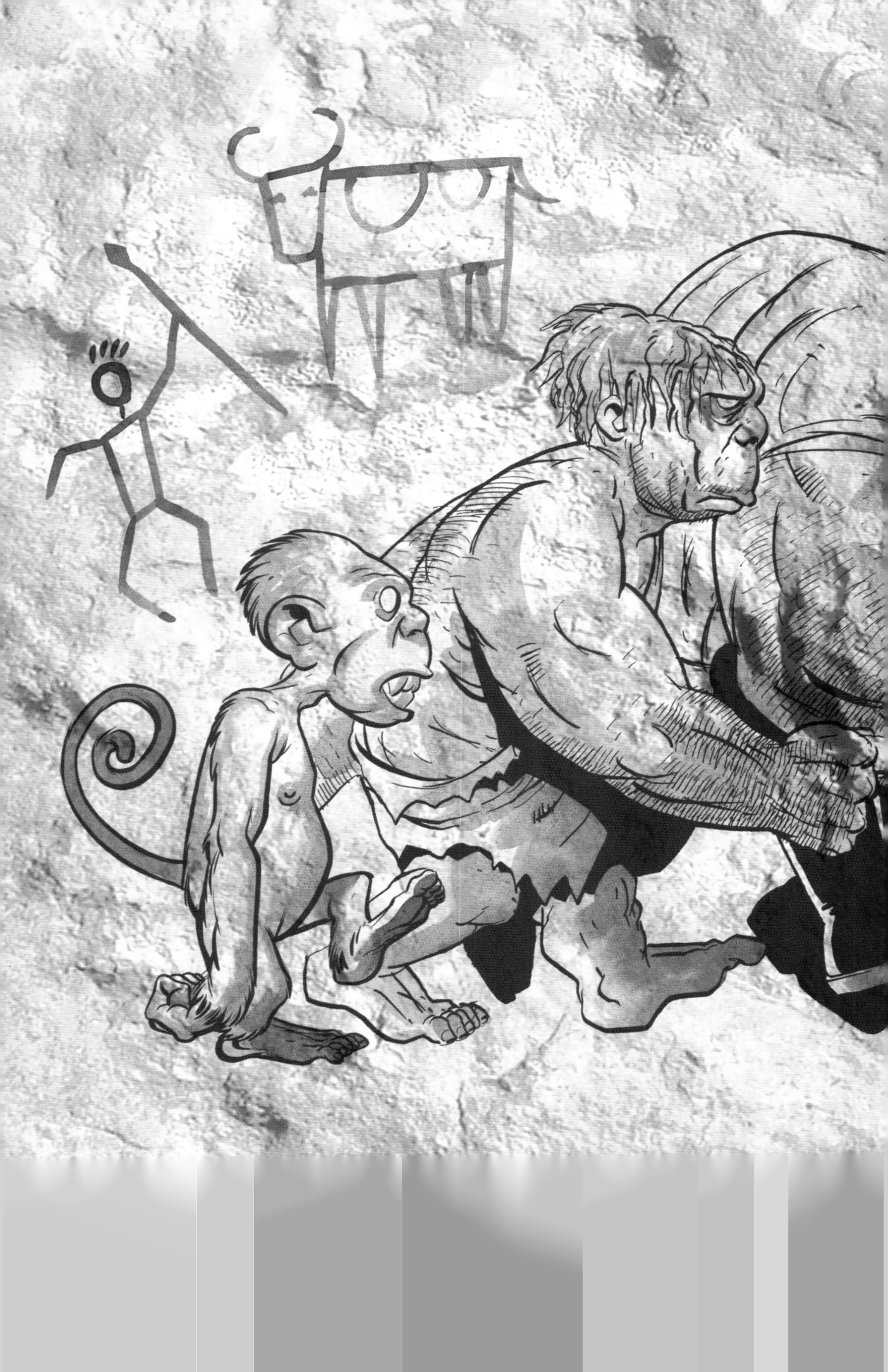

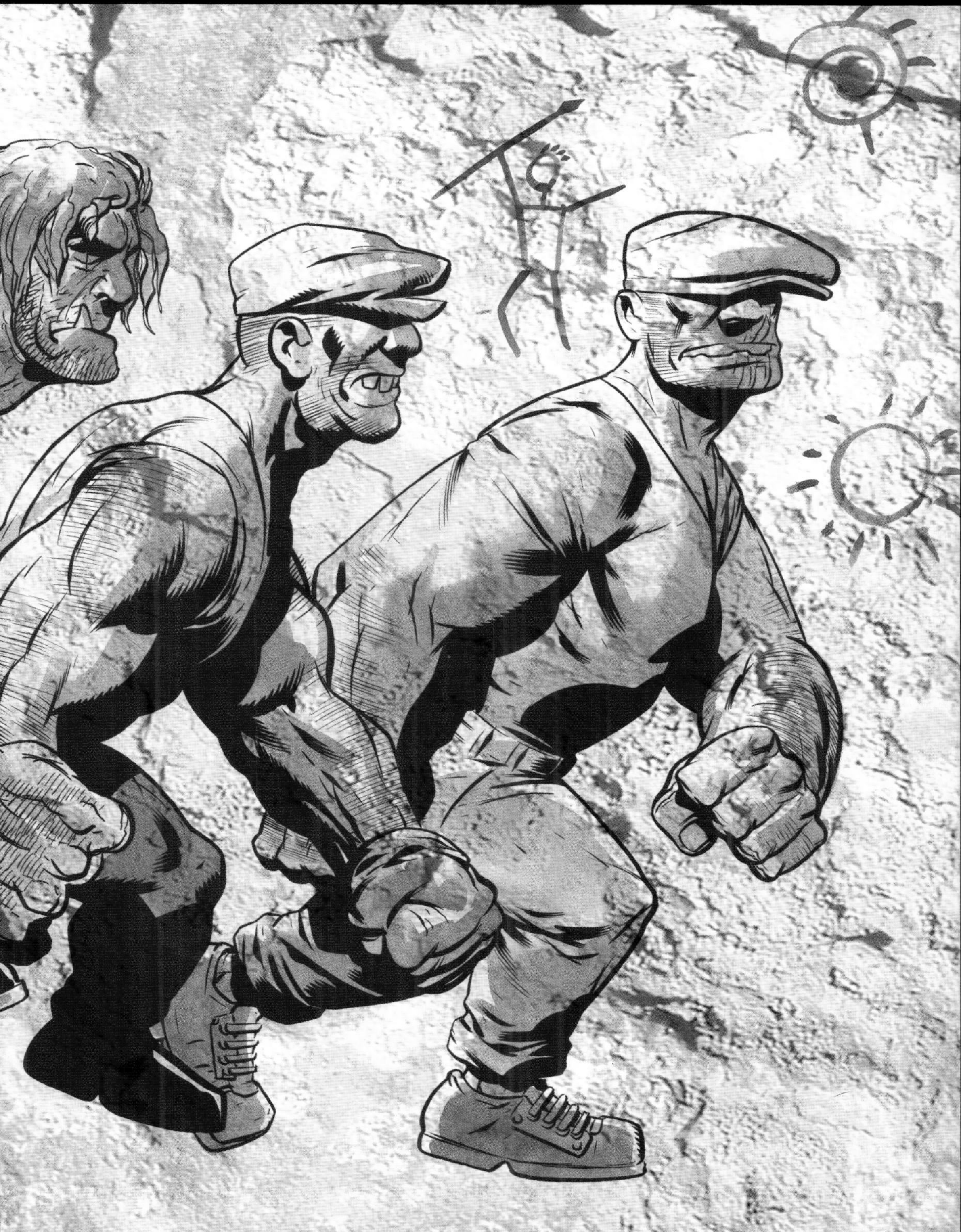

OF THE GOON

**Believe it or not, this is where the Goon began.**

**I was trying to come up with something to pitch around to the smaller publishers, since I was having no luck getting anywhere with the big boys (and for good reason—I sucked). I was watching a cartoon where a mouse turned into a Mr. Hyde-type creature. It was your typical cartoon monster, with long arms dragging on the ground and short stumpy legs. I've always loved the big thuggish characters, and the design inspired me. I came up with this idea of a kid monster named Mog—sort of a mix between a rat and a gorilla—living in the real world and going to school with normal kids. It was a really weak idea.**

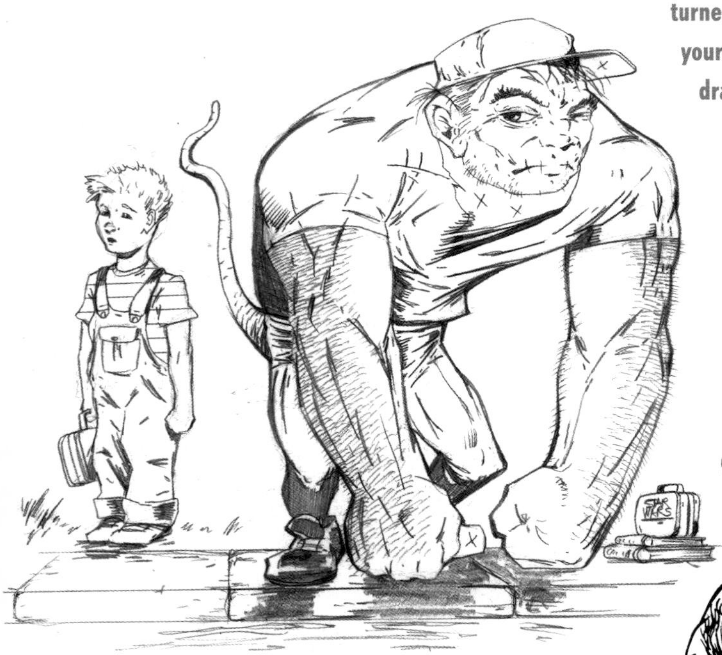

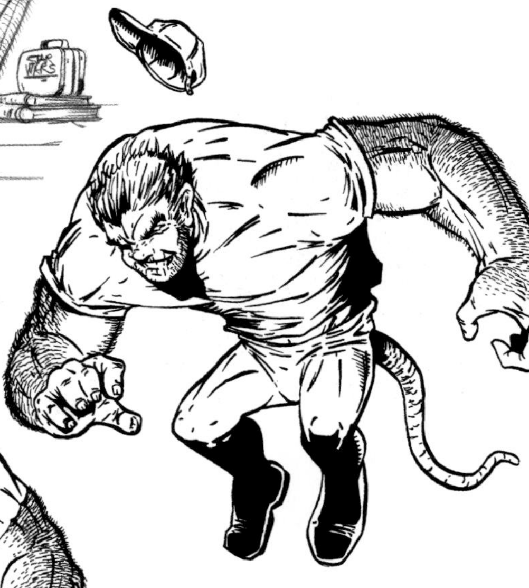

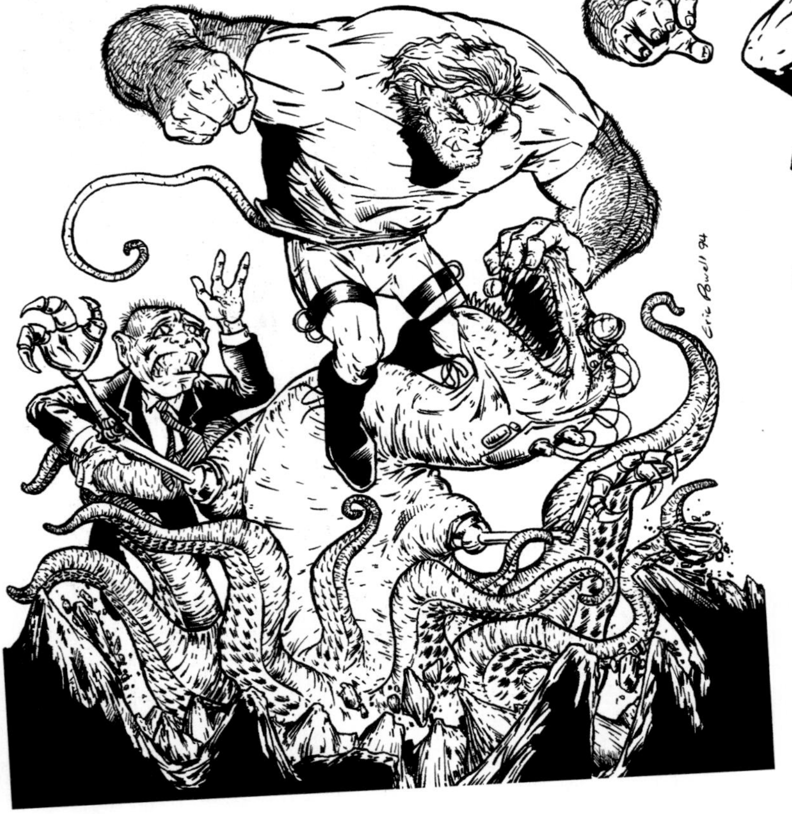

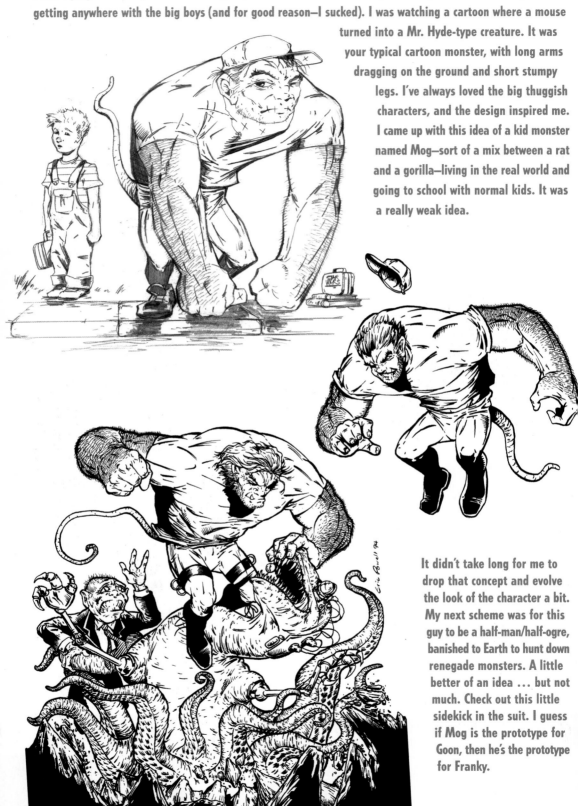

**It didn't take long for me to drop that concept and evolve the look of the character a bit. My next scheme was for this guy to be a half-man/half-ogre, banished to Earth to hunt down renegade monsters. A little better of an idea ... but not much. Check out this little sidekick in the suit. I guess if Mog is the prototype for Goon, then he's the prototype for Franky.**

In 1994, I met a couple of local guys named Chuck Angel and Larry Underwood, who were self-publishing a horror comic. I approached them about putting a Mog story in one, and I did a short in their book *Best Cellars*. Other than this image, used in a series of trading cards featuring small press comic characters, that was the only time Mog saw print.

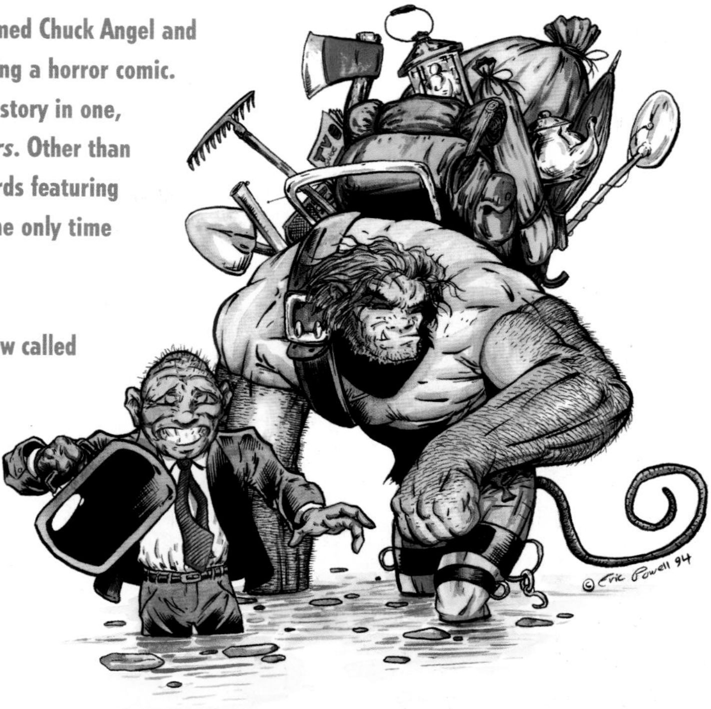
© Eric Powell 94

Chuck and Larry now have a television show called *Chiller Cinema* that airs late-night Thursdays on UPN in the middle Tennessee area as well as a few select cities across the country.

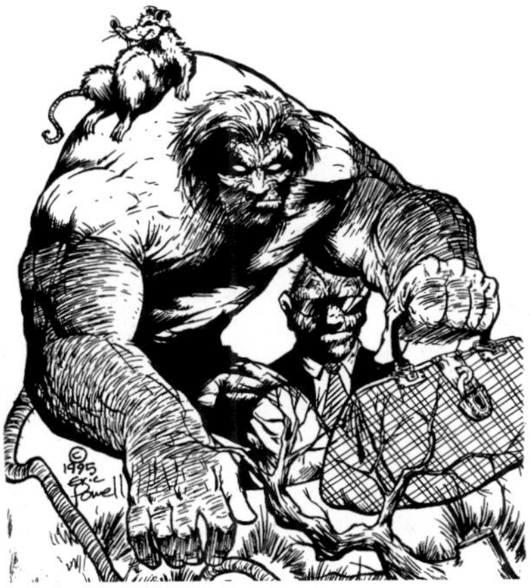
© 1995 Eric Powell

This pencil page was done when I received several rejection letters from publishers saying I should "pencil or ink … not both." Now that I'm a working professional, I can say with all honesty that it was one of the stupidest things I've ever heard. I've only been able to continue working in this business because of my versatility, allowing me to take any type of work that came my way. Telling an artist that he should train himself in only one medium is moronic.

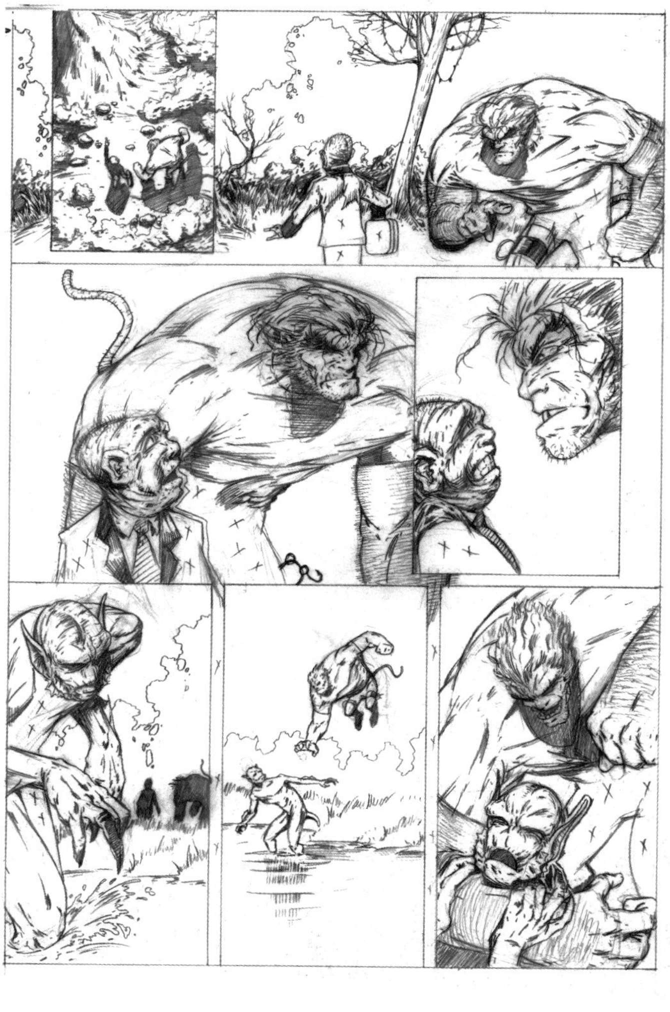

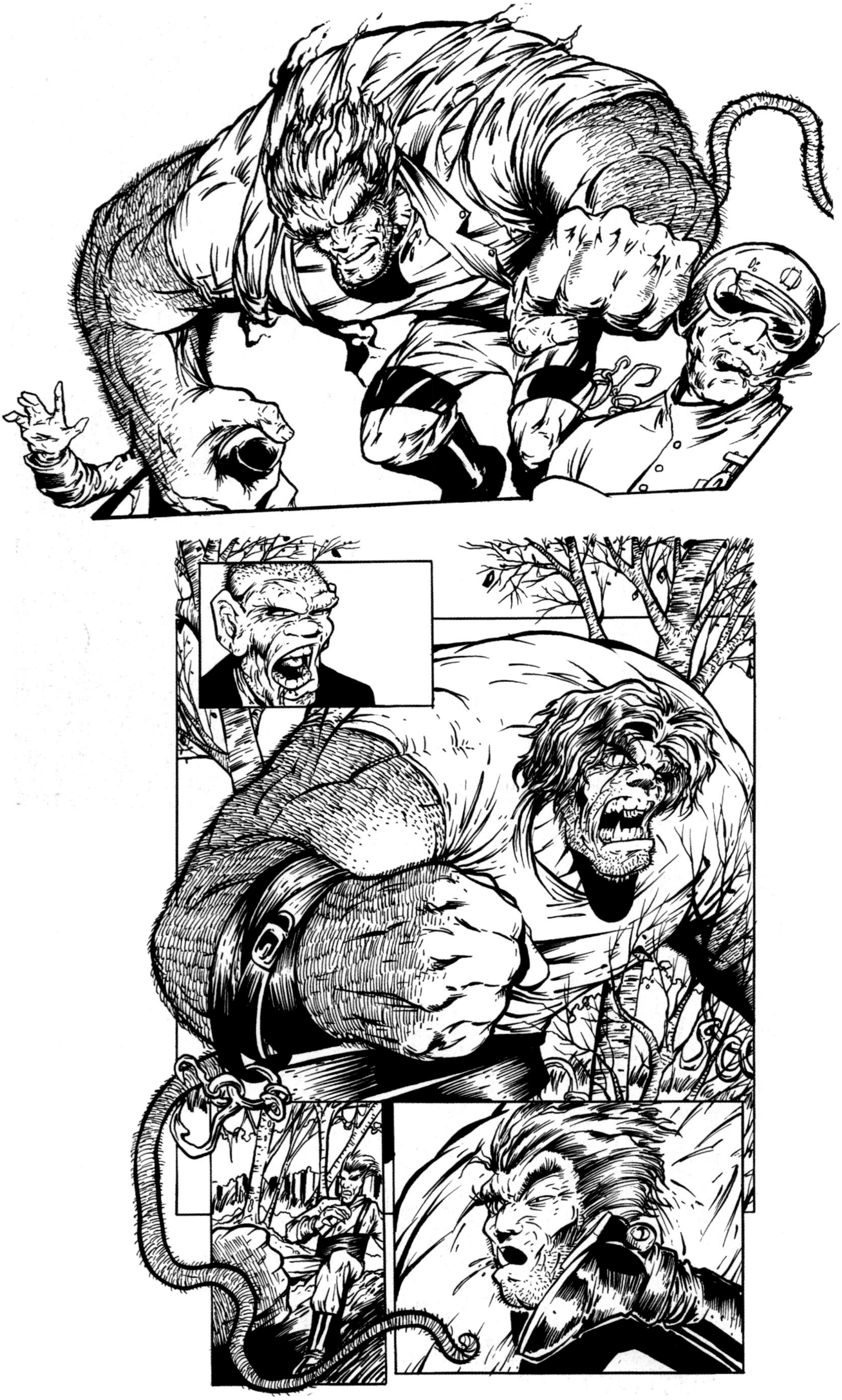

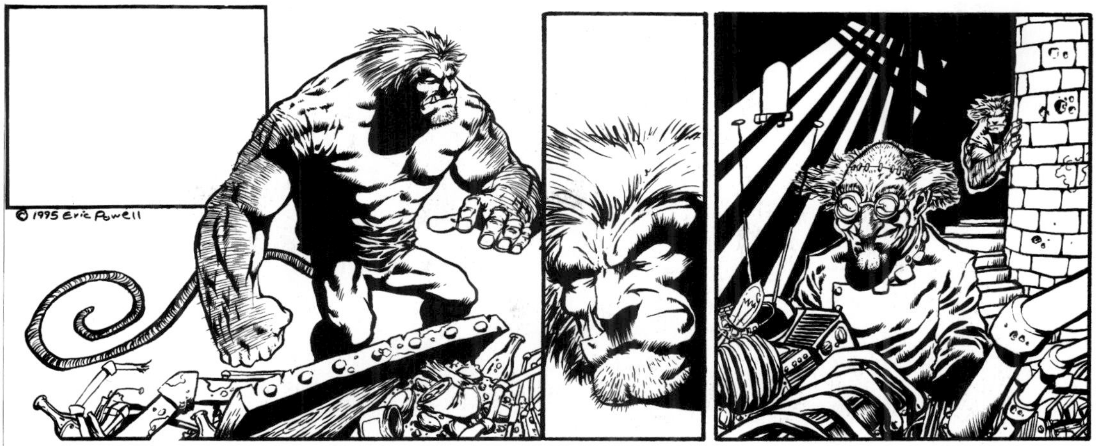
© 1995 Eric Powell

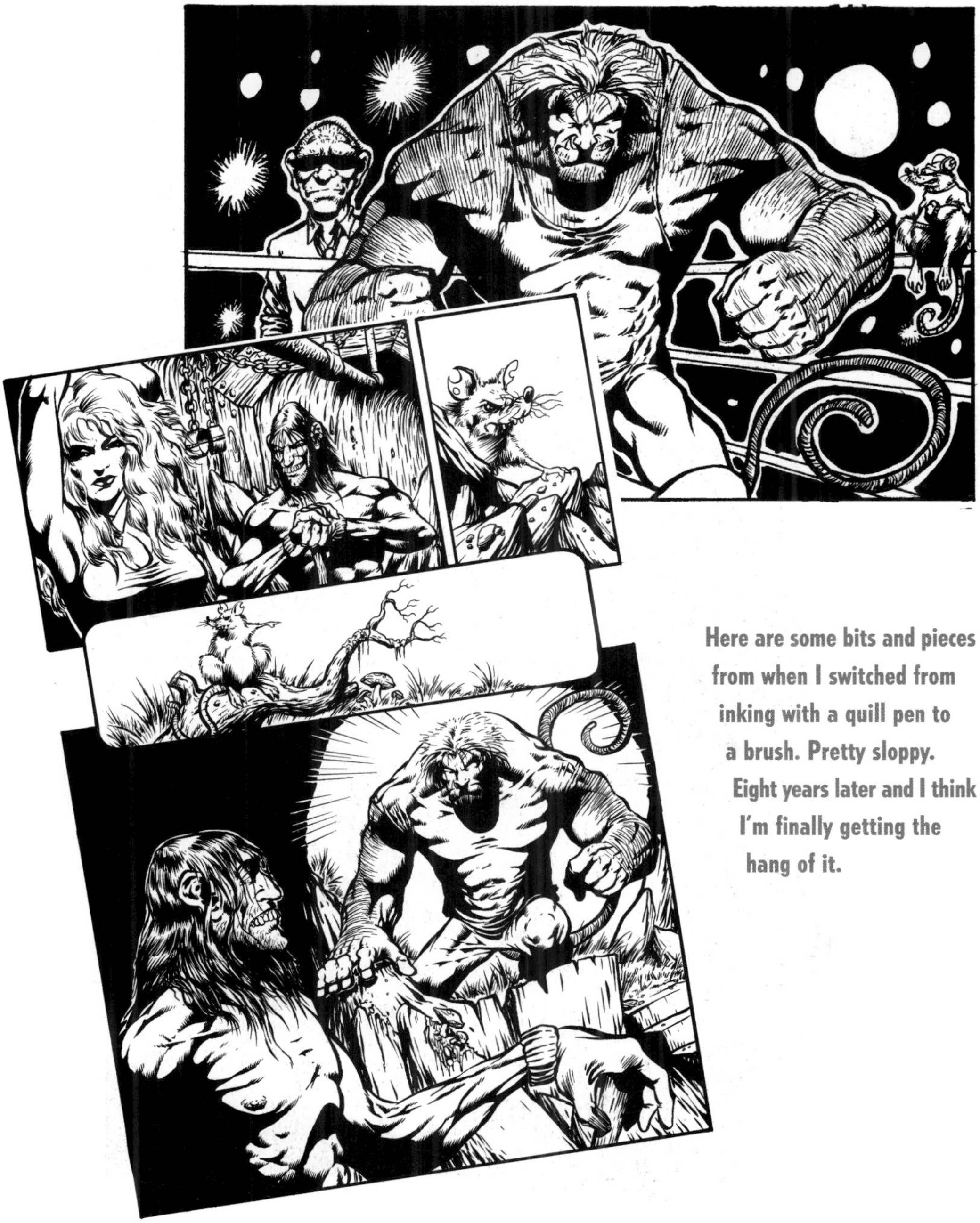

Here are some bits and pieces from when I switched from inking with a quill pen to a brush. Pretty sloppy. Eight years later and I think I'm finally getting the hang of it.

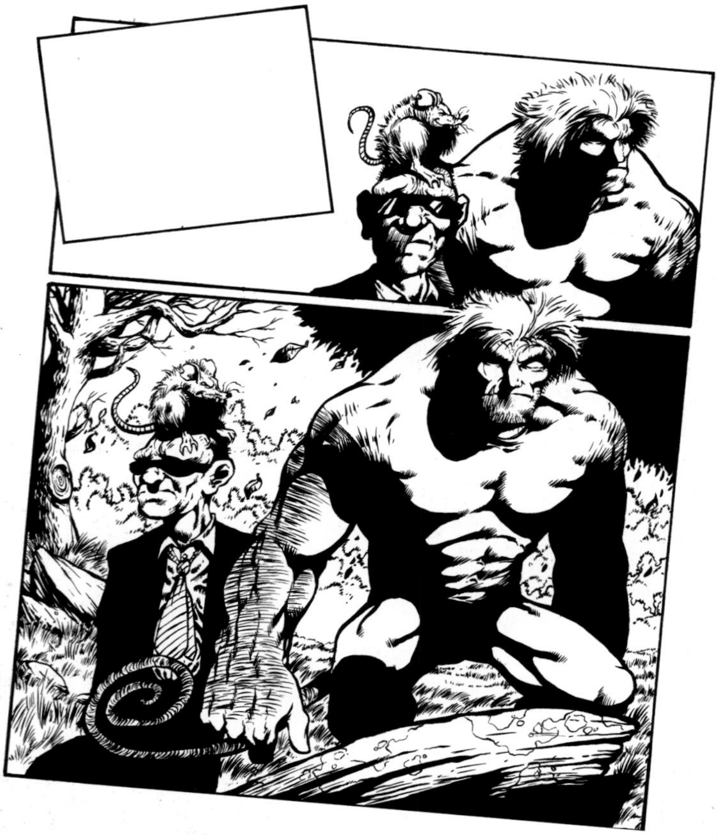

Some "Goon" finally starts to come through here. This was my first use of the cap.

I may have to use these mutated rednecks in *The Goon* sometime. They still look kinda cool.

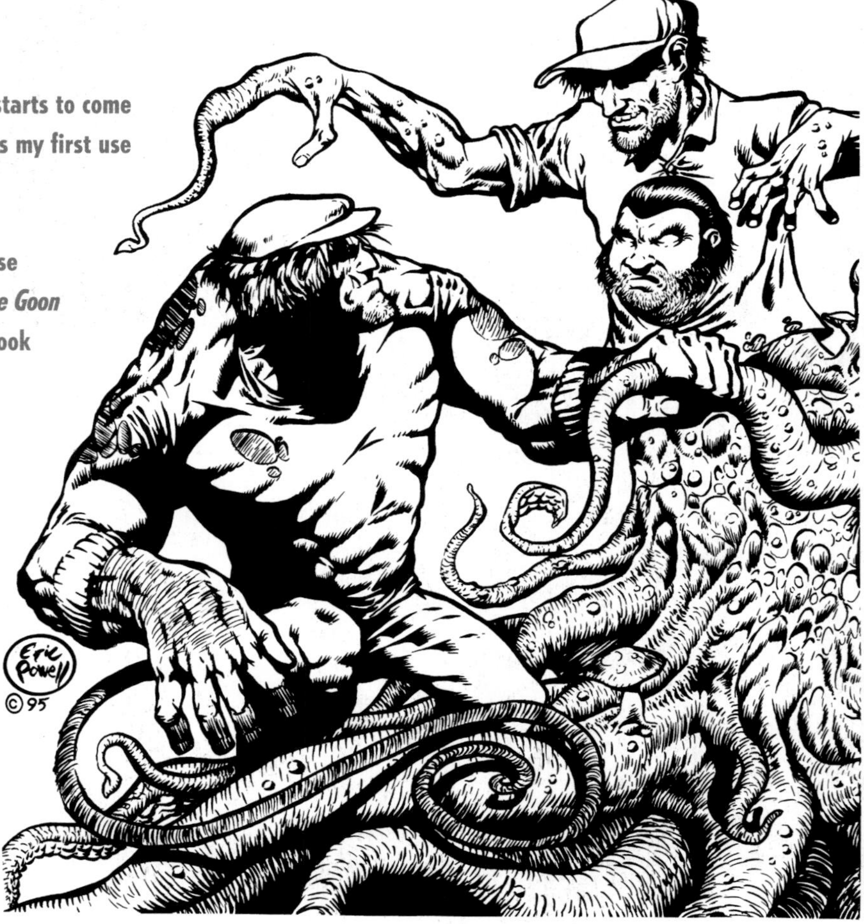
Eric Powell
©95

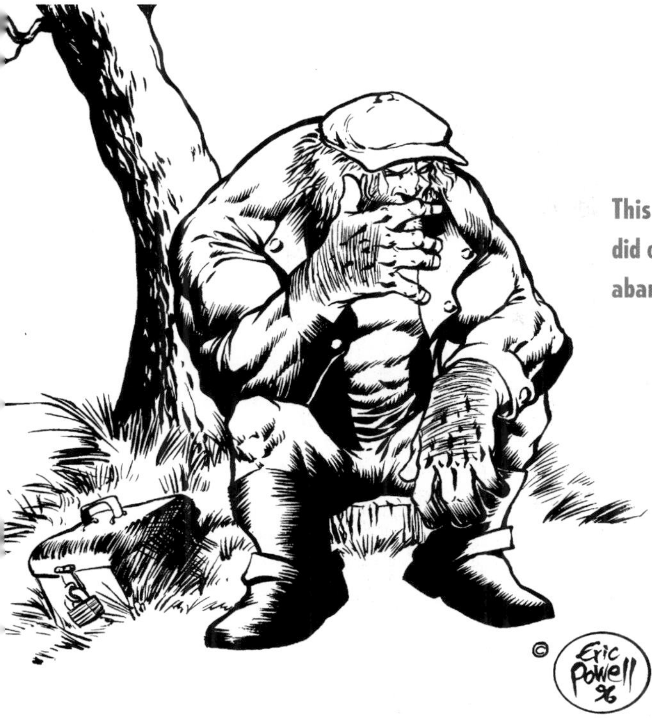
© Eric Powell 96

This was the last drawing I did of Mog before completely abandoning the concept.

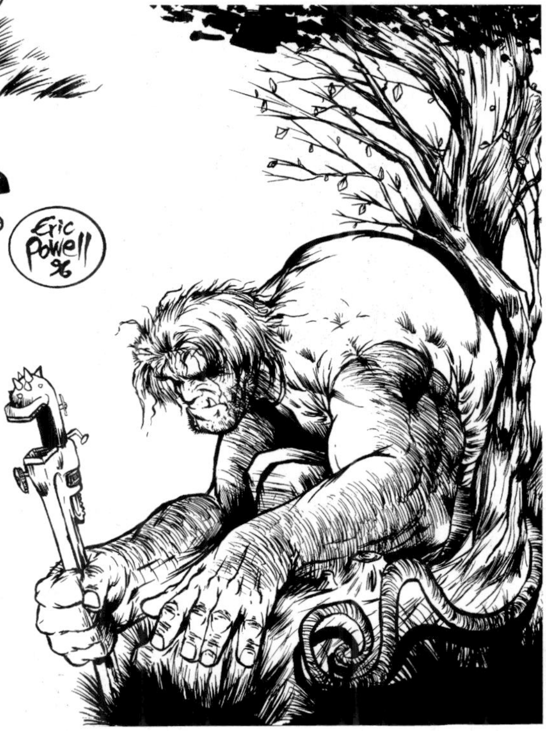

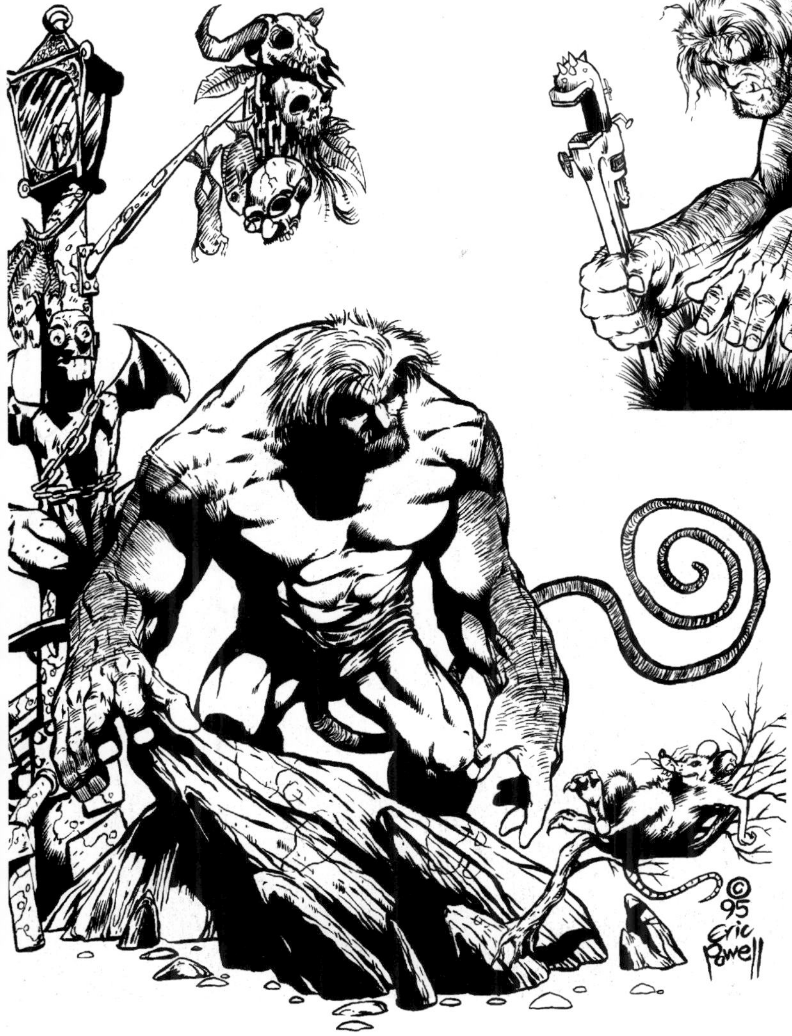
© 95 Eric Powell

I started getting some work-for-hire jobs, but I still wanted to try my own thing. I decided Mog wasn't good enough, but I didn't have anything else in mind. I just knew I still wanted to do something with monsters.

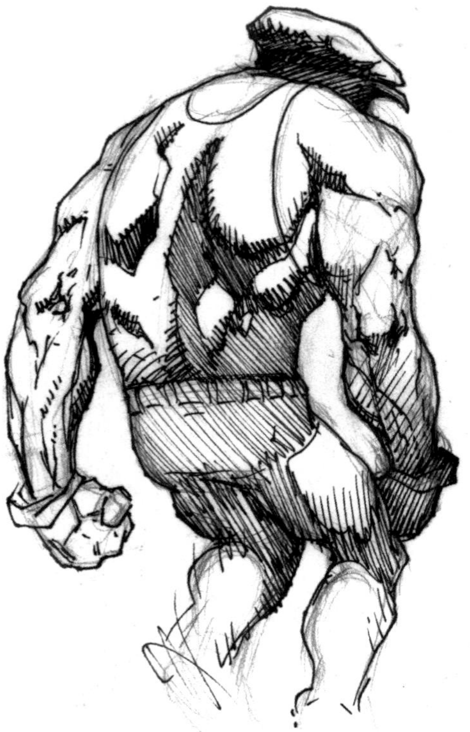

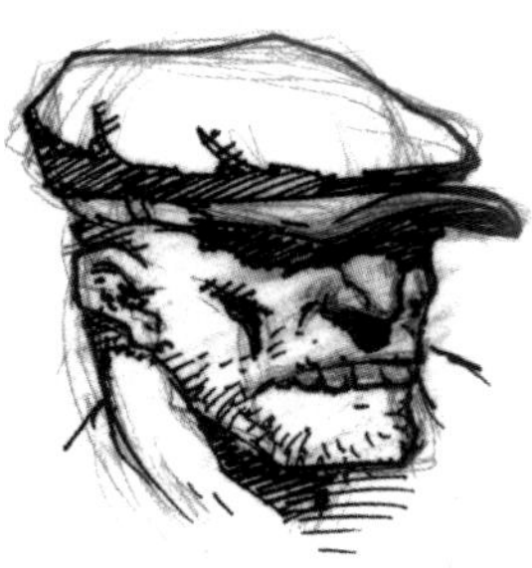

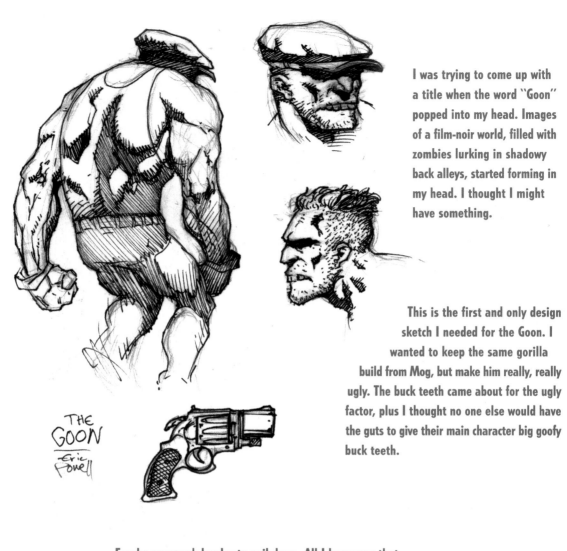

I was trying to come up with a title when the word "Goon" popped into my head. Images of a film-noir world, filled with zombies lurking in shadowy back alleys, started forming in my head. I thought I might have something.

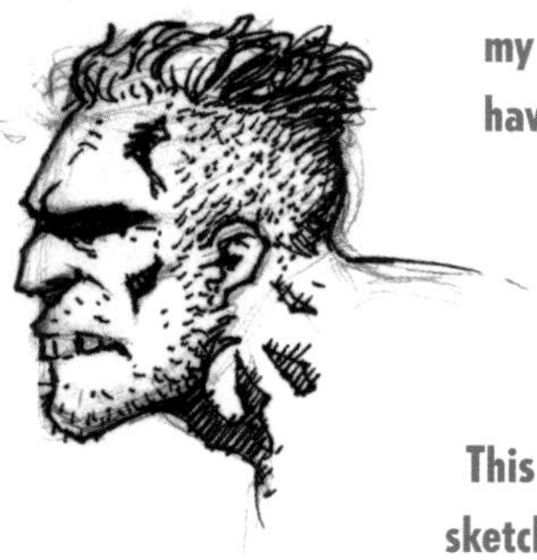

This is the first and only design sketch I needed for the Goon. I wanted to keep the same gorilla build from Mog, but make him really, really ugly. The buck teeth came about for the ugly factor, plus I thought no one else would have the guts to give their main character big goofy buck teeth.

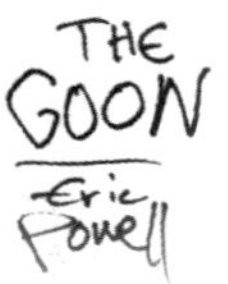
THE GOON
Eric Powell

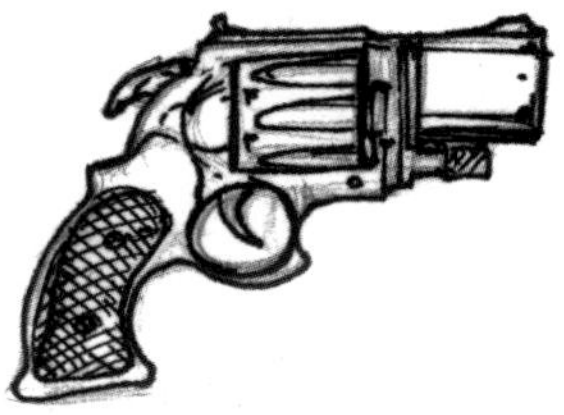

Franky was much harder to nail down. All I knew was that I wanted the Goon to have a little maniacal sidekick. It always came out too crazy looking. I finally came to the peanut head that we all know and love.

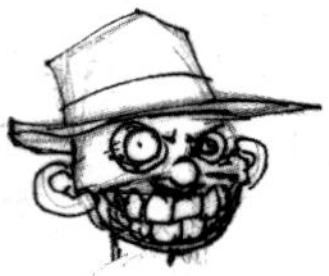

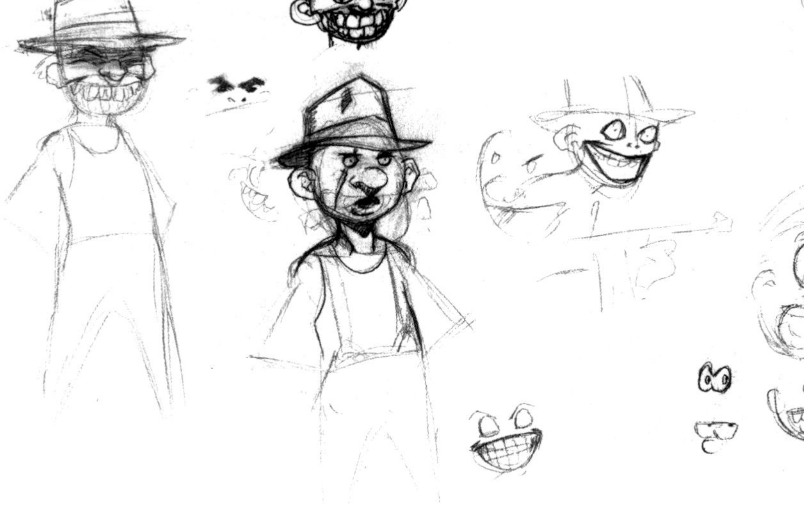

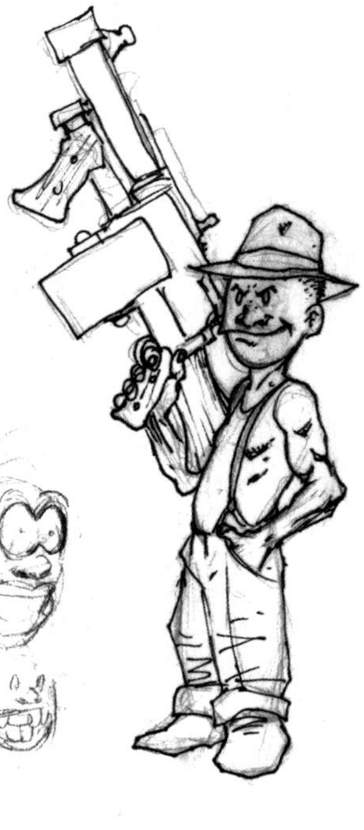

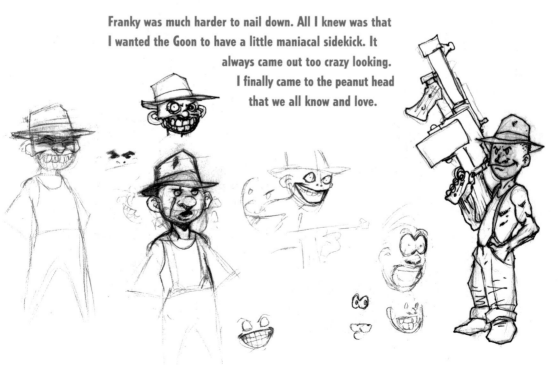

The zombie priest was always pictured as a severely anorexic George C. Scott.

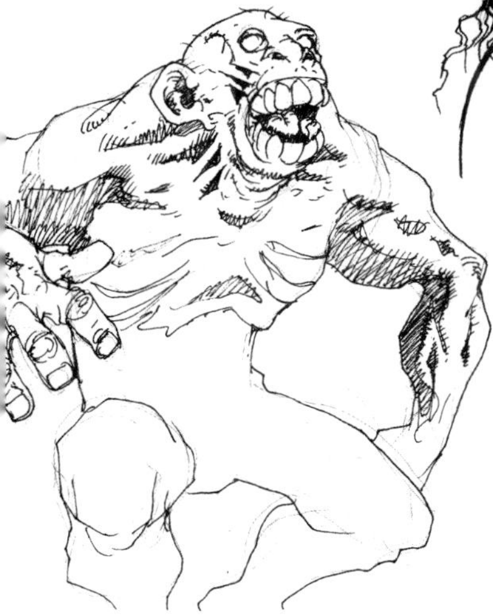

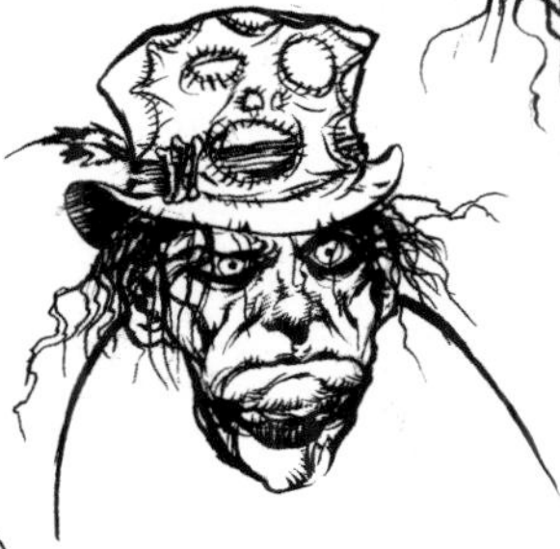

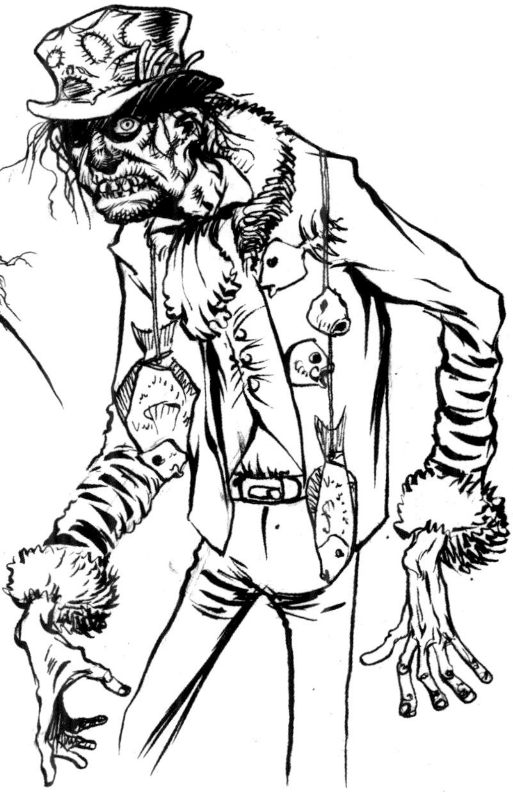

Joe the Ball came about in one of my many bizarre phone conversations with Tom Sniegoski. I believe we were discussing what would happen to a midget baby if it got its hand stuck in a bowling ball and couldn't get it out. Why, it would grow up with one gigantic arm of course.

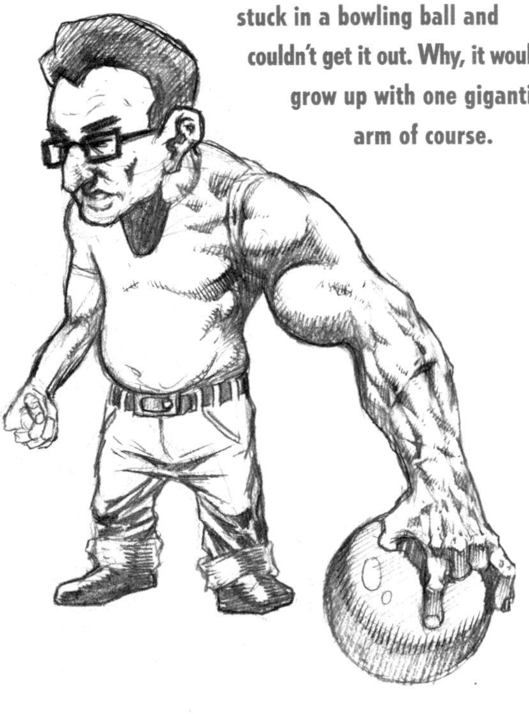

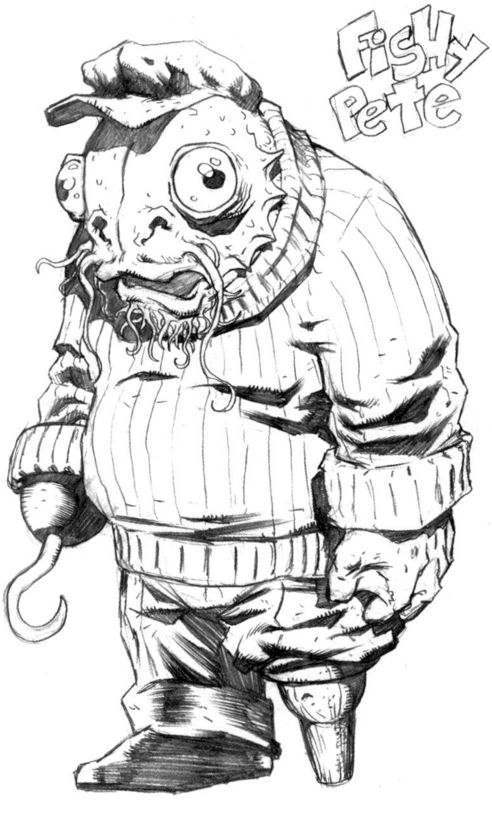
Fishy Pete

This is the first finished piece I did of the Goon ... and all the other characters for that matter.

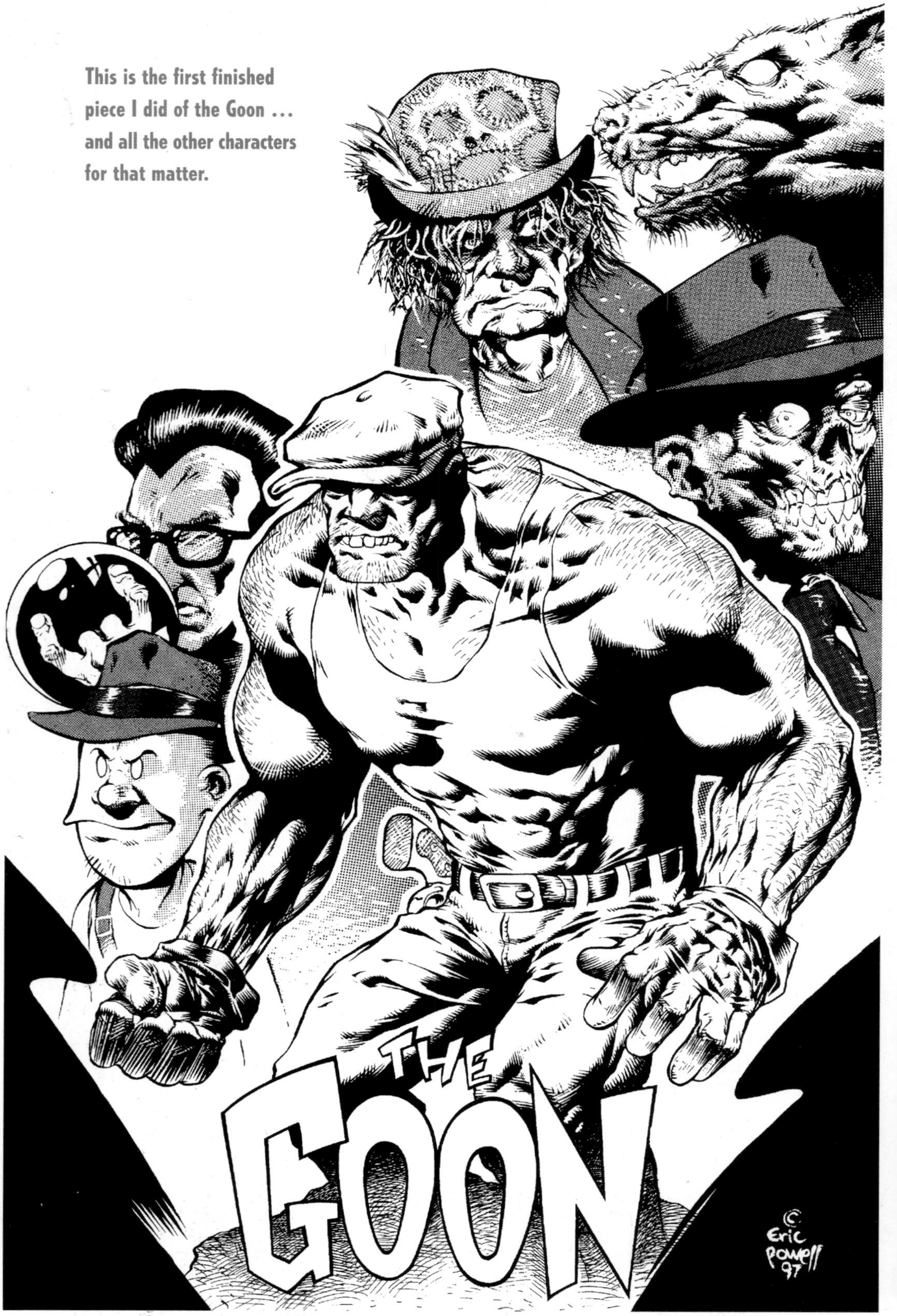
THE
GOON
© Eric Powell '97

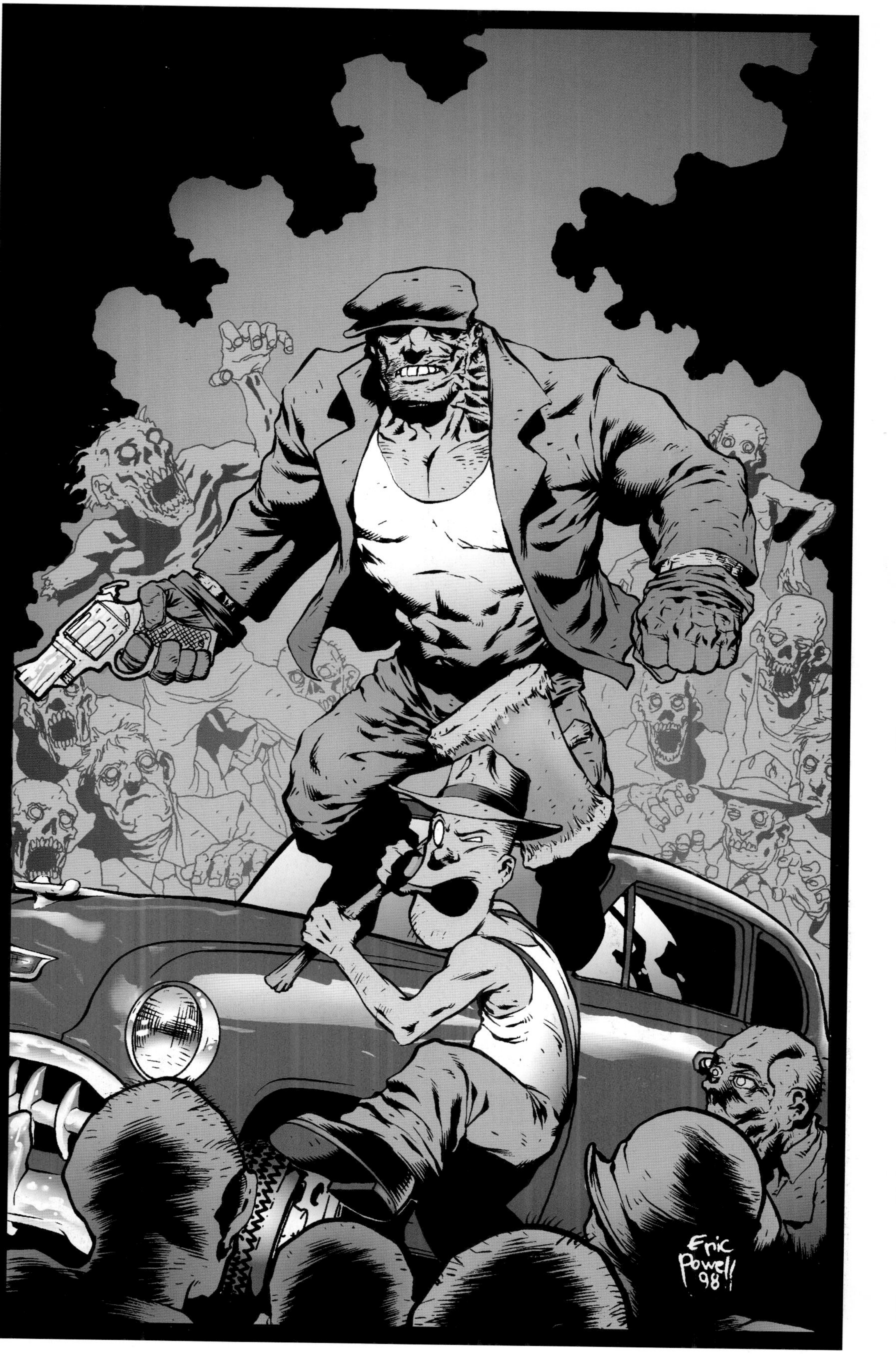
Eric Powell 98

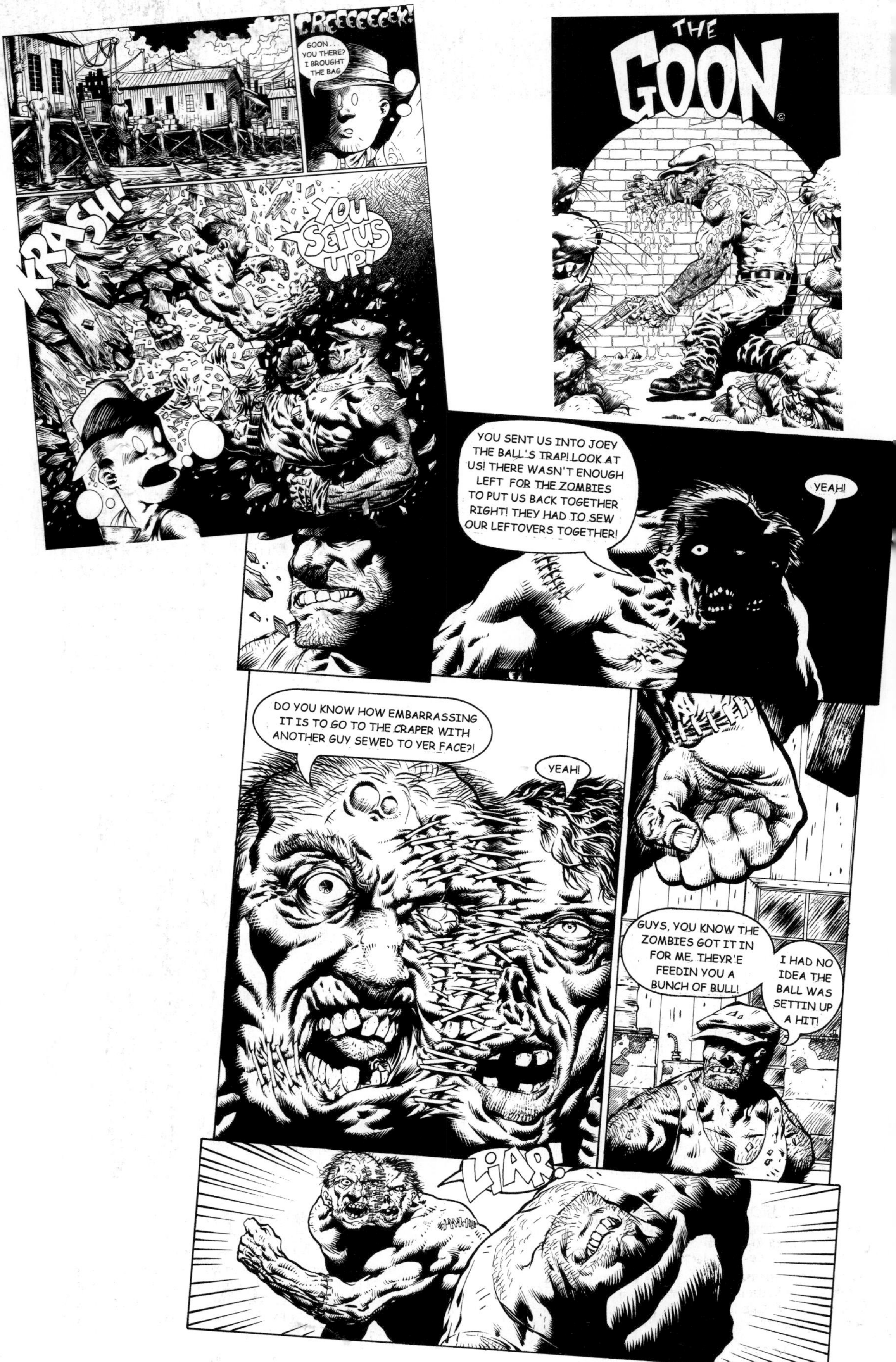
CREEEEEEEEK!
GOON... YOU THERE? I BROUGHT THE BAG
KRASH!
YOU SET US UP!
THE GOON
YOU SENT US INTO JOEY THE BALL'S TRAP! LOOK AT US! THERE WASN'T ENOUGH LEFT FOR THE ZOMBIES TO PUT US BACK TOGETHER RIGHT! THEY HAD TO SEW OUR LEFTOVERS TOGETHER!
YEAH!
DO YOU KNOW HOW EMBARRASSING IT IS TO GO TO THE CRAPER WITH ANOTHER GUY SEWED TO YER FACE?!
YEAH!
GUYS, YOU KNOW THE ZOMBIES GOT IT IN FOR ME. THEYR'E FEEDIN YOU A BUNCH OF BULL!
I HAD NO IDEA THE BALL WAS SETTIN UP A HIT!
LIAR!

# ALSO FROM DARK HORSE COMICS!

THE GOON
NOTHIN' BUT MISERY
by Eric Powell

**THE GOON, VOLUME 1: NOTHIN' BUT MISERY**
*By Eric Powell*

An insane priest is building an army of the undead, and only one man can put them in their place: the Goon. This volume collects *The Goon* issues 1-4 and *The Goon Color Special*, originally published by Albatross Exploding Funny Books; presented in full-color for the first time.

Wizard Magazine says, "Every comic should be this much fun to read!"

Soft cover, 136 pages, Full color
$15.95, ISBN: 1-56971-998-5

THE GOON
MY MURDEROUS CHILDHOOD
(and other grievous yarns)
by Eric Powell

**THE GOON, VOLUME 2: MY MURDEROUS CHILDHOOD (AND OTHER GRIEVOUS YARNS)**
*By Eric Powell*

Goon and Franky battle a family of grave robbers eager to supply the Zombie Priest with fixin's for his army of the dead. Things get bad for everyone when they wind up in Hobo Jungle, where the destitute have given up train hopping for a feral life of cannibalism in the wild. Will the Goon end up in a hobo stew?

Soft cover, 128 pages, Full color
$13.95, ISBN: 1-56971-999-3

MIKE MIGNOLA'S
HELLBOY
WEIRD TALES
Volume One

**HELLBOY: WEIRD TALES VOLUME ONE**
*By Joe Casey, John Cassaday, Steve Lieber, Alex Maleev, Eric Powell, Leinil Francis Yu, and many more!*
*Cover by Mike Mignola*

Some of the top writers and artists in today's world of comics provide their take on Hellboy and the B.P.R.D. Old-fashioned pulp fun featuring one of the greatest heroes of modern comics.

Soft cover, 128 pages, Full color
$17.95, ISBN: 1-56971-622-6

ANGEL
HUNTING GROUND
Christopher Golden
Tom Sniegoski
Brian Horton
Paul Lee
Eric Powell

**ANGEL: HUNTING GROUND TP**
*By Christopher Golden, Tom Sniegoski, Eric Powell, Brian Horton, and Paul Lee*

There's a killer tossing dead bodies out of L.A. sewers like hot potatoes, and all the evidence points Detective Kate Lockley towards Angel. But Angel knows there are a lot more monsters in LA—he just doesn't know which one's trying to set him up.

Soft Cover, 80 pages, Full color
$9.95, ISBN: 1-56971-547-5

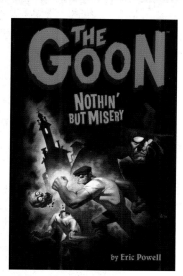

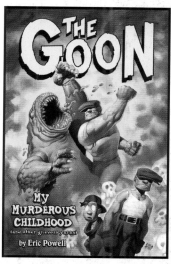

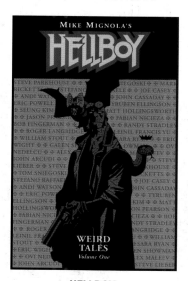

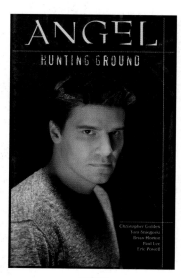

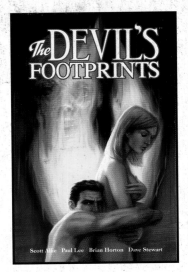

## THE DARK HORSE BOOK OF HAUNTINGS HC

*Featuring Mike Mignola, P. Craig Russell, Paul Chadwick, Evan Dorkin, Jill Thompson, and others. Cover by Gary Gianni*

Mike Mignola's Hellboy investigates a haunted house and discovers his own unexpected connection to the spirits within. P. Craig Russell and Mike Richardson tell the story of a child who vanishes into an abandoned house, and Paul Chadwick and Randy Stradley team up for a creepy short about a haunted suit. Jill Thompson and Evan Dorkin recount the legend of a haunted doghouse.

Hard cover, 96 pages, Full color
$14.95, ISBN: 1-56971-958-6

## THE DEVIL'S FOOTPRINTS

*By Scott Allie, Paul Lee, Brian Horton, and Dave Stewart*

Brandon Waite investigates his dead father's study of witchcraft. But his desire to protect loved ones forces him to cover up his own tentative steps into the black arts, leading him to mix deception with demon conjuration, isolating himself in a terrible world where his soul hangs in the balance.

Soft cover, 144 pages, Full color
$14.95, ISBN: 1-56971-933-0

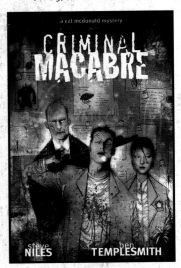

## CRIMINAL MACABRE
## A Cal McDonald Mystery

*By Steve Niles and Ben Templesmith*

The creative team behind *30 Days of Night* launch a new series of occult detective stories featuring the monstrously hard-boiled Cal McDonald, a pill-popping alcoholic, the only line of defense between Los Angeles and a growing horde of zombies, vampires, and werewolves. The best-selling comics series is collected in this massive graphic novel.

Soft cover, 170 pages, Full color
$17.95, ISBN: 1-56971-935-7

## THE BLACKBURNE COVENANT

*By Fabian Nicieza and Stefano Raffaele*

Someone is following novelist Richard Kaine. Someone interested in finding out how Richard came up with his best-selling first novel. Because unbeknownst to Richard, his fantasy novel was non-fiction. Could Richard have written about an event that had been meticulously eradicated from human history? Who are the Blackburne Covenant? Why are they willing to kill Richard Kaine in order to keep him quiet?

Soft cover, 104 pages, Full color
$11.95, ISBN: 1-56971-889-X

**DARK HORSE COMICS**™ *drawing on your right mar*